Currency Boards: Analysis, Risks and Benefits

Currency Boards: Analysis, Risks and Benefits

Brian Lawrence

Clanrye International
www.clanryeinternational.com

Clanrye International,
750 Third Avenue, 9th Floor,
New York, NY 10017, USA

ISBN: 978-1-64726-637-0

Cataloging-in-Publication Data

Currency boards : analysis, risks and benefits / Brian Lawrence.
p. cm.
Includes bibliographical references and index.
ISBN 978-1-64726-637-0
1. Currency boards. 2. Monetary policy. I. Lawrence, Brian.

HG230.5 .C87 2023
332.46--dc23

For information on all Clanrye International publications visit our website at www.clanryeinternational.com

CLANRYE INTERNATIONAL

Contents

Preface

This book aims to highlight the current researches and provides a platform to further the scope of innovations in this area. This book is a product of the combined efforts of many researchers and scientists, after going through thorough studies and analysis from different parts of the world. The objective of this book is to provide the readers with the latest information of the field.

A currency board is a country's monetary authority that is tasked with sustaining a fixed exchange rate along with a foreign currency. The control of the money supply and exchange rate is delegated to a monetary authority by a currency board. This monetary authority then makes decisions concerning the currency valuation of a country. The currency board permits limitless exchange of the domestic currency with foreign currency to the agents. It provides stable exchange rates that facilitate investment and trade. Currency boards are also well-known for controlling inflation. However, there are certain risks associated with the currency boards. In a crisis, the investors can quickly exchange their domestic currency for foreign currency, leading to an increase in the interest rates. This can severely impact the reserve and liquidity requirements of the banks. This book analyses the risks and benefits associated with currency boards. It is appropriate for students seeking detailed information in this area of study as well as for experts.

I would like to express my sincere thanks to the authors for their dedicated efforts in the completion of this book. I acknowledge the efforts of the publisher for providing constant support. Lastly, I would like to thank my family for their support in all academic endeavors.

Brian Lawrence

1

Currency Boards: An Introduction

In 1991 Argentina introduced a currency board to stabilize its troubled economy, plagued by hyperinflation reaching up to 20,000%. This represented the revival of an old monetary arrangement that had gone out of fashion a long time ago. For the first time for almost 20 years—not considering Hong Kong's 1983 return to the currency board system abandoned in 1974—a country had decided to adopt a currency board as its exchange rate arrangement.

The Argentinean currency board proved to be very effective in achieving monetary stabilization. Inflation was brought down to single digit rates within two years—a level of monetary stability that had not been achieved in Argentina for fifty years—and economic growth quickly rebounded.

The outstanding stabilization success of the Argentinean currency board, coupled with the administrative simplicity of setting up and operating a currency board, made it a very attractive monetary arrangement for transition and post-chaos countries. Four countries have eventually followed the Argentinean example and set up their own currency boards; all of them located in eastern Europe. Estonia was the first transition country to adopt a currency board briefly after gaining independence from the Soviet Union. In 1992 it introduced a sovereign currency, the kroon, which was pegged to the Deutsche mark by means of a currency board, and replaced the ruble as legal tender. Lithuania followed the successful example of its Baltic neighbor in 1994, and introduced a currency board with the US dollar as the anchor currency. In 1997 Bulgaria and Bosnia and Herzegovina also introduced currency boards, both pegging the value of their domestic currencies to the Deutsche mark.

The successful revival of the currency board system, which had been spread throughout the whole world during its heyday in the first half of the twentieth century, prompted increased interest of economists in the topic. Some currency board advocates even propagated the allegedly beneficiary adherence to early twentieth century currency board design.[1] The sudden popularity of currency boards, and repeated proposals to introduce them in a variety of countries facing monetary destabilization, even led some authors to ask, whether currency boards offered a "cure for all monetary problems" (Enoch and Gulde 1998, part of paper title), and were the "ultimate fix" (Gosh, Gulde, and Wolf 1998, part of paper title).

They were not. In the late 1990s it became apparent that currency boards, while unquestionably successful in monetary stabilization, were not a tool to overcome all economic problems, and exposed countries to the risk of real economy imbalances. This risk was dramatically highlighted by the Argentinean debt default and subsequent currency board exit in early 2002, which had a devastating effect on the domestic economy.

Most of the literature concerned with the potential benefits and risks of currency boards draws on the arguments of the standard fix versus float discussion, or the theory of optimum currency areas. Yet, only few models exist that consider some of the essential design features of currency boards, most specifically the strong legal commitment, by which the currency board rules are set forth in law.

This thesis examines in great detail the potential benefits, but also the risks of introducing a currency board, by employing a modified second generation currency crises model. The model underlines the important role of legal and political commitment to the currency for the stabilization process, but also highlights the adverse role such commitment may play, once the currency board economy faces real imbalances, such as high unemployment. Furthermore, the thesis studies the potential effects that the presence of foreign-currency denominated debt—often a byproduct of currency board introduction, particularly when following monetary destabilization and hyperinflation—may have on the stability of the currency board and the performance of the economy.

The thesis is structured as follows: Chapter 2 presents a general currency board definition by emphasizing the essential design features of currency boards, and by showing how a currency board differs from a central bank. Further, a short overview over the literature on currency board is given, highlighting the characteristics, pros, and cons of currency boards, such as the ability to lend policy credibility and achieve monetary stabilization, or the importance of fiscal austerity.

Chapter 3 outlines the history of currency boards and introduces to a selection of present-day currency boards. Studying the history of currency boards illustrates how the currency board system has evolved over time.

[1] See the discussion of currency board design in subsection 2.1.3.

The primary rationale for introducing a currency board has changed over time, from having a simple monetary regime that easily provides a domestic currency, to achieving monetary stabilization and gaining policy credibility. The introduction to modern present-day currency boards, exemplified by the cases of Hong Kong, Argentina, Estonia, Lithuania, and Bulgaria, serves to provide an overview over the different currency board designs countries have opted for, and to show how the respective economies performed under the currency board. For each country, separate subsections are devoted to the lead-up to the currency board, to the currency board design, to economic performance under the currency board, and, in the case of Argentina, to the exit from the currency board.

Chapter 4 examines the benefits and risks of having a currency board by applying a modified second generation currency crises model. First, an overview over the basic features and properties of second generation currency crises models is given, and the differences to first generation models are illustrated. Following the introduction of the modified model, exchange rate decisions, stability of the currency board, and the loss from a currency board exit are examined. The following section then extends the model to include the effects from foreign-currency denominated debt, after briefly surveying the literature regarding that topic. That section serves to demonstrate how the model results differ from the previous results, due to the presence of foreign-currency denominated debt.

Finally, chapter 5 presents the policy implications that can be derived from the model examination, taking into account also the results from chapters 3 and 4, and concludes.

2

Design and Characteristics of Currency Boards

This chapter is intended to give a very brief overview over currency board design and characteristics. Section 2.1 explains the basic design features of currency boards and what distinguishes them from central banks. Section 2.2 then shortly examines the pros and cons as well as prerequisites for successfully operating a currency board.

2.1 Basic Features of a Currency Board

2.1.1 Definition of a Currency Board

A currency board (CB) is a very simple, strictly rule-bound institution for supplying an economy with a domestic currency. In the past, currency boards have usually been operating in place of a central bank, although more recent currency boards, starting with Argentina 1991, have usually been set up within previously existing central banks.

A typical currency board is defined by the four following central features:

Fixed exchange rate The value of the domestic currency is strictly tied to the value of an anchor currency at a fixed rate of exchange. Until the second half of the 20th century, the predominant anchor currency was the British pound sterling, although there have been pegs to other currencies and even gold, as well. Recent currency boards have either chosen the US dollar or the Deutsche mark, respectively the euro since the introduction of the common European currency, as an anchor.

Backing requirement A typical currency board is required to fully back the monetary base with foreign exchange reserves. Foreign exchange reserves held by the board must at all times be sufficient to, at least theoretically, convert all notes and coins in circulation, as well as all domestic currency deposits held with the currency board, into the anchor currency at the fixed exchange rate. Domestic currency can only be issued in exchange for the respective amount of foreign exchange. The reserves of the currency board are to be held in foreign cash, and in foreign, liquid, interest-bearing assets denominated in the anchor currency. In practice, most currency boards hold reserves exceeding 100% of base money in order to guard against the risk that the market value of their assets will diminish.

Unrestricted convertibility A typical currency board is a passive monetary institution. It exchanges the anchor currency into domestic currency and vice versa on demand and unlimited, so that the supply of base money always matches the demand for it.

Legal commitment The rules of the currency board, i.e. the choice of an anchor currency and the exchange rate, the backing requirement, and the convertibility undertaking are usually set down in law. This practice serves to prevent the currency board from becoming subject to short-term changes and to signal stability and reliability to economic agents. The currency board rules might be included in the constitution or in basic law, to achieve highest legal rigidity, or be set down in the law governing the central bank, or a special currency credibility law, as is the case with most current currency boards.[1]

A currency board with all these features implemented is a very simple, yet stable, strictly rule-bound institution for supplying an economy with a domestic currency. It is one step short of officially dollarizing[2] the economy, but the local currency is retained, yet only as a token for the anchor currency.

The various motives for introduction of a currency board, which will be discussed in further detail in section 3.1, highlight some characteristics of currency boards. The earliest currency boards were introduced in British colonies in the second half of the 19th century as a simple, yet reliable source

[1]Hong Kong, while not having any special statutory provisions that require the Hong Kong Monetary Authority (HKMA) to adhere to currency board rules, has codified a backing requirement into its basic law, that obliges the HKMA to maintain sufficient reserves to fully back all bank notes in circulation.

[2]In this context the term "dollarization" refers to replacing the domestic currency with any other foreign currency. The chosen currency could be the US dollar, but could as well be the euro or any other currency deemed appropriate.

of domestic money. Prior methods of supplying money had failed, proven unreliable, or led to abuse, such as the free issue of notes through private banks or the issue of unbacked money by colonial governments. Currency boards, in turn, offered a stable and easily administrable way of supplying domestic money that did neither require many nor highly skilled staff.

Later currency boards, such as the West African Currency Board established in 1913, added another motive for currency board introduction. Rather than using British notes and coins as money, colonial governments wanted to use their own currencies that would earn them income from seigniorage. Introducing a currency board, therefore, proved a suitable solution. On the one hand, the domestic currency, backed by the British pound sterling, was merely a token for the anchor currency, on the other hand, the currency boards earned interest on the reserves they held, which would be transferred to the colonial government.

Current currency boards, starting with Hong Kong's re-introduction of its currency board in 1983, and, most notably, the Argentinean currency board established in 1991, introduced yet another motive for currency board selection. These countries sought to achieve economic stabilization by introducing a credible nominal anchor. As a currency board is the most rigid form of fixing the exchange rate vis a vis an anchor currency, short of dollarizing the economy, these countries opted for a currency board to reconstitute trust in their domestic currencies. In the case of Hong Kong, the exchange rate had gotten under pressure and the Hong Kong dollar was rapidly losing value prior to the introduction of the currency board. Argentina introduced the currency board to put a stop to rampant hyperinflation.

2.1.2 Currency Boards vs Central Banks

A currency board is not only an exchange rate system, but a different monetary system. It differs essentially from any other exchange rate system under a central bank in the most important aspect that almost no discretionary monetary policy is possible under a currency board. In the most extreme case, the currency board is not only subject to a total backing rule, but also to a marginal backing rule. While the total backing rule specifies that at all times the foreign exchange reserves have to fully cover the monetary base, the marginal backing rule goes one step further and requires that every change in the monetary base has to be accompanied by a corresponding change in foreign exchange reserves. With a marginal backing rule in place there is no way for the monetary authority to actively change the money supply, except through changes in reserve requirements for commercial banks. With only a total backing requirement in place some scope for monetary policy exists, yet limited to the extent of foreign exchange reserves exceeding the monetary base.

Currency Board

Assets	Liabilities
Liquid reserve-currency assets	Notes & coins in circulation
	(Deposits of commercial banks)
	Net worth

Central Bank

Assets	Liabilities
Liquid reserve-currency assets	Notes & coins in circulation
Domestic assets (government debt)	Deposits of commercial banks
	Net worth

Source: Williamson (1995, p. 3)

Figure 2.1: Stylized T-accounts of a currency board and a central bank.

Consider figure 2.1, where the stylized T-accounts of a currency board and a central bank are shown. The assets of a currency board consist only of its foreign exchange reserves. The liabilities of the currency board are the monetary base, consisting of notes and coins in circulation and, if applicable, deposits of commercial banks, containing for example the required reserves of the banking sector.[3] Unlike in a central bank system, many currency boards allow or even require commercial banks to hold their reserves in the anchor currency (Williamson 1995, p. 2). The net worth of the currency board, representing its excess reserves, has to be either zero or positive in order not to violate the backing requirement.

[3]Note that many historical currency boards, as well as orthodox currency boards advocated by Hanke and Schuler (which will be discussed in more detail in the following subsection), were not allowed to keep deposits.

The key difference between a currency board and a central bank is the fact that a central bank is allowed to also hold domestic assets, including loans, of which the most important part normally is government debt. This enables the central bank to pursue a discretionary monetary policy, systematically influencing the supply of domestic money. The central bank can increase the money supply by buying domestic assets. It may, in turn, reduce the supply by selling such assets. If the central bank is required to sell foreign exchange to defend the exchange rate, it may offset, or sterilize, the ensuing reduction of the monetary base by buying domestic assets. Also, the central bank may act as a lender of last resort (LoLR) during a liquidity crisis affecting the banking system, by granting loans to banks or by buying assets from them through a discount operation (Williamson 1995, pp. 3–4).

These options are not available under a pure currency board. The monetary base is solely determined by demand. If the public sells foreign exchange to the currency board, the monetary base increases, and if the public sells domestic currency in exchange for foreign exchange, the monetary base decreases.

2.1.3 Flexibility in Design

While the key currency board features described in subsection 2.1.1 represent a definition of an ideal type of currency board most economist could agree on[4], such a definition still fails to capture every aspect and nuance of a monetary arrangement that has existed and evolved for more than 150 years.

As a pure currency board characterized by the four key features described in subsection 2.1.1 enforces extreme rigidity concerning monetary policy, most present-day currency boards have decided to introduce some flexibility in their currency board design to retain at least some scope for discretionary monetary policy. Of the five modern currency boards discussed in chapter 3, none adheres to the marginal backing rule, which would preclude any discretionary change in the monetary base without a corresponding change in foreign exchange reserves. These currency board countries have opted for such flexibility, primarily to gain the ability to engage in LoLR operations. While LoLR support is in all cases restricted to the extent of excess reserves of the monetary authority, the ability to extend at least such limited support in the case of a liquidity crisis in the banking system was deemed necessary. Yet, the scope for discretionary monetary policy is not only restricted to LoLR support. While Bulgaria's currency board has the least scope for dis-

[4]See for example Baliño and Enoch (1997, pp. 1–4), Bennett (1994, pp. 2-6), Gulde (1999, p. 5), Schwartz (1993, pp. 147–148), and Williamson (1995, pp. 2–5).

cretion and may only change reserve requirements to affect the money supply, the Lithuanian currency board has almost all monetary policy instruments of a full-fledged central bank at its disposal, among them issuing Treasury-bills or engaging in open market operations.

Some of the five currency boards do not even adhere fully to the total backing requirement. While all currency boards are obliged to fully back the monetary base, not all of them are obliged to do so by exclusively holding foreign cash and foreign assets. The Argentinean and the Lithuanian currency board are[5] both allowed to hold domestic anchor-currency denominated government bonds as reserves. While this does not violate the 100% backing requirement—the monetary base is still fully covered by anchor-currency denominated assets—it introduces some scope for discretionary monetary policy, as the monetary base can be expanded without a reduction of the domestically available foreign exchange.

Further deviations from typical currency board design may be observed concerning unrestricted convertibility. While all five currency boards are obliged to sell foreign exchange against the domestic currency at, or very close to the official exchange rate, some of them, specifically Argentina, Hong Kong, and Lithuania, are not required to sell domestic currency against foreign exchange on demand at the official exchange rate, even though in practice they usually do.[6] Also, the extent of legal commitment varies greatly among the five currency board countries. While both Argentina and Bulgaria have set down in respective laws all three central elements, backing requirement and composition of reserves, anchor currency and exchange rate, and convertibility, Estonia does not specify the exchange rate, and Lithuania specifies neither the exchange rate nor the anchor currency. Yet, regarding low legal commitment, Hong Kong is in a class of its own. While the HKMA has shown great commitment towards the currency board, there are barely any statutory provisions that oblige the HKMA to operate a currency board. Only Hong Kong basic law requires the HKMA to keep bank notes in circulation fully backed, but otherwise no provisions are made concerning the exchange rate, the anchor currency, or convertibility.

---

[5]The Argentinean currency board was abandoned in early 2002. Nevertheless, it still represents an example of a modern present-day currency board. If referred to in present-tense throughout this thesis, this will be for the sake of uniformity.

[6]This one-way convertibility poses no threat to the credibility of the currency board, though. It guarantees to agents the exchange of their domestic cash holdings into foreign exchange anytime, which is an important pillar of currency board credibility. The failure to exchange foreign exchange into domestic money may only pose a problem if agents feared the domestic currency might be revalued. Consequently, a lack of two-way convertibility may hinder arbitrage mechanisms to function properly in situations of upward pressures to the currency, but does not lessen the credibility of the currency board.

Despite all these deviations from the four key features, these currency boards are generally—and in the context of this thesis—considered to be currency boards. They are still, by and large, rule-bound monetary institutions, fully backing the monetary base, and pledging to convert on demand domestic currency into foreign exchange at a fixed exchange rate.

Yet, some economist disagree. According to one of the strictest and most voiced definitions of a currency board, strongly advocated by Steve Hanke and Kurt Schuler, these five present-day currency boards are merely "currency board-like systems" (Hanke and Schuler 2000, chapter 3, section 5).[7] The authors base their definition of what they call an *orthodox currency board* on the design of historical currency boards, most notably the West African Currency Board, established in 1913 (Schuler 1992, chapter 4, paragraph 1).[8] According to their definition, which includes but exceeds the key features described in subsection 2.1.1, a currency board's *sole* purpose must be to be a passive device for conversion of the anchor into the domestic currency and vice versa. The currency board must not pursue any other ends in monetary policy nor should any other state-owned or state-controlled institution do so. Consequently, any scope for discretionary monetary policy, lending to the government, LoLR support, or financial regulation and supervision by the currency board are explicitly ruled out. The currency board must not accept deposits from commercial banks (which consequently rules out reserve requirements for banks) or the government. Complementary, to ensure the functioning of the monetary arrangement and the adjustment process of the whole economy, regulation of goods, factors, and financial markets should be liberal, markets should be open and integrated with world markets (Schuler 1999, pp. 5–6).

While this definition has been voiced often, it is not generally agreed upon. The insistence on orthodoxy, based on a design almost a century ago, seems to suggest that properly mimicking today the features and peculiarities of the currency board systems existing during the first half of the twentieth century will also lead to the indisputable stability and growth that the economies hosting these systems enjoyed. Yet, this would obviously be an oversimplification, as "the notion that [currency boards] can be revived to function as they did in the past idealizes them and neglects the change in economic fundamentals in current circumstances as well as the need for pre-

[7]For Hanke and Schuler's definition of currency boards see for example Hanke and Schuler (1992, 1993, 2000), Hanke, Jonung, and Schuler (1993), Hanke (1999, 2000), and Schuler (1992, 1999). Kurt Schuler also maintains a site on the internet dedicated to currency boards and dollarization at `http://www.dollarization.org`.

[8]The West African Currency Board will be discussed in great detail in subsection 3.1.4.

commitment by governments and their constituencies to the discipline these institutions exact" (Schwartz 1993, p. 183).

2.2 Currency Board Characteristics

Section 2.1 has shown that a currency board is a very simple monetary arrangement that is rather easily set up and operated. Little skills in monetary policy are required. The main tasks of a pure currency board are the exchange of domestic currency into foreign exchange and vice versa, which requires few and not overly skilled staff, and the investment and management of reserves, which requires few but expert staff. The operation of the currency board is easily carried out and easily understood by the public. This makes currency boards particulary attractive for post-chaos countries—such as Bosnia—or for small countries that have recently attained independence—such as Estonia and Lithuania—and wish to create their own currency for motives of seigniorage as well as national identity (Hanke, Jonung, and Schuler 1993, p. 106; Baliño and Enoch 1997, p. 6).

Besides such simplicity of administration and operation, the main reason why currency boards have been set up in recent years was their effectiveness in stabilizing economies, in which the credibility and value of the domestic currency have been threatened or destroyed and where high inflation and marked devaluations of the domestic currency have disrupted the functioning of the economy. This essential benefit of stabilization, and how it can be explained will be discussed in subsection 2.2.1.

Yet, the introduction of a currency board is no magic cure for a destabilized economy, which offers benefits without drawbacks. For the currency board to function properly and to be sustainable a number of prerequisites have to be met and potential disadvantages have to be considered before introducing it. One essential prerequisite are flexible factor and goods markets, as will be shown in subsection 2.2.2. Without the exchange rate providing for external adjustment, domestic prices need to adjust instead. If prices are inflexible, though, adjustment will have to come by potentially costly adjustments of the real economy, through consumption and incomes. The choice of an adequate anchor currency is equally important as the introduction of a currency board effectively implies importing the monetary policy of the anchor currency country, as will be shown in subsection 2.2.3. Yet, if e.g. business cycles in the anchor country are completely unrelated to cycles in the host country economy, monetary policy in the anchor country may exert unnecessary stress on the host country. Further, the introduction of a currency board presupposes a robust banking sector. As lender of last resort (LoLR) support is limited or even non-existent under the currency board, banks have to be able to cope with higher levels of financial system stress than they might have been used to before. This point will be explored in subsection 2.2.4. Finally, subsection 2.2.5 stresses that the policymaker needs to be aware of the implications the currency board has on fiscal policy. Under a currency board fiscal deficits cannot be monetized any longer, but have to be financed by financial markets. Therefore, fiscal policy needs to be austere, closely watching government deficit and debt levels.

2.2.1 Credibility and Macroeconomic Stability

The main reason why recent modern currency boards have been introduced, has been the aim to institute a credible exchange rate mechanism and credible monetary policy, and thereby to import the low inflation and interest rates of the anchor currency country. For example, countries as Argentina, Bulgaria, and Lithuania were all experiencing high to hyperinflation combined with, or driven by large government budget deficits prior to introduction of their currency boards. The introduction of a currency board was seen as an extreme emergency measure to regain trust in their currencies and to achieve stabilization of their respective economies.

By choosing a currency board, policymakers signal their willingness and determination to subject themselves to the strict discipline imposed by the currency board. The scope for discretionary monetary policy is removed, and with it the ability of the central bank to monetize the government budget deficit, one main source of inflationary pressures. Government expenses become subject to a hard budget constraint, forcing the government to increase fiscal discipline and to reduce or eliminate the budget deficit.

Yet, the introduction of a fixed exchange rate and the announcement of tight fiscal and monetary policy alone are not sufficient for economic stabilization, as long as they lack credibility. This point, which distinguishes currency boards from regular pegs, has been made by Kydland and Prescott (1977) in their seminal paper on the time-inconsistency of optimal plans, and will also become very clear from the model in chapter 4.[9] Under a regular fixed exchange rate, if the public trust in the policymaker's announcement of low inflation and therefore adjust their inflation expectations accordingly, the policymaker is presented with an incentive to cheat on his commitment and to generate surprise inflation, thereby lowering unemployment. But, if the public form their expectations rationally, they are aware of this incentive to

[9]The problem of time-inconsistency and how a currency board may help overcome it, will be discussed in more detail in subsection 4.2.3.

cheat and will consequently form high inflation expectations. Consequently, the lack of credibility will leave the policymaker with two undesirable options: Either stick to the low-inflation policy and accept higher unemployment, or keep unemployment constant by generating inflation.

Such lack of credibility can be overcome by a currency board. Its operating principle is simple and transparent, making it easily understandable for the public. Second, the choice of a currency board signals the policymaker's willingness to subject his policy actions to the strict requirements of the currency board. Third, the legal commitment, by which the currency board rules are normally set down in law, assures economic agents that no short-term changes to the arrangement are possible.

In theory, a fully credible currency board operating in an economy with flexible markets should then lead to inflation and interest rates similar to those in the anchor currency country (Baliño and Enoch 1997, pp.8–9). In practice, though, as chapter 3 will show, rates are often, but not necessarily, close to those in the anchor currency country. Inflation may, for example, be higher due to higher productivity growth in the currency board country—the Balassa-Samuelson effect, to which some economist attribute relatively high levels of inflation in Estonia and Lithuania[10]. It may be lower due to inflexible labor and goods market, leading to a protracted period of adjustment after a shock, possibly entailing deflation, as has been the case in Argentina in the late 1990s. Interest rates also tend to remain above those in the anchor currency country, as the exchange rate risk is greatly but not completely reduced. For example, in Argentina domestic interest rates on dollar transactions have constantly been below interest rates on peso transactions throughout the currency board period (see figure 3.20).

Few attempts have been made to assess the impact of exchange rate regimes on economic performance, specifically inflation and growth, by examining historical data, and the overall results of these studies have generally been contradictory. For example, Schuler (1996, pp. 24–26) concludes that developing countries with central banks have, both under the Bretton Woods

[10]The assertion is based on the assumption that the large share of labor productivity growth is taking place in the tradeables sector, where prices are determined by international markets. Assuming the exchange rate remains constant, labor productivity growth in the tradeables sectors will increase wages in the tradeables sector. On the other hand, wages in the non-tradeables sector cannot be completely disconnected from wages in the tradeables sector. Consequently, wages in the non-tradeables sector will rise as well. Yet, if we assume, as is often done, that productivity growth in the non-tradeables sector is slow, the increase in wages in the non-tradeables sectors needs to be financed by increases in prices of non-tradeables. As a result, high but uneven productivity growth can by itself lead to inflation. Yet, as this inflation is an expression of adjusting relative prices, it does not affect a country's competitiveness or the real exchange rate.

monetary system, as well as after it, on average experienced less growth and markedly higher inflation, compared to developed countries and developing countries with alternative monetary systems, most notably currency boards. This result is partly confirmed by another study by Gosh et al. (1997, p. 2), which also finds that inflation has been lower and more stable under fixed exchange rate regimes—which would entail currency boards—but fails to find a notable difference in growth between fixed and flexible exchange rate regimes. Contrary to these two studies, Levy-Yeyati and Sturzenegger (2001b, 2002c), using their own classification of exchange rate regimes, not the IMF standard classification[11], find no significant difference in inflation between fixed and flexible exchange rate regimes, but markedly better inflation performance of both regimes compared to intermediate exchange rate regimes. Regarding growth performance, they find that flexible exchange rate regimes have outperformed fixed exchange rate regimes, while the latter have also been subject to higher growth volatility.

2.2.2 The Adjustment Process and Market Flexibility

With the exchange rate fixed, any country adopting a currency board gives up the buffer-function of nominal exchange adjustments to adapt to external imbalances. Consequently, any misalignments of the real exchange rate, be it overvaluation due to higher domestic inflation compared to the anchor currency country, or overvaluation due to an adverse macroeconomic external shock hitting the economy, or a sudden reduction in capital inflows, have to be adjusted through changes in domestic prices, wages, incomes, and consumption. If markets are sufficiently flexible, such adjustment can be borne by prices and the real economy alike. The less flexible markets are, though, the higher the share of adjustment that has to be borne by the real economy.

To illustrate this adjustment process, this subsection employs the standard dependent economy model, initially developed by Swan (1960, 1963) and Salter (1959) for the Australian economy, which is often used, for example, to examine exchange rate policies in transition countries.[12]

The model economy, which is assumed to be a small country relative to the rest of the world, produces two kinds of goods: tradeables and non-tradeables, which are imperfect substitutes.[13] Prices of tradeables are deter-

[11]The authors base their classification on de-facto behavior of exchange rate regimes and not on the officially announced exchange rate regime. For more details on this classification see Levy-Yeyati and Sturzenegger (2002a).

[12]This section draws heavily on Gerloff (2001, pp. 78–92).

[13]For simplification, the term "goods" is used for both, goods and services. Also, reference to the trade balance includes both, the balance of trade and the balance of services.

mined by world markets, while prices for non-tradeables are determined by domestic supply and demand.

The domestic supply of both tradeables (Y_T) and non-tradeables (Y_N) depends on the real exchange rate (RER), which is defined as the price of tradeables (in domestic currency units) divided by the domestic price of non-tradeables. An increase (decrease) of the price of tradeables (non-tradeables), which represents a real depreciation, i.e. an increase of the RER, increases the domestic supply of tradeables and decreases the supply of non-tradeables. Similarly, an increase (decrease) in the price of non-tradeables (tradeables), representing a real appreciation, a decrease of the RER, increases the supply of non-tradeables and decreases the supply of tradeables. Algebraical:[14]

$$Y_T = Y_T(R\overset{+}{E}R) \tag{2.1}$$

$$Y_N = Y_N(R\overset{-}{E}R) \tag{2.2}$$

Domestic demand for tradeables (D_T) depends on the RER and real absorption (A), i.e. private and public consumption and investment, which is measured in tradeable goods. Demand for tradeables increases with lower values of the RER (appreciation), as tradeables become less expensive relative to non-tradeables (substitution effect), and as a lower RER increases the real income of households (income effect). Further, demand for tradeables increases with real absorption:

$$D_T = D_T(R\overset{-}{E}R, \overset{+}{A}) \tag{2.3}$$

Similarly, demand for non-tradeables (D_N) depends on the RER and real absorption, too. While an increase in absorption unequivocally raises demand for non-tradeables, the effect of changes in the RER is undetermined: While an increase in the RER (depreciation) increases the prices of tradeables relative to non-tradeables, leading to a shift in demand from tradeables to non-tradeables (substitution effect), the increase in the RER also reduces real income, which tends to reduce demand for non-tradeables (income effect). Consequently, the overall effect cannot be determined. Yet, we will assume that the substitution effect dominates the income effect, i.e. real depreciation leads to increased demand for non-tradeables:

$$D_N = D_N(R\overset{?/+}{E}R, \overset{+}{A}) \tag{2.4}$$

[14]A plus or minus above variables indicates whether the first partial derivative of the function respect to that variable is positive or negative.

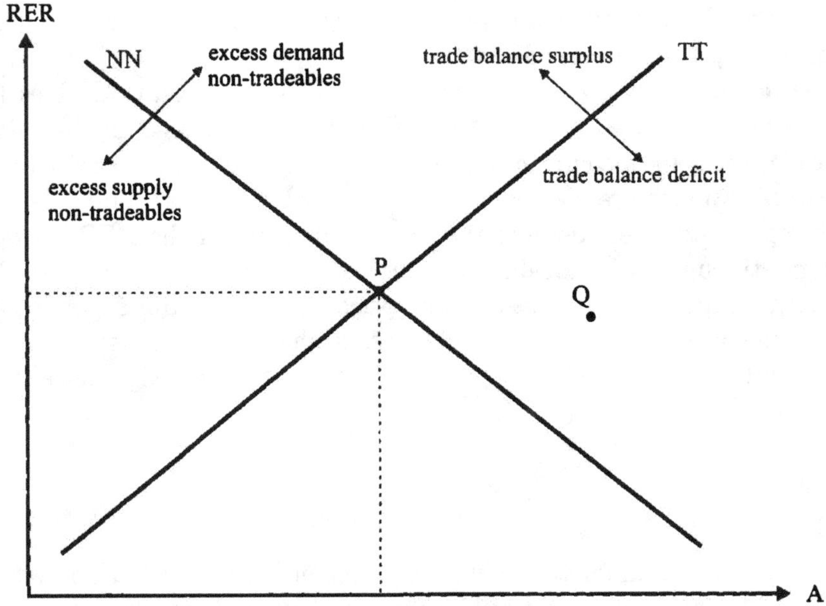

Source: Swan (1963, p. 387)

Figure 2.2: Internal and external equilibrium in the dependent economy model.

Equating equations 2.1 and 2.3, and 2.2 and 2.4 yields the conditions for external and internal equilibrium, respectively. External equilibria are represented by the TT-curve in figure 2.2, which is upward-sloping.[15] Increases in real absorption lead to excess demand for tradeables that can only be balanced by an increase in the RER, which increases supply and lowers demand for tradeables. Similarly, internal equilibria are represented by the NN-curve, which is downward-sloping, as increased demand for non-tradeables through higher absorption has to be balanced by appreciation of the RER, which increases supply and lowers demand.

The economy is in full equilibrium when both external and internal equilibrium are achieved. This is the case in point P in figure 2.2. Points that are not on the TT-curve represent external disequilibria, points that are not on the NN-curve represent internal disequilibria. As indicated in the figure, any point to the right of the TT-curve leads to a trade balance deficit, demand for

[15]For simplicity, curves are assumed to be linear. Actually, the slope of the TT-curve would have to be increasing, as higher absorption would require ever higher devaluations to balance the trade balance (Swan 1963, p. 386). Yet, qualitative results of the analysis remain unchanged by assuming linear curves.

tradeables exceeds domestic supply for tradeables. Points to the left of the TT-curve represent a trade balance surplus. Similarly, points to the right of the NN-curve lead to excess demand for non-tradeables, tending to push up prices for non-tradeables, while points to the left are associated with excess supply of non-tradeables. For example, realization of point Q leads to excess demand for non-tradeables and a deficit of the trade balance. Note, though, that the dependent economy model assumes flexible domestic prices. Therefore, the economy will always be in internal equilibrium, as excess supply or demand of non-tradeables are immediately translated into price changes, which will eventually clear the market. Consequently, the excess demand for non-tradeables in Q will immediately prompt prices for non-tradeables to rise, driving the RER down and resulting in internal equilibrium.

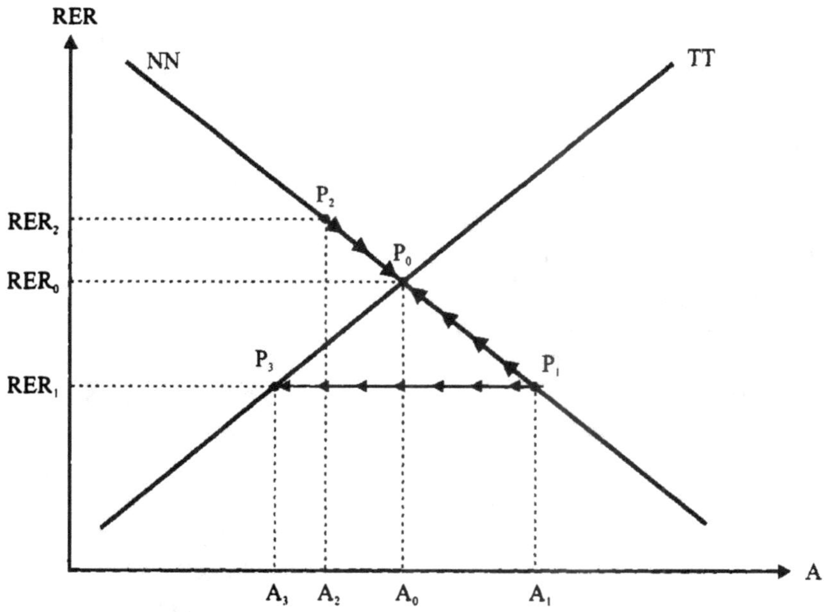

Source: Gerloff (2001, p. 90)

Figure 2.3: Adjustment in the dependent economy model.

Let us now consider the adjustments needed to balance external disequilibrium. Assume that for some reason, e.g. due to inflation persistence after the introduction of the currency board, which has often been the case, the RER is overvalued. This situation corresponds to point P_1 in figure 2.3. While the market for non-tradeables is in equilibrium, the market for tradeables is not. The relatively high level of non-tradeables prices lead to misallocation of resources: Too many factors of production are devoted to the production of non-tradeables, while the production of tradeables is neglected.

The trade deficit in P_1 leads to an excess demand for foreign exchange and excess supply of domestic currency. Since the exchange rate is fixed under a currency board, this imbalance cannot be adjusted through changes of the price of domestic currency, i.e. of the nominal exchange rate. The consequence is an outflow of foreign exchange and the inevitable contraction of the monetary base, as residents exchange domestic currency for foreign exchange to finance the trade deficit, and as monetary authorities have no ability to influence the money supply under the currency board. The contraction of the monetary base, in turn, leads to a reduction in real absorption.[16] As a reduction of absorption reduces the demand for non-tradeables, excess supply of non-tradeables is the result, which is immediately compensated by a reduction in the prices of non-tradeables, though. Fallen prices of non-tradeables, in turn, increase the RER, which reduces the trade deficit further. Eventually, adjustment proceeds along the NN-curve, reducing absorption from A_1 to A_0 and increasing the RER from RER_1 to RER_0, until full equilibrium is reached in P_0.[17]

Now, assume that prior to adopting the currency board the exchange rate was devalued by more than was necessary to achieve the equilibrium RER rate. Such a situation would correspond to P_2. The resulting trade balance surplus leads to an inflow of foreign exchange, expanding the monetary base and, therefore, expanding real absorption, which reduces the trade surplus. The expansion of absorption also leads to excess demand for non-tradeables, which is immediately accommodated through increases in non-tradeables prices, appreciating the RER and reducing the trade balance surplus further. Eventually, the balance of trade is balanced by increased absorption and inflation, leading to full equilibrium in P_0. Consequently, introducing a currency board and setting the nominal exchange rate such that it results in in real undervaluation of the domestic currency may undermine the stabilization effects of the currency board, as the resulting balance of trade surplus eventually inflates away the real exchange rate misalignment.

The adjustment processes considered so far, especially the adjustment process resulting from overvaluation of the RER, were based on the underlying assumption of flexible prices in the non-tradeables sector, i.e. if required, prices could sink to reach the equilibrium RER. Yet, how does adjustment differ, if goods prices (and, underlying, factor, specifically labor prices) are

---

[16] Gerloff (2001, pp. 87–88) points out that generally, authors employing the dependent economy model assume a positive correlation between the monetary base and real absorption, without modelling it, and provides a possible way to model such an interrelationship.

[17] This does not necessarily indicate that adjustment requires deflation in the non-tradeables sector, rather inflation in non-tradeables has to be below (foreign) inflation in tradeables.

not flexible?[18] Consider again the situation represented by P_1: The trade balance deficit corresponding to P_1 leads to an outflow of foreign exchange, which reduces the monetary base under a currency board. The resulting reduction in real absorption reduces the trade balance deficit and leads to excess supply of non-tradeables. Yet, as goods and labor prices are not downward flexible, the prices of non-tradeables cannot sink to accomplish internal equilibrium, and furthermore, the RER does not increase, which would otherwise reduce the trade deficit further. Consequently, the trade deficit can only be reduced by reductions in real absorption, which will have to be higher than in the case of goods and labor prices flexibility. Eventually, the adjustment process proceeds from P_1 to P_3. The RER remains constant at RER_1 due to inflexible goods and labor prices, while real absorption has to be reduced from A_1 to A_3, exceeding the reduction under flexible prices. The inflexibility of prices leads to excess supply of non-tradeables that cannot be accommodated by price reductions, and, therefore, unemployment. The inability to achieve some of the required adjustment via prices and wages, therefore, puts a higher adjustment burden on the real economy, such as consumption, incomes, and employment.

These results highlight one of the central prerequisites for introducing a currency board: flexible goods and labor markets. The easier markets are able to accommodate especially negative real external shocks, which require a depreciation of the RER, the more sustainable and beneficial the introduction of a currency board for the host country. If markets are not sufficiently flexible, an overvalued RER, whether stemming from persistent inflation, external shocks, or a reduction of capital flows[19], puts a high burden on the real economy, as consumption, investment, and incomes have to be lowered by more than necessary, and as unemployment results from failure to achieve internal equilibrium (Corden 1997, p. 3; Fischer 1997, pp. 20–21).

2.2.3 Anchor Currency Selection—A Theory of Optimum Currency Areas Perspective

As has been argued before, a currency board is just one step short of forming a currency union with the anchor country. Therefore, when opting for the introduction of a currency board, policymakers should consider how suitable such a peg is, especially when selecting the anchor currency.

[18] Gerloff (2001, p. 92) points out that this approach, while widely used in the literature, would actually require a re-specification of the supply functions.

[19] See Wohlmann (1998, pp. 57–62) for a detailed description of how different types of capital inflows affect the dependent economy model.

Generally, the Mundell-Fleming-Dornbusch model implies that in the presence of nominal shocks, fixed exchange rates avoid real cost of adjustment, since they eliminate the possibility of money supply shocks and immediately accommodate any money demand shocks. On the other hand, flexible exchange rates are well suited to accommodate real shocks through changes in the nominal exchange rate, rather than requiring adjustment through domestic prices or absorption, as in the case of fixed exchange rates. Consequently, flexible exchange rates are prescribed for economies mainly facing real shocks, while fixed exchange rates are considered appropriate for economies facing nominal shocks (Levy-Yeyati and Sturzenegger 2001a, pp. 5–6).

Similarly, the theory of optimum currency areas, introduced by Mundell (1961) and later expanded by McKinnon (1963) and Kenen (1969), seeks to identify under what conditions it is optimal for countries to enter into a monetary union, and under what conditions it is better to retain nominal exchange rate flexibility.[20] The central questions of the theory are: To what extent are two countries exposed to asymmetric real shocks, how well can they cope with such real shocks under a fixed exchange rate, and how well could a flexible exchange rate serve to alleviate such shocks?

In general it may be said, the less countries are hit by asymmetric shocks, i.e. shocks that affect the countries in question differently, the more suitable is a common currency. This also applies to the correlation of business cycles. If business cycles are not synchronized, monetary policy in the anchor currency country can be devastating for the currency board country. Argentina provides an example: In late 1998 Argentina entered into a severe and protracted recession, while the US was still enjoying strong growth. Consequently, monetary policy in the US was tight, interest rates were relatively high, and the exchange rate of the dollar vis a vis other currencies continued to appreciate—exactly the opposite of what the Argentinean economy was needing (Roubini 2001, pp. 28–29).

One important factor determining countries' ability to cope with asymmetric shocks is the extent of labor mobility. While Mundell's initial example was explicitly aimed at labor mobility between the countries in question, Eichengreen (1994, p. 83) suggests that that the term should be considered as a proxy for labor market flexibility generally.

[20] Initially Mundell asked "What is the appropriate domain of a currency area?" (Mundell 1961, p. 657), implying that optimum currency areas might be limited to parts only of a nations state, or to parts of two or more nation states. Yet, so far political reality dictates that newly founded monetary unions consist of nation states. Currently, it does not seem plausible for regions of separate nation states to have a common currency while some regions of at least one of the countries does not. Therefore, the theory of optimum currency areas is usually applied to nation states.

Let us examine the simple example used by Mundell (1961, pp. 658–659): Assume two countries A and B, initially in balance of payments equilibrium and full employment, share a common currency, or one country has pegged the value of its domestic currency to the value of the other country's currency by means of a currency board. The equilibrium is disturbed by a shift in demand from goods of country B to goods from country A. Under a flexible exchange rate equilibrium can be restored through a change in the terms of trade by adjusting the nominal exchange rate; an option that is foreclosed under a currency board. Instead, domestic adjustment in country B is needed. If prices and wages are sticky, adjustment requires a reduction of incomes and employment in country B, as has been shown in subsection 2.2.2. Yet, the cost of adjustment can be lowered by labor market flexibility: If workers migrate from country B to country A, this reduces unemployment and the adjustment burden in country B, and, additionally, reduces the inflationary pressure in country A. Alternatively, if wages in country B are downward flexible this avoids unemployment and alleviates the cost of adjustment in country B, without a need for real international factor mobility. Therefore, the more flexible labor markets are—either in the sense of how easily reductions in nominal wages can be achieved, or in the sense of how easily workers may migrate between the countries in question—the better equipped are countries for monetary union, and the more suitable a fixed exchange rate among them.

Another factor favoring a common currency or fixed exchange rates is the degree of openness, in this context measured as the tradeables sector's share of production relative to the non-tradeables sector's share. One argument for a fixed exchange rate can be made based on transaction costs: The higher the share of trade with the anchor currency country, the more the tradeables sector can benefit from a fixed exchange rate, reducing price volatility and exchange rate risk (Eichengreen 1994, p. 80). Also, a higher degree of trade integration with the anchor currency country implies greater synchronization of the business cycle (Roubini 2001, p. 29).

Additionally, it is often argued that the nominal exchange rate becomes a less effective tool to achieve real exchange rate (RER) realignment, the more open the economy: the higher the degree of openness, the higher the pass-through of exchange rate depreciation on domestic prices, therefore, the less the change in the RER, but the more adverse the effect on price stability. Also, under a fixed exchange rate, the reduction of absorption required to restore external balance has as smaller impact on unemployment and production, the higher the degree of openness (McKinnon 1963, pp. 719–720). On the other hand, the required change in the RER to achieve external balance is also smaller in a more open economy, which compensates for the reduced effectiveness of devaluations under flexible exchange rate regimes. (Eichengreen 1994, p. pp. 80–81; Roubini 2001, p. 30).

The implications of the theory of optimum currency areas have recently lost some of their importance for the decision whether to dollarize (or introduce a currency board) or not, since many countries considering such a super-peg do not do so for shielding their economies from shocks, but, even more basic, to regain credibility of their currencies and policies. Yet, even if optimum currency area considerations are disregarded when deciding to fix the exchange rate, they should still play an important role when deciding which currency to chose as anchor currency (Levy-Yeyati and Sturzenegger 2001a, pp. 7–8). In the short-term credibility may be gained just from the fact that the currency is pegged by means of a currency board; in the medium-term, though, the peg has to be sustained, which makes the implications of the theory of optimum currency areas an important factor to consider.

From the viewpoint of the theory of optimum currency areas, a currency board country, when deciding on the anchor currency, should consider the degree of trade integration and synchronization of business cycles, as well as the exposure to shocks it has in common with the anchor currency country. While trade integration and synchronization of business cycles may increase after pegging the domestic currency, such a process may be painful and involve real economic cost. For example, both Argentina and Lithuania have suffered from the economic boom and the appreciating dollar in the US in the late 1990s. The extent of cost and length of adjustment is crucially determined by the flexibility of markets, most importantly labor markets. The easier adjustments can be made through reductions in prices and wages, the lower the required reduction in expenditure and incomes.

2.2.4 Monetary Policy, Lender of Last Resort Support, and Financial Fragility

As has been mentioned before, a pure currency board has no scope for monetary policy and no way of influencing the money supply, except maybe for changing reserve requirements. Obviously, as this is the fundamental idea of having a currency board, this cannot be considered a drawback of the system, since the most important stabilizing element of a currency board is the removal of monetary policy discretion, which is usually the driving force behind inflation. Yet, many authors have worried about the currency board's resulting inability to act as a LoLR in the case of a looming banking crisis. For example, the combination of a currency board and no LoLR capabilities contributed to the failure of all domestic banks in Djibouti in the 1980s (Santiprabhob 1997, pp. 4–5). On the other hand, as Williamson (1995, p. 25) and Fischer (1997, p. 20) point out, the lack of a LoLR should be considered only a mixed curse. In dealing with crises that originated from outside the banking system the lack of a LoLR is a real loss. On the other hand, for crises originating within the banking system, resulting from poor bank management and supervision, it may be a gain not to have a LoLR, in order not to bail out banks when those bailouts would be a mistake.

Further, all of the modern currency boards discussed in chapter 3 have made provisions allowing their currency boards to provide at least limited LoLR support up to the extent of excess reserves of the currency boards. Such LoLR support has repeatedly been used in dealing with banking crises in four of the five currency board countries[21], and while the toll on the economy has been large at times, this cannot generally be ascribed to the presence of a currency board or limited LoLR support. For example, Estonia, which allowed two smaller banks to go bankrupt and rescued one medium-size bank during its banking crisis, emerged from the crisis with the banking system largely intact. On the other hand, Lithuania and Bulgaria (prior to the introduction of the currency board) experienced more dramatic crises. In Lithuania the crisis can partly be ascribed to lax banking supervision, and weak and questionable commitment to the currency board arrangement. Eventually, a large number of banks failed and the government (not the central bank) ended up compensating depositors in failed banks and recapitalizing other banks, costing an estimated 3.5% of GDP. Similarly, in Bulgaria the banking crisis resulted mainly from weak and not-enforced banking supervision. Abundant LoLR support from the Bulgarian National Bank (BNB), combined with an excessive government deficit monetized by the BNB, eventually led to hyperinflation and then the introduction of the currency board to stop it.

The lack of full LoLR support underlines the importance of a sound banking system. The absence of a LoLR poses the highest risk in countries with high capital mobility, but where banks have limited access to foreign funds or where the banking system is weak (Baliño and Enoch 1997, p. 15). Consequently, strong banking supervision and enforcement of regulations are essential in currency board economies. The presence of foreign banks may also provide emergency liquidity, as the local branches could resort to their headquarters for emergency liquidity support (Santiprabhob 1997, p. 4). On the other hand, the experience of Argentina has shown that foreign banks may well leave their domestic branches to cope with liquidity shocks on their own if risks are considered too high (Williamson 1997, p. 8).

[21]The banking crisis in Bulgaria preceded the introduction of the currency board.

2.2.5 Fiscal Policy

A currency board requires fiscal discipline. As the currency board should not be allowed to hold domestic assets[22], the government budget deficit cannot be monetized anymore, imposing a hard budget constraint on the government: the budget deficit can only be financed by raising funds in financial markets. While it is often very hard for a government to reduce its expenses, the currency board may provide a credible excuse for doing so (Avramov 1999, p. 10).

The importance of moderated government spending is also highlighted by the dependent economy model employed in subsection 2.2.2. Excessive government spending increases real absorption, tending to increase prices in the non-tradeables sector and appreciating the real exchange rate. This increases the need for adjustment, which is particularly severe if prices are inflexible and the needed reduction of absorption is higher than the initial increase in government spending, as RER depreciation is only slowly taking place. On the other hand, fiscal policy can support necessary adjustment by reducing expenses when a reduction of real absorption is required to achieve external equilibrium.

A currency board requires, but cannot really enforce fiscal discipline. Governments introducing a currency board should be well aware of the importance of fiscal discipline, and should be willing to subordinate spending to this necessity. Budget deficits can only be financed through financial markets, borrowing by the government will tend to raise interest rates and crowd out private investment. While this might work as long as government debt levels and interest rates are low, increases in both may endanger the sustainability of government finances, and eventually of the whole currency board arrangement. The case of Argentina proves to be a good point: While budget deficits had never been excessive, they eventually led to a build-up of government debt. As long as the economy was growing, this had not been a problem, but when the economy entered into a protracted recession in late-1998, government debt levels and the inability to reduce the budget deficit became a problem: interest rates on government debt rose, increasing

[22]Some currency boards are nevertheless allowed to do so. For example, the Argentinean currency board was allowed to hold up to 30% of its reserves in domestic dollar denominated government securities, and the Lithuanian currency board is also allowed to buy government securities on the secondary market. On first sight, this might not pose a threat to the currency board, as long as the government is in a position to serve its debt. But if the credit standing of the government is questionable and the value of government securities deteriorates, this might result in insufficient backing of the monetary base, which would in turn undermine the credibility of the currency board and increase the exchange rate risk.

the debt service and worsening budget deficits. This, in turn, raised interest rates further for fear of a government default. Argentina had been caught in a debt trap that eventually led to government default and the exit from the currency board.

2.3 Conclusion

A currency board can be a very effective monetary arrangement to stabilize an economy that suffers from high inflation, where confidence in the domestic currency has eroded, and government policies are not credible anymore. All five currency boards discussed in chapter 3 were introduced to achieve economic stabilization. Introducing a currency board does not require many skills nor many staff, increasing the attractiveness of currency boards further. Still, the following three general restrictions need to be considered before introduction of a currency board:

First, stabilization comes at a price and countries intending to introduce a currency board should be willing to adhere to the requirements necessary that facilitate the operation of the currency board. Fixing the nominal exchange rate implies that RER misalignments have to be adjusted by changes in domestic prices, wages, and incomes, as the nominal exchange rate loses its buffer function for real shocks. To facilitate such adjustment, goods and labor markets should be as flexible as possible, otherwise adjustment may be painfully long and have a deeper impact on incomes and employment.

Second, introducing a currency board implies largely giving up control over the domestic money supply. The resulting lack or limitation of LoLR capabilities therefore requires a sound banking system, achieved through strong and strict banking regulation and supervision, so that banks are in a position to weather through phases of tight liquidity on their own. Otherwise, banking crises may turn out to be worse, as even a modern currency board with some LoLR capabilities may be unable to restore trust in the banking sector.

Third, fiscal policy needs to be subordinated to the stabilization efforts of the currency board. Under a currency board, the budget deficit cannot be monetized through the central bank through direct lending to the government or by buying government securities. Instead, excess spending is limited to the ability to raise funds on financial markets. Therefore, government spending has to be curtailed and budget deficits need to be reduced. Otherwise, increasing levels of government debt tend to compromise the stability of the economy by raising interest rates and perhaps even putting the government in a debt trap that will ultimately lead to the abandonment of the currency board.

3

Evolution of Currency Boards

This chapter is intended to give a detailed overview over past and present currency boards. Section 3.1 examines the history of currency boards, how they evolved, and why they were instituted. It shows how the currency board system achieved worldwide presence between the first halves of the nineteenth and twentieth century, and how and why it almost disappeared afterwards.

Sections 3.2 to 3.5 examine in detail five modern present-day currency boards: Hong Kong, Argentina, Estonia, Lithuania, and Bulgaria. Each section describes the reasons for currency board introduction, inspects the design specifics of the particular currency board, and examines the economic performance under the currency board. The different design features of these five currency boards are then summarized in table 3.1, and, in more detail, in table B.1.

3.1 History of Currency Boards

To understand currency boards today it is helpful to know how and why they evolved and also, how they performed.[1] This section is subdivided into two parts: Subsection 3.1.1 gives a broad general overview of the history of currency boards and how the rationale for establishing them changed over time. Subsections 3.1.2 to 3.1.5 then examine in more detail different epochs of currency boards, starting with the intellectual foundations and followed by an examination of general features of currency boards at different times.[2]

[1]This section draws heavily on the works of Schuler (1992) and Schwartz (1993).

[2]For a very detailed and profound survey on the history of currency boards see Schuler (1992).

Additionally, an overview over all countries operating or participating in a currency board, with date of establishment, date of exit and anchor currency, can be found in appendix A.

3.1.1 General Overview

Currency boards came to life about 150 years ago. First existing only in small numbers, they gained broad popularity in the second decade of the 20th century, only to almost completely disappear forty years later. Recently, interest in currency boards has been revived, after first Argentina and then a couple of eastern-European states adopted currency boards; the first newly founded currency boards for almost 20 years.[3]

The rise and fall of the currency board system is depicted in figure 3.1, which charts the number of states and territories operating or participating in a currency board over time.[4] As can be seen, currency boards have been in existence for more than 150 years and have enjoyed wide popularity especially in the 1940s and 1950s, while rapidly declining in number thereafter.

The history of currency boards dates back to 1849 when the first currency board was established in Mauritius as a mean to guarantee a stable and secure supply of domestic money. Before, the British colony had relied on competitive note issue by commercial banks, but had experienced economic troubles as bank failures and inappropriate British banking regulation had repeatedly disrupted the domestic money supply. One possible solution, unrestricted money issue by the colonial government itself, had been considered undesirable as other British colonies had abused this monetary arrangement before. Therefore, the currency board had been devised as a simple and effective remedy to the problem.

Generally, two goals drove the institution of early currency boards, those founded before 1913: First, to guarantee states a stable supply of domestic money through monopoly note issue by a central authority while avoiding potential abuse of unrestricted note issue. Second, to tie colonial currencies to the currency of their colonial power in order to avoid exchange rate fluctu-

[3]Excluding Hong Kong's 1983 return to the currency board it had abandoned in 1974.

[4]Historic currency boards often supplied several member states with a common currency. Therefore, the number of states does not directly correspond to the number of currency boards in existence.

Further, states are recorded according to their historic borders. For example, British Somaliland and Italian Somaliland, at times members of different currency boards, at times members of the same currency board, are considered two sperate states, even though they are both part of present-day's Somalia.

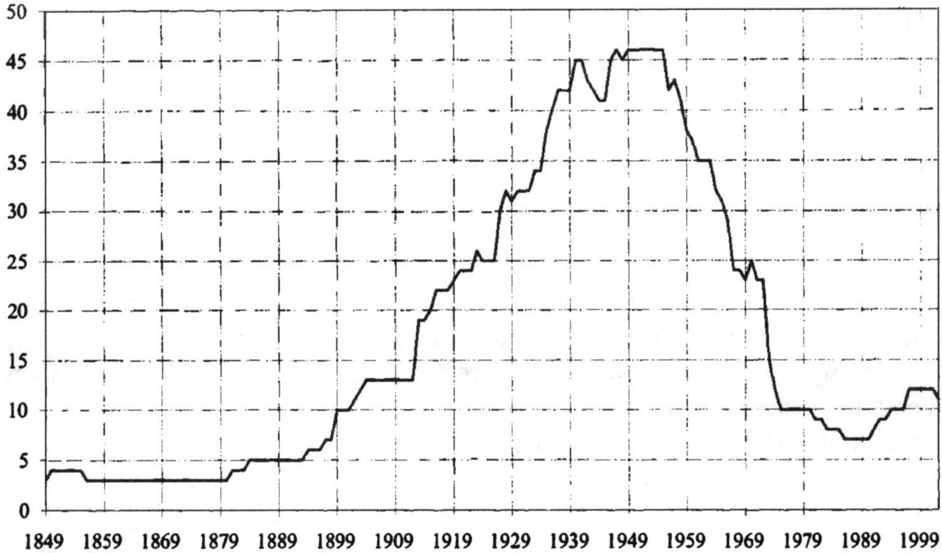

Sources: Schuler (1992, appendix), Gosh, Gulde, and Wolf (1998, p. 8), own calculation

Figure 3.1: Number of countries having or participating in a currency board in particular year.

ations as they often occurred among states on different exchange standards, such as the gold vs. the silver standard, respectively.

A new rationale for establishing a currency board was introduced in 1913, when the West African Currency Board was set up—according to Schuler (1992, p. 26), the "first modern orthodox currency board". One explicit objective of this board was to capture seigniorage from the currency circulating within its member states. Before, member states of the board had mainly used British silver coins as money, but when West-African colonies had demanded to participate in the earnings generated through seigniorage in Britain, the British government had refused to share its revenues. As a consequence, the West African Currency Board had been set up to bolster the participating colonies' budgets with their own income from seigniorage.

The success of the West African Currency Board in providing a stable exchange rate on the one hand and generating income from seigniorage on the other hand, made it an attractive monetary arrangement for other states and colonies worldwide. The administrative simplicity of the arrangement meant that even states with little administrative capabilities could implement it. Additionally, in 1930 the British Colonial Office drew up a model currency board statue based on the constitution of the West African currency board, making the institution of such a monetary arrangement even easier for British colonies.

Many states followed the West-African example, most of them British colonies. The spread of the currency board system reached its peak during the period from 1949–1955, when 46 countries participated in a currency board or even had their own.

The following twenty years witnessed the rapid decline of currency boards, reducing the number of countries with a currency board to 10 by 1975. The reasons for this decline are manifold, but two aspects seem to have been of special importance: After World War II, decolonization gave independence to an increasing number of colonies. Many of the newly independent states that had so far had a currency board, considered it a vestige of colonialism. A central bank, providing the ability to pursue an independent monetary policy and allowing greater ease of increasing government spending, was seen as an expression of national sovereignty (Schuler 1992, p. 60). Therefore, most currency boards were replaced by central banks shortly after independence. This general development was furthered by the prevailing trend in economics that favored central banks for independent states, considering them the more modern, flexible and advantageous arrangement. Also, various conferences of the League of Nations[5] had repeatedly issued statements that all developed countries should have central banks (Schwartz 1993, pp. 169–172).

Until 1974, currency boards had been a monetary arrangement mainly used in colonial states, as demonstrated by figure 3.2. Of the countries operating or participating in a currency board between 1849 and 1974 only 10 had been independent countries, while the vast majority had been British colonies. The reason for this has been pointed out before: Colonies could easily tie the value of their currencies to the currency of their colonial master—usually also their main trading partner—while at the same time enjoying many of the benefits of a domestic currency, such as the income from seigniorage. Also, many of the independent countries with a currency board were small states, often depending economically or politically on a greater power in their vicinity.

Within the group of colonial states with currency boards, the vast majority had been part of the British dominion, where currency boards had originated. All currency boards within the Italian and French domain and many independent ones had existed in states neighboring British colonies with currency boards or had been influenced by British currency board experiences. The early Argentine currency board (1902–1914, 1927–1927) seems to have

[5]Brussels 1920, Genoa 1922 and London, 1933.

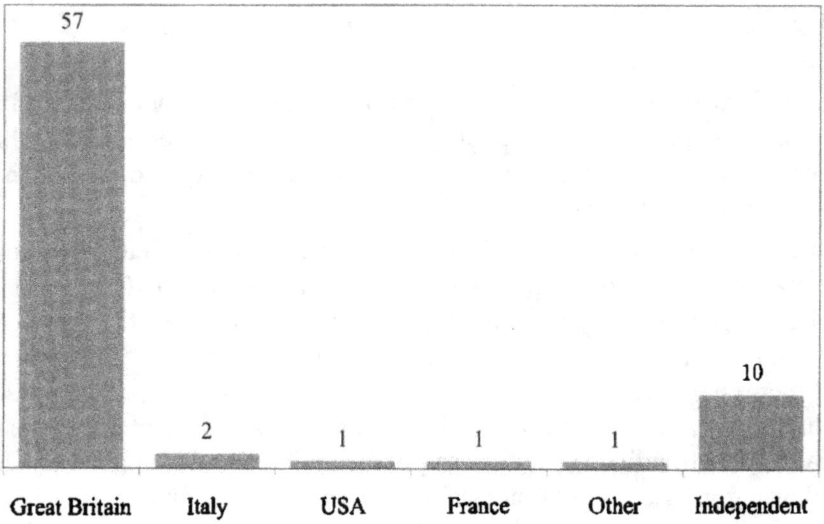

Sources: Schuler (1992, appendix), Gosh, Gulde, and Wolf (1998, p. 8), own calculation

Figure 3.2: Number of currency board-countries pertaining to realm of particular colonial power. 1849–1974.

been the only example of a currency board developing independently within an independent state.

There had also been a regional concentration of currency boards, as figure 3.3 demonstrates. Africa and Arabia had had the highest share of countries participating in a currency board, in absolute as well as relative terms. Also many island states in the Caribbean had had currency boards. All these regions were extensively colonized by Great Britain.

By 1975 the steep decline of the currency board system had reduced it to a monetary arrangement of marginal importance. The only states that had retained their currency boards were tiny states, most of them small island states, such as Gibraltar or the Falkland Islands.

Interest in currency boards revived in the late 1980s and early 1990s, when in 1983 Hong Kong re-instated the currency board it had abandoned in 1974, and when in 1991 Argentina set up a currency board to bring down hyperinflation. These two currency boards introduced a new rationale for installing a currency board: as a means of stabilizing an economy plagued with high inflation and/or intensive pressure on the external value of its currency. Their examples were soon followed by four East-European countries, which, besides facing a troubled economy, also lacked experience in central banking and monetary policy due to their socialist past: Estonia (1992),

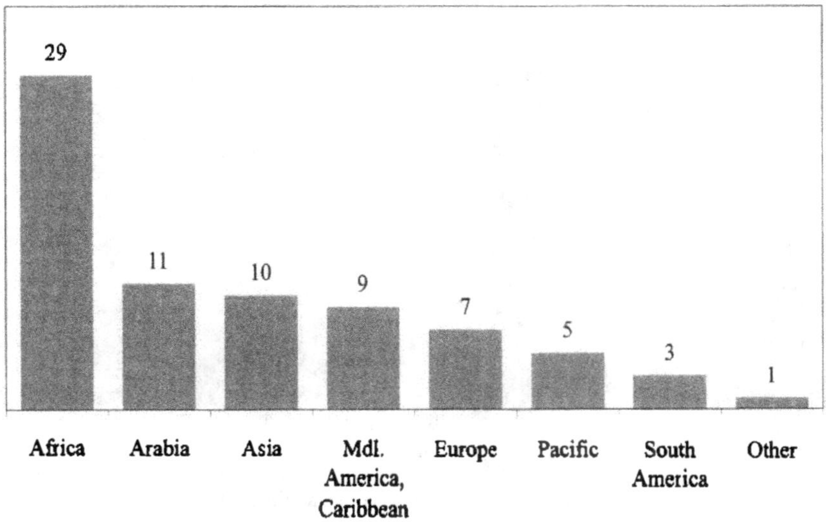

Sources: Schuler (1992, appendix), Gosh, Gulde, and Wolf (1998, p. 8), own calculation

Figure 3.3: Location of currency boards. 1849–2001.

Lithuania (1994), Bulgaria (1997) and Bosnia (1997). Most of these recent currency boards will be described in more detail in the following sections of this chapter.

Another aspect of the history of currency boards is revealed, when examining the choice of anchor currencies at different times, as shown in figure 3.4. As might have been guessed from the preceding paragraphs, the British pound sterling was the main anchor currency until the mid-1960s, as the majority of countries with a currency board then were within the British dominion. Other currencies, such as the US dollar, the New Zealand pound or gold played only minor roles.

Today's picture is quite different. The British pound has completely lost its predominance[6], while newly-founded currency boards have either selected the US dollar or the Deutsche mark / euro, as their anchor currencies, the main currencies in international trade.[7]

In summary, it has become clear that at different times there have been very different rationales for introducing a currency board. These often reflected the economic necessities of the time or of the country concerned. As the currency board system evolved and thrived almost exclusively within the

[6] Only Gibraltar and the Falkland Island still use the British pound as reserve currency.

[7] Note that the exit from the Argentinean currency board early 2002, as well as Lithuania's switch from the dollar to the euro in 2002 are not reflected in the figure.

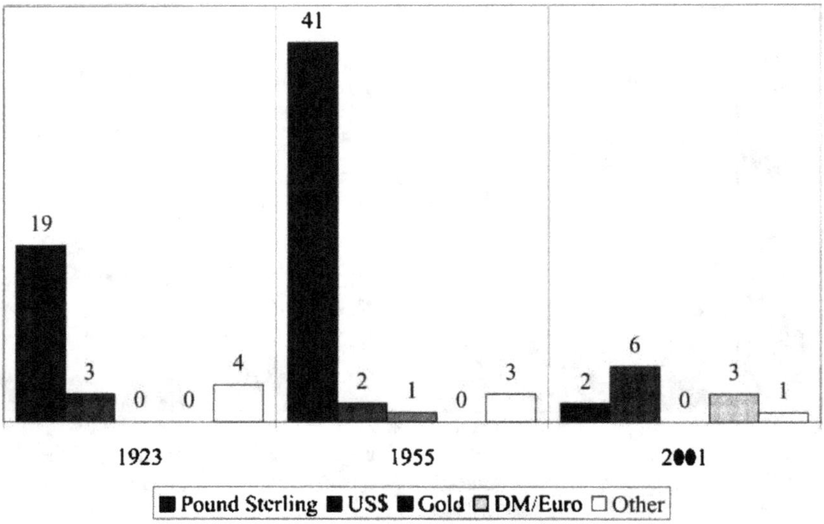

Sources: Schuler (1992, appendix), Gosh, Gulde, and Wolf (1998, p. 8), own calculation

Figure 3.4: Number of currency board countries with particular anchor currency, 1923, 1955, 2001.

British dominion, design features of orthodox currency boards often reflect economic thought and needs within the British Empire at that time. As a consequence, the decline of the Empire led to the simultaneous decline of the currency board system. Only recently have currency boards been rediscovered as a means of monetary stabilization.

While this subsection intended to give a broad overview over the development of currency boards and their features over time, the following subsections will describe in more detail how currency boards evolved. At first, the intellectual underpinning of currency boards will be illustrated, followed by a review of different currency board-periods.

3.1.2 Foundations

The intellectual foundations for currency boards were laid in Great Britain. In 1844 the Bank Charter Act, known as Peel's Act, after the Prime Minister who got it enacted, monopolized note issue, giving the Bank of England the sole right to issue bank notes. Before, there had been competitive note issue by privately owned banks: banks had issued their own bank notes, which were convertible into a fixed amount of gold. But repeated suspension of convertibility, depreciation of notes and financial crises had led to a questioning of the established system of notes issue and finally to a replacement thereof through the Bank Charter Act (Schwartz 1993, p. 158).

The prevailing intellectual sentiment of that time can be summarized by a statement of Jevons(1889, pp. 341–342, cited from Schuler 1992, p. 16):

> "[..] Each kingdom should have one uniform paper circulation, issued from a single state department, more resembling a mint than a bank [..] the paper circulation should be made to increase and diminish with the amount of gold deposited in exchange for it. At the same time, no thought need be given about the amount so issued. The purpose [..] is not to govern the amount, but to leave that amount to vary according to the natural law of supply and demand."

The Bank Charter Act split the Bank of England into an Issue and a Banking Department. The Issue Department was responsible for note issue only. Note issue beyond the hard core of circulation[8] had to be backed 100 percent by silver and gold reserves. The Banking Department was to handle all other operations of the Bank of England.[9]

Despite the 100 percent marginal backing rule of the Issue Department, the Bank of England did not constitute a currency board, since the Banking Department faced no reserve requirements for the deposits it accepted and was not an independent institution. From the standpoint of other banks notes and deposits were essentially equivalent, and the Bank of England as a whole was able to sterilize capital flows in and out of the banking system (Schuler 1992, p. 15). Nevertheless, the establishment of monopoly note issue in Great Britain was an essential precondition for the spread of currency boards, especially in British colonies.

3.1.3 The First Currency Boards (1849–1912)

During the beginning and middle of the nineteenth century, most non-self governing British colonies had, as Great Britain at that time, competitive

[8]The hard core of circulation is the expected amount of notes which will never be redeemed, as it is necessary for the functioning of the economy.

[9]In this respect to the backing requirement the Bank of England was somewhat similar to a currency board. For example, the Hong Kong Monetary Authority is also required to keep 100 percent reserves against bank notes in circulation, while neither a fixed exchange rate nor a convertibility undertaking are required by law. Nevertheless, the HKMA is de facto adhering to currency board rules. Note also that Estonia and Bulgaria have copied this institutional setup of the Bank of England. Their central banks are divided into an Issue Department, which operates the currency board, and a Banking Department, which may engage in monetary policy as excess reserves of the currency board allow.

note issue by private banks. There had been a number of colonies with unrestricted note issue by colonial governments in the eighteenth and at the beginning of the nineteenth century, but as these notes had often been used to finance government debt and had in some cases been depreciated, the British government had decided to suppress note issue by colonial governments.

Competitive note issue prevented such abuse but caused other problems. British banking regulation at that time required imperial and locally chartered banks wanting to issue notes in British colonies to limit their overall note issue to the paid-in capital of the bank. This limitation in turn led to artificial note shortage in some colonies. Further, repeated bank failures in colonies or Great Britain at times led to disruption of note issue and losses for note holders.

It was in response to such a failure of a commercial bank, that the first currency board was established in 1849 in *Mauritius*, a non-self governing British colony.[10] A currency board was deemed an appropriate instrument to overcome the problems caused by colonial note issue, while at the same time, by being extremely restrictive in design, avoiding the dangers of unrestricted note issue by colonial governments.

The Mauritius currency board adhered to the silver standard. It issued 5 and 10 rupee notes redeemable on demand in Indian silver rupee coins.[11] Notes issued had to be fully backed by the currency board reserves, of which at least 1/3, ideally 1/2 had to be in coins. The rest of the reserves was to be invested in interest earning securities. Initially, only local securities were held but over time an increasing share of reserves was invested in British securities. In 1864 the colonial government officially limited the share of local securities to at most 50 percent of total securities (Schuler 1992, p. 20). The transactions of the board were carried out by a commercial bank in Port Louis, the capital.

In 1865 the currency board set up a depreciation fund to provide protection against a drop in value of the securities held by the board. Every year one percent of circulation was to be set aside from the profits of the board

[10] According to Randall (2003, p. 2) British colonies could be subdivided into those possessing responsible government and those not possessing responsible government. In self governing colonies—including for example Canada, South Africa, New Zealand, and Australia—the crown only reserved the power of disallowing legislation and the Secretary of State for the Colonies had no control over any public officer except the Governor. In all matters affecting the internal affairs of such a colony the governor acted on the advice of ministers who were responsible to the legislature. In contrast to that, in non-self governing colonies the administration was carried out by public officers under the control of the Secretary of State for the Colonies.

[11] The Indian silver rupee was widespread means of payment in the territories bordering the Indian Ocean.

until an adequate amount, supposedly 10 percent, was reached (Schwartz 1993, pp. 152–153).

Since Mauritius was on the silver standard, while Great Britain was on the gold standard, fluctuations in the price of silver relative to the price of gold repeatedly troubled the Mauritius currency board in the period from the 1860s up to the 1930s. As a consequence, the currency board eventually switched to the sterling exchange standard in 1934, fixing its currency directly to the pound sterling. Additionally, the board changed the composition of its reserves, excluding local securities from its reserves and holding sterling securities exclusively.

The Mauritius currency board operated until 1967, when the country, shortly after gaining independence, replaced it by a central bank.

While the Mauritius currency board was a pragmatic response to a disruption in the supply of bank notes, the establishment of the *New Zealand* currency board in 1850 was prompted by the influence of the intellectual debates in Great Britain that favored the monopoly of note issue and led to the passing of the Bank Charter Act. The currency board was short lived, though. After becoming a self governed colony in 1856, and driven by distrust in government notes issue due to bad experiences before the CBs operations, the board was dissolved and replaced by competitive note issue, which was in turn replaced by a central bank in 1934.

The period from 1849 to 1912 witnessed the establishment of about a dozen currency boards, all of them in British colonies, except for the boards in Argentina, the Philippines, and Panama.

The Philippines established what might be called a currency board in 1903. The territory had fallen to the United States of America in 1898, which were on the gold standard then, while the Philippines were on the silver standard. As the US suddenly became the Philippines main partner in trade and investment, fluctuations in the price of silver resulted in large variations in the terms of trade for the Philippines. To prevent these fluctuations, the US decided to establish a gold-exchange standard for the Philippines. Actual peso coins were still to consist of silver but law provided that they were redeemable into gold worth $0.50. To secure convertibility, the Gold Standard Fund was set up to hold in gold and US Dollars at least 15 percent of the face value of all silver peso coins in circulation—a rough approximation of the difference between the rate of exchange into gold and the actual metal value of peso coins.(Schwartz 1993, pp. 164–165).

The Philippine currency board did not exactly constitute a currency board. As domestic coins were made of silver but redeemable into gold, the reserves of the Gold Standard Fund, depending on the price of silver, covered at times more and at times less than the difference between the exchange rate and the metal value of coins. The general operating principle, though, was currency board like.

As in the case of Mauritius, the hybrid status of the currency board eventually caused troubles. Fluctuations in the relative price of silver led to hoarding and a shortage of peso coins. Additionally, mismanagement of reserves, including a provision that allowed holding domestic bonds, led to the eventual breakdown of the currency board and an ensuing currency crisis and deflation from 1919 to 1922.

In 1923 the currency board arrangement was reinstalled, returning to the the original framework set forth in 1903. The government borrowed funds to reconstitute the Gold Standard Fund. The Philippine currency board continued its operations until 1948—with a short interruption during Japanese occupation from 1942 to 1945—and was then replaced by a central bank (Schwartz 1993, p. 166).

Prior to its 1991–2002 currency board, *Argentina* had also had two previous currency board stints. In 1899 the pre-existing Caja de Conversión, which had been intended to maintain the value of the peso after a government debt default, but had nevertheless mainly served as an institution for issue of fiat money, was ordered to back any additional issue of domestic currency by an equal worth of gold. Obviously, such an arrangement did not represent an ideal currency board, since the majority of the monetary base remained unbacked. But at least on the margin it operated like one. Over time, increasing prosperity led to a rise in demand for notes and gold reserves grew from 0.11 percent of notes in circulation in 1902 to almost 73 percent in 1913. With the outbreak of World War I Argentina suspended the Gold standard for fear of large outflows of gold out of the country and ensuing deflation, and prohibited the export of gold. This effectively ended the currency board system. In response to wide swings in the exchange rate of the peso vs the US Dollar Argentina reinstated the gold standard and the currency board in 1927. The revival was short-lived, though. Rising interest rates in the United States led to significant capital outflows, which amounted to 40 percent of combined reserves of the Caja and banks within 18 months. The gold standard was once again suspended, as it appears, once again for the fear of deflation, at the end of 1929 (Schuler 1992, p. 36). In 1935 Argentina established a central bank to replace the Caja.

3.1.4 The West African Currency Board (1913)

The West African Currency Board is considered to have been the first modern orthodox currency board. It had a significant impact on the design of many later currency boards , especially in British colonial territories, as the model currency board statute devised by the British Colonial Office in 1930 was based on the statute of the West African Currency Board (Schwartz 1993, p. 159).

The main reason to introduce a currency board for the West African colonies of the British Empire was the colonies desire to capture seigniorage revenues for their budgets from the currency circulating in their domain while at the same time avoiding the danger of a depreciation of their domestic currency against the pound sterling.[12]

Before the CB was introduced, use of British silver coins was widespread in the colonies, as the £1 gold coins and bank notes were too high in value to be useful for transactions and furthermore bank notes were too perishable for the climate. Falling silver prices had increased the seigniorage from minting silver coins, which amounted to 165% gross seigniorage in 1912, but the imperial government refused to share the revenue from coins circulating in the West African colonies.

Therefore, the West African Currency Board was set up in 1913, issuing the West African pound (WA£) as currency, which was fixed to the pound sterling at a rate of one to one. At first, the board issued only silver coins, but in 1916 started issuing bank notes as well, which did not become legal tender until 1919, however.

The CB had its headquarters in London, where it held its reserves, and had its coins and bank notes produced. Instead of setting up offices, it used the Bank of British West Africa and the London Joint Stock Bank as its agents. In principle, business with the CB was open to the public, but practically the high minimum amount required for exchange meant that the board was only dealing with banks.[13] For exchanges the board demanded a commission varying between 1/2% and 1-1/2% to cover its expenses.

From the beginning on the boards reserves were close to, but not quite 100% of the currency in circulation.[14] The reserves first exceeded 100% in 1926. Gold and securities were held as reserves, most of the securities issued or guaranteed by the British government and municipalities, and none of them issued locally. Further, to guard itself against losses in the value of its securities, the board accumulated an extra 10% of reserves.

[12]Initially, the currency board provided a common currency for today's Gambia, Ghana, Sierra Leone and Nigeria. After World War I today's Togo and the western part of Cameroon (then British Cameroon) joined the West African currency board.

[13]The initial minimum accepted for exchange was WA£100, later it was raised to WA£10000.

[14]Against silver coins the board held only reserves equivalent to the difference between the nominal and the metal value of these coins. In 1920 a rise in the price of silver led the colonies to start replacing silver coins by token coins, selling the silver at a profit.

The operating costs of the West African Currency Board were around WA£4000 per year. It started distributing seigniorage to its member countries in 1920 and the overall seigniorage generated during its years of operation amounts to around WA£37 million (Schuler 1992, p. 29).

The circulation of the WA£ varied according to economic activity in the region. While in 1920 there were WA£13.59 million in circulation, a depression reduced circulation to WA£7.27 two years later. In 1957 circulation of notes and coins reached its peak at more than WA£125 million. After that circulation constantly declined, as more and more member countries of the board became independent and founded their own central banks, issuing their own domestic currency.

Even though the West African Currency Board is often referred to as the first modern orthodox currency board, and even though its design largely reflects the definition of subsection 2.1.1, it lacked one central feature considered important for today's currency boards: a clear, outspoken legal commitment to the currency board principles. The West African Currency Board statute, and therefore the statutes of all other CBs based on it, did neither set exact reserve requirements nor restrict the types of assets that could be held as securities. It merely required reserves to be "more than sufficient to secure the convertibility of the note and coin issue, and to provide a reasonable reserve against possible depreciation" (de Loynes 1962, pp. 42-43, cited from Schuler 1992, p. 50) and securities to be from any government within the British Empire or otherwise to be approved of by the British Secretary of State for the Colonies. The strict adherence of the West African Currency Board to currency board rules was instead enforced by administrative regulation, which until 1955 e.g. required British currency boards to invest at least 70 percent of reserves into British national and municipal securities and up to 30 percent into colonial securities except for domestic ones. Only after that were CBs allowed to invest in domestic securities, but the West African Currency Board did barely take advantage of this allowance.

Practically, the West African Currency Board ceased its operation in 1971, after the last member country had achieved independence from Great Britain and established a central bank. The last seven years of its existence the board had been operating as the Gambia Currency Board for the only remaining member country. Still, despite not issuing West African pounds anymore, the board continued to redeem notes and coins until 1973.

3.1.5 The Peak and Decline of the Currency Board System (1913–1974)

The West African Currency Board provided a well-functioning example of a stable and reliable currency arrangement for other colonies within the British dominion, and inspired the founding of similar arrangements based upon it in many British colonies. As these currency boards were basically based on the West African Currency Board in design and operation, only a few of them will be described in brief in this section. There also existed some, though not many, later non-British currency boards after 1913.

The *East African Currency Board* was founded in 1919 to stop ongoing fluctuations in the exchange rate between the pound sterling and the Indian silver rupee, the currency mainly used for transactions in the British East African colonies. It's currency, the East African pound (EA£), was tied at a one to one rate to the pound sterling and during the first years the board exchanged Indian silver rupees and German silver coins according to their metal value for the new currency. The East African CB was explicitly modelled after the West African Currency Board and even shared directors with it (Schuler 1992, p. 30). It was initially founded to provide the EA£ for the colonies of Kenya and Uganda, but there was a steady flow of countries joining and exiting it.[15] The currency board existed until 1965, when the last remaining member countries achieved independence and founded their own central banks.

The East African Currency Board's experience and performance were very different from the West African. A rapid decline in the price of silver, composing a large share of reserves, inflicted a significant loss on the board's reserves. Reserves were further reduced during the depression year 1932 and reached a low of 9.9 percent. Only in 1950 did reserves reach 100 percent, and the board paid seigniorage to its member countries for the first time (Schuler 1992, p. 31). Additionally, the currency board took full advantage of the option to hold domestic assets. In 1965, 28.2 percent of its reserves were invested in local, partly short-term assets. Further, the board had moved its headquarters from London to Nairobi, established a clearing system, and had finally even signalled its intent to act as a lender of last resort.

The third currency board in Africa was the *Southern Rhodesia Currency Board*, which was later renamed to *Central African Currency Board*. It

[15] Joining: Tanganyika, part of today's Tanzania, 1920, Zanzibar, 1936, Italian Somaliland, British Somaliland, Eritrea, Ethiopia and Aden during WW II. Leaving: Ethopia, 1945, Italian Somaliland, 1950, British Somaliland, 1960, Aden 1964.

served the colonies of Southern and Northern Rhodesia and Nyasaland.[16] and operated from 1939–1956, when it was replaced by a central bank.

Besides Africa, the Middle East was the second region with a high share of British currency boards. The *Palestine Currency Board*, established in 1927, provided the Palestine pound, which was fixed to the pound sterling, as a currency for Palestine and Transjordan.[17] It operated until 1948 in Israel, until 1951 in the Gaza Strip and until 1964 in Jordan. The *Iraq Currency Board*, set up as a transitional institution, operated from 1931 till 1949, when a central bank replaced it. Other boards in the region were located in *Kuwait*, 1961–1969, *Yemen Arab Republic*, 1964–1971, *Aden*, 1965–1972, *Bahrain*, 1965–1973, *Quatar/Dubai*, 1966–1973 and *Oman*, 1970–1974.

Another two major British currency boards were located in Asia. The *Burma Currency Board* was established in 1947. It issued the Burmese rupee, fixed to the pound sterling. In 1952, a central bank replaced the board. It is worth noticing that during this period the Burmese board managed to maintain its fixed exchange rate vis a vis the pound sterling despite an ongoing civil war.

The second major British currency board in Asia was that of *Hong Kong*. It operated from 1935–1974, with a three years intermission during Japanese occupancy in World War II. Hong Kong reintroduced a currency board in 1983, which is still in operation today and will be discussed in more detail in section 3.2.

From 1913 to 1974 there have also been some currency boards not under British governance. Still, many of these have at least been influenced by currency boards examples and experiences in British colonies. Africa witnessed the existence of some non-British boards, like the CB in *Italian Somaliland*[18], which was set up under Italian rule in 1950, after the country had given up its membership in the East African Currency Board. The board was replaced by a central bank in 1960. *Sudan* and *Libya* had a similar history of currency boards, operating from 1956–1960 and 1951–1955, respectively.

In general, many currency boards established during the 1950s and 1960s had been intended as intermediate institutions only, preparing newly independent nations, with a lack of expertise and qualified personnel in the field of monetary policy, for the introduction of a central bank, while already allowing for issue of a national currency, thanks to the simplicity of operating a currency board. For example, a 1952 IMF report clearly stated that the Libyan currency board would serve as a good way-point in establishing a

[16] Today's Zimbabwe, Zambia and Malawi, respectively.

[17] Present-day Israel and Jordan.

[18] The southern part of today's Somalia.

central bank, since, initially, given the economic and administrative conditions in Libya at that time, a central bank would offer no advantage over a currency board while at the same time carrying more risk (Blowers and McLeod 1952, pp. 447–448).

Three other historic currency boards have been located in Europe or its vicinity; North Russia 1918–1919, Danzig 1923–1924, and Ireland 1927–1943. The *North Russian* currency board deserves to be mentioned, as it apparently provides the only example of a currency board becoming insolvent. The board, whose details had been thought up by John Maynard Keynes, had been set up by the World War I Allies to provide a reliable currency for their forces deployed in North Russia, in order to support the White, anti-Bolshevik forces in the Russian civil war (Williamson 1995, p. 6). The board was held its (sterling) reserves in London. It stopped operating when the allied forces decided to withdraw in fall 1919. Soon thereafter, the North Russian government collapsed, rendering the boards 25 percent of reserves consisting of North Russian government bonds worthless, thus inflicting a loss on local note holders that had not managed to redeem their notes in time, and on the British government that had purchased the major share of North Russian rubles (Schuler 1992, pp. 87–88).

3.2 Hong Kong (1983)

Of the present-day currency boards discussed in this chapter, Hong Kong's has the longest history. The monetary system of Hong Kong has undergone remarkable changes in the last seventy years, during which Honk Kong had three currency board periods, one period of free floating, and one silver standard period (Kwan and Lui 1999, p. 406). Today's currency board possesses and exercises extensive monetary policy discretion, which make it an unusual example of a currency board. Yet, extensive foreign exchange reserves allow for such discretion without violating the backing requirements of a currency board.

3.2.1 Lead-Up to the Currency Board

Before the first institution of a currency board in 1935, Hong Kong was on the silver standard. In that year China nationalized all holdings of silver, which lead to a hoarding of silver by the public in Hong Kong. To avoid a shortage of silver, Hong Kong declared Hong Kong dollar (HK$) bank notes to be legal tender and nationalized all private holding of silver, as well, which were turned over to an Exchange Fund as backing for bank and government notes.

In exchange for their silver, three note-issuing banks—no other banks had the right to issue—received noninterest-bearing Certificates of Indebtedness (CI). To issue more notes, the banks had to buy more CIs (Schuler 1992, pp. 62–63; Schwartz 1993, p. 173).

The arrangement said nothing about a currency board system. No fixed exchange rate was specified, nor was a reserve requirement for the Exchange Fund set. The fund had no legal obligation to repurchase CIs. It was authorized to invest the silver reserves and future earning in any currency, gold, silver, or approved securities. The exchange rate initially ranged from HK$15.36 to HK$16.45 per UK£. Yet, in practice, Hong Kong settled into a currency board system. The Exchange Fund kept almost all reserves, which were from the start above 100 percent of the monetary base, in sterling securities or bank deposits. In 1939 the fund officially established the exchange rate link with the pound sterling, by offering to buy or sell unlimited amounts of CIs at HK$ 16.20 and HK$ 16.00 per UK£, respectively (Schuler 1992, pp. 63–64; Schwartz 1993, p. 173).

Unique to Hong Kong's currency board was the fact that notes were not issued by the currency board but by the three banks that had the right of issue.[19] Other banks could purchase bank notes at a spread around the Exchange Fund's rates.

The currency board's operation was halted from December 1941 to August 1945, under Japanese occupation. The Japanese spent unissued notes in bank vaults, amounting to almost 50 percent of currency circulation, but did not get a hold on the Exchange Fund's assets, which were held in London. The illegally spent notes, called duress notes, were honored at face value in 1946, when the currency resumed operation, as were limited amounts of the military yen the Japanese had issued (Schuler 1992, pp. 64–65; Schwartz 1993, p. 174).

The HK$ remained fixed vis a vis the pound sterling. Following a devaluation of the pound in 1967, the currency board revalued the HK$ against the pound to compensate to some extent for the devaluation against the US dollar. When Britain, in 1972, floated the pound sterling against the US$, Hong Kong uncoupled the Hong Kong dollar from the pound and fixed it to the dollar instead, at a central rate of HK$ 5.65 = US$ 1 and within a band of 2.25 percent of either side of the central rate. The Exchange Fund had already in 1971 begun to shift its assets from sterling to dollar securities, but still incurred a substantial loss from the sterling's float against the dollar, as it still held substantial sterling assets (Schuler 1992, p. 65).

[19]The Hongkong and Shanghai Banking Corporation (HSBC), the Chartered Bank of India, Australia, and China, and the Mercantile Bank of India, Australia and China.

With the switch of the anchor currency the fund also allowed banks to purchase CIs with Honk Kong dollars, instead of US dollars, as should be the case under a currency board.

A depreciation of the US dollar in 1973 was offset by revaluing the HK$, and speculation against the US dollar led to capital inflows into Hong Kong, inflating the monetary base. Eventually, in order to preserve price stability, the HK$ was floated against the US dollar in 1974.

The Hong Kong dollar floated for nine years. The economy performed well during the early part of this period: it recovered speedily from the oil crisis, achieving growth rates of over 10% coupled with moderate inflation of 4–6%. In the late 1970s signs of overheating became apparent, though, fuelled by public construction projects and a booming property market: growth of broad money supply and domestic loans reached 35–43%, inflation surged to over 15%, and the exchange rate depreciated quickly, as shown by figure 3.5 (Chiu 2001, p. 2; HKMA 2000a, pp. 28–29).

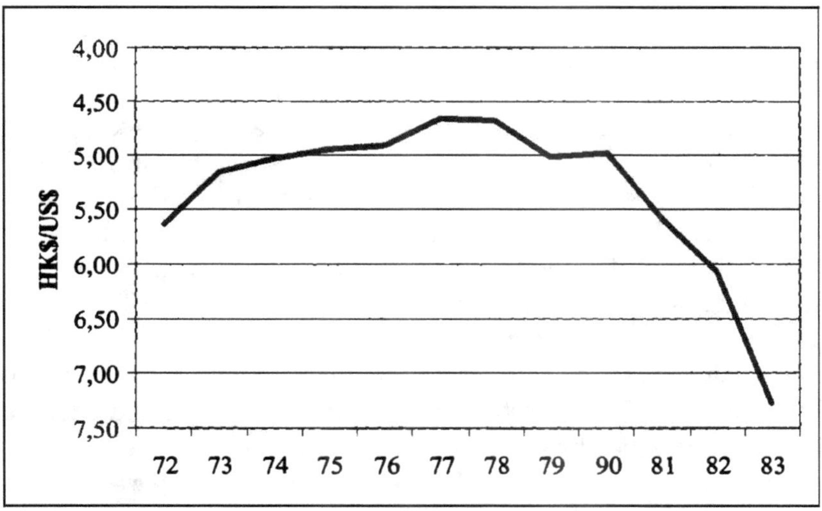

Source: IMF (2002c)

Figure 3.5: Exchange rate HK$ per US$, 1972–1983.

Part of this downturn was due to the lack of a monetary anchor, an ill-defined objective of monetary policy and the lack of monetary instruments to implement monetary policy. CIs could still be purchased with Hong Kong dollars. The receipts of these purchases were transferred to accounts the Exchange Fund held with the note-issuing banks. Effectively, the purchase of CIs with HK$ only led to an accounting transfer within the banks; the banks lost no reserves. Even though the Exchange Fund required the banks to keep 100-percent liquid-asset cover against the funds short-term deposits, this requirement did not limit the creation of Hong Kong dollar credit, as the banks could borrow foreign currency to obtain liquid assets (Chiu 2001, p. 3; Schwartz 1993, pp. 174–175).

The situation escalated when British-Chinese talks on the future of Hong Kong began in 1982. The uncertainties surrounding Hong Kong's political transition led to the burst of the stock market and property bubble, and runs on small banks engaged in the property market. The HK$ fell to a low of HK$ 9.55 per US$ on September 24, 1983. On the following day the government proclaimed in a stopgap announcement the intention to re-introduce a currency board. On October 15 the government fixed the exchange rate at HK$ 7.80 = US$ 1. The Exchange Fund was required to hold dollar reserves equal to 105% of base money, and CIs were to be obtained only in exchange for US$. Yet, still only the note-issuing banks could acquire US$ at the official rate. (Chiu 2001, pp. 3–4; Schuler 1992, p. 67; HKMA 2000b, p. 8; Walters 1993, p. 5).

3.2.2 Currency Board Design

Today's Hong Kong currency board is maintained and operated by the Hong Kong Monetary Authority (HKMA), which was established in 1993 by merging the Office of the Exchange Fund with the Office of the Commissioner of Banking (HKMA 1999b, p. 1). The currency board has inherited many peculiarities from past Hong Kong monetary arrangements, but has also undergone comprehensive reform since its establishment in 1983.

The reserves of the currency board are held and managed by the Exchange Fund. Yet, the assets of the fund not only comprise of the currency board reserves, but in 1976 the assets of the Coinage Security Fund (holding the backing for coins issued by the government) and the bulk of foreign currency assets held in the Government's General Revenue Account were transferred to the fund. Additionally, from 1976 onwards, the government began to transfer its fiscal reserves to the fund. In 1998 the assets of the Land Fund were merged with the Exchange Fund (HKMA 1999a, pp. 1–2). By law, the Exchange Fund is under control of the financial secretary, in consultation with the Exchange Fund Advisory Committee. The fund's assets may be invested in gold, silver, HK$, foreign exchange, and any securities and assets considered appropriate. The assets of the funds shall be used for purposes directly or indirectly affecting the exchange value of the currency, and to maintain the stability and integrity of the monetary and financial systems of Hong Kong with a view to maintaining Hong Kong as an international financial center (Government of Hong Kong 1997, section 3).

In practice, though, the fund is managed by the HKMA. It's assets are split into two separate portfolios: a backing portfolio, holding short-term, highly liquid US$ denominated securities to fully back the monetary base, and an investment portfolio engaging in longer-term investments to preserve the fund's value. In 1999 the Exchange Fund adopted a new investment benchmark stating that 80% of the fund's assets shall be held in bonds and 20% in equities, with a currency composition of 80% US$, 15% European currencies and 5% yen. Resulting from stock market intervention in 1998 to fend off speculative pressure, the fund also holds a substantial portfolio of Hong Kong equities, which are managed by a separate entity as a long-term investment portfolio (HKMA 1999a, pp. 1–2; HKMA 1999c, p. 2). At the end of July 2002 the fund's total assets at US$ 110 billion covered roughly 3.6 times the monetary base and 7.4 times notes and coins in circulation (HKMA 2002, tables 7.2 and 7.3).

Currency notes are not issued by the HKMA itself, but still by three commercial banks.[20] To issue notes the banks have to hold an equivalent amount of CIs, which can be sold and bought from the HKMA at the fixed rate of HK$ 7.80 to US$ 1. Consequently, the convertibility undertaking applies to CIs but not to bank notes. No convertibility is guaranteed for the other component of the monetary base, the aggregate balance, i.e. the sum of the balances in the clearing accounts maintained by the banks with the HKMA for settling interbank payments and payments between banks and the HKMA (Yam 1998, pp. 78–79).

A holder of bank notes is not able to exchange these at the fixed exchange rate. Instead, the level of the exchange rate in the foreign exchange market is determined by market forces. Initially, there was a general belief that the possibility of banknote arbitrage alone would keep the exchange rate very close to HK$ 7.80, but the arbitrage mechanism was eventually considered to not work effectively, prompting reforms to enhance the monetary policy options of the then Exchange Fund (Chiu 2001, pp. 5–6). Regardless, exchange rate volatility has been very moderate, as figure 3.6 reveals.

Quasi-dollarization, often a by-product of having a currency board, is high in Hong Kong, yet not officially encouraged. Half of the money supply in Hong Kong is in foreign currencies and much of its external trade is settled in US dollars. (Tsang and Ma 2002, p. 56; Xu 1998).

The Hong Kong currency board, after several reforms, has extensive rights and instruments to exercise discretionary monetary policy. For example, in 1988 it acquired power to conduct open-market operations, in 1990 it

[20]The Hongkong and Shanghai Banking Corporation Limited (HSBC), Standard Chartered Bank, and the Bank of China (Government of Hong Kong 2001, Schedule).

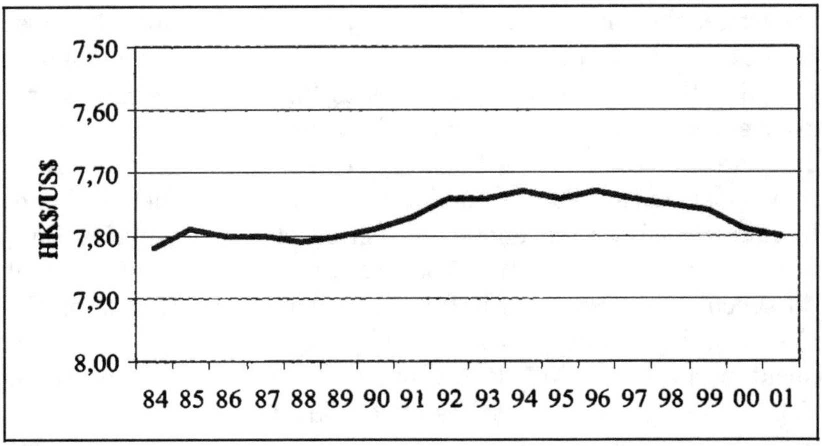

Source: IMF (2002c)

Figure 3.6: Exchange rate HK$ per US$, 1984–2001.

started to issue three-month treasury bills, and in 1992 it opened up a limited discount window. With ample excess reserves at its hands, the HKMA may in many respects act like a normal central bank, without having adopted the status of one (Schwartz 1993, p. 176).

Also, over time, design flaws of the system were eliminated and the HKMA increased it's active role in monetary policy.

Until 1996 interbank clearing and settlement was arranged through a private bank, HSBC. Consequently, an important component of the monetary base, the aggregate balance, was not on the currency board's balance sheet, and could not be subjected to the discipline of a currency board. There was, therefore, a risk that market operations, such as a sale of dollars by the fund to support the exchange rate, could be undermined by increased lending of HSBC to other banks. In 1988 the Exchange Fund put a cap on interbank liquidity HSCB could create by requiring the bank to hold an account with the fund, and devising an incentive system for the bank to manage net clearing balances at a level not exceeding the balance in this account, which was determined by the government. In 1996, on the occasion of the introduction of the real time gross settlement system, HSBC was stripped of it's role as clearing institution and instead each bank had to directly keep a clearing account with the HKMA. After this, the currency board adhered largley, but with exceptions, to the monetary rule in respect of the aggregate balance (Chiu 2001, pp. 5–7; Yam 1998, p. 27).

To cushion occasional liquidity shocks that might result from tighter control over interbank liquidity, the Exchange Fund introduced the Liquidity

Adjustment Facility (LAF) in 1992. Banks short of Hong Kong dollar liquidity could use Exchange Fund paper and other eligible debt instruments as repo securities to obtain overnight funds at the LAF offer rate. Banks with surplus liquidity could deposit it at the LAF bid rate. While the LAF was intended for limited and very restrictive provision of liquidity to ensure the smooth functioning of the interbank payment system, the repeated speculation[21] against the currency board in the aftermath of the Asian crisis 1997, during which lack of liquidity led to overnight interest rates of over 300% at one time, eventually led to the introduction of a fully-fledged discount window in September 1998. The discount rate is set with reference to a pre-announced formula that is based on the US Fed funds target rate and Hong Kong dollar interbank interest rates (Chiu 2001, pp. 7–13; Yam 1998, pp. 36–37).

At the same time the HKMA introduced a discretionary one-way convertibility undertaking to all licensed banks. The HKMA may, whenever deemed necessary, trigger convertibility for domestic currency at or near the fixed exchange rate. Once convertibility has been triggered, the HKMA takes a passive stance, taking in whatever amounts of HK$ banks want to exchange. Initially, after the attacks on the currency board, this rate was 7.75. A 500-day transition period took place between April 1999 and August 2000 when the rate was moved by one pip per day to converge to the linked rate of 7.80 (Chiu 2001, pp. 11-12; Yam 1998, p. 28).

Even though the HKMA's commitment to the currency board is great, the legal foundations of the currency board are weak. The HKMA's main functions and responsibilities are set forth by the Exchange Fund Ordinance (Government of Hong Kong 1997), governing the operations of the Exchange Fund, and the Banking Ordinance (Government of Hong Kong 2002), governing banking supervision and regulation. The Exchange Fund Ordinance states that the main purpose of the Exchange Fund is to control the exchange rate. Yet, it contains no provisions for the existence of a currency board, not even a fixed exchange rate or a specific level of the exchange rate. There is no legal barrier to abandoning the currency board at an instant (Tsang 2000, p. 7).

Overall, the HKMA operates a de-facto but unorthodox currency board. While adhering to the basic currency board rules in most respects, the HKMA possesses and exercises extensive discretion in monetary policy. Yet, while this is very unusual for a currency board, the ample reserves of the Exchange Fund allow for such discretion without violating the backing requirements of the currency board.

[21]There were attacks in October 1997, January 1998 and June 1998.

3.2.3 Currency Board Performance

The performance of the Hong Kong currency board has generally been considered a success. The currency board has provided the desired economic stability and has even successfully weathered periods of great duress, as in the aftermath of the Asian crisis, 1997-1998.

As shown by figures 3.6 and 3.7, the deviations of the market exchange rate from the fixed exchange rate of HK$ 7.80 = 1 US$ have been minimal, even during the crisis years 1997 and 1998. Especially during the early years of the currency board inflation has been relatively high compared to inflation in the US. Yet, these differences are mainly related to inflation of the prices of non-tradeable goods, which in turn results from high productivity growth in the tradeable goods sector relative to the non-tradeable goods sector (Walters 1997, p. 12; Schwartz 1993, p. 176). Lately, though, Hong Kong has experienced deflation as the economy is still recovering from the recession caused by the Asian crisis.

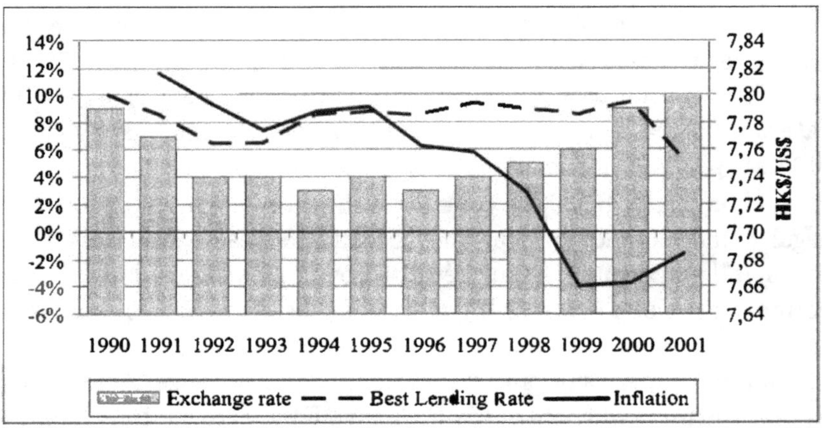

Source: IMF (2002c), own calculation

Figure 3.7: Exchange rate, best lending rate, and inflation, Hong Kong, 1990–2001.

Under the currency board, interest rates in Hong Kong generally fluctuated around the level of US interest rates. This is demonstrated by figure 3.8, which shows the interest rate differential between Hong Kong treasury bills and US treasury bills. Again, the notable exception is the Asian crisis period from mid 1997 to mid 1998, during which speculation against the Hong Kong dollar led to a liquidity crunch and drove interest rates up. Yet, within one year after the crisis interest rates returned to their previous level.

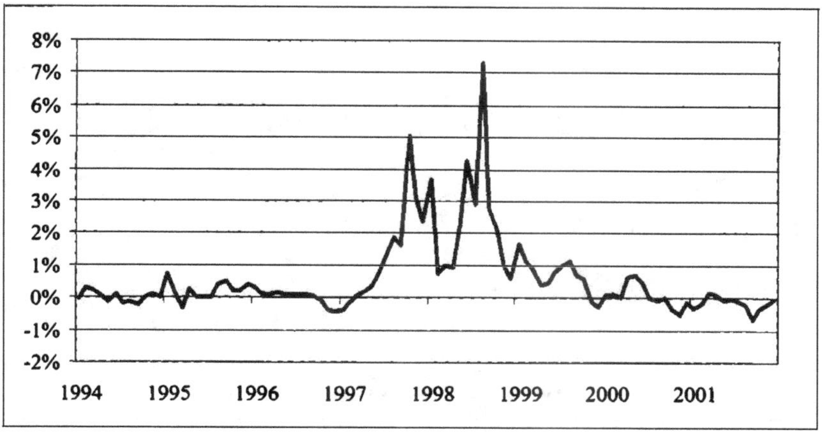

Source: IMF (2002c), own calculation

Figure 3.8: Interest rate differential Hong Kong vs USA, (Hong Kong treasury bills rate / USA treasury bills rate), 1994–2001.

Economic activity performance of Hong Kong has been very sound, as demonstrated by figure 3.9. Throughout the whole currency board period from 1984–2001 Hong Kong has witnessed strong growth and exceptionally low unemployment. During the period from 1986 to 1997 average growth was at 5.8% and average unemployment at 2.0%. Yet, speculative attacks against the Hong Kong dollar and the stock market in 1997 and 1998 led to a sharp contraction in economic activity and a steep rise in unemployment. While growth resumed in 2000, reaching more than 10%, the economy fell back into recession in the second half of 2001 from which it has not yet recovered (Hong Kong Census & Statistics Department 2002).[22]

It becomes clear that Hong Kong's experience with a currency board has been a success until 1997. With the onset of the Asian crisis the country was thrown into a severe recession and unemployment reached the highest levels in two decades, exposing one of the fundamental problems of having a fixed exchange rate: in case of a shock or a speculative attack hitting a fixed-exchange rate country, the exchange rate cannot provide a nominal cushion against the shock, thus requiring accommodation of the shock through changes in prices and incomes, which can be very painful. Even though a fully-backed currency board can, as a matter of principle, not fail, the resulting contraction of base money leads to a credit crunch in the banking system, causing liquidity problems for banks with poor balance sheets, maybe even a run on the banking system. Higher and more volatile short-

[22]September 2002.

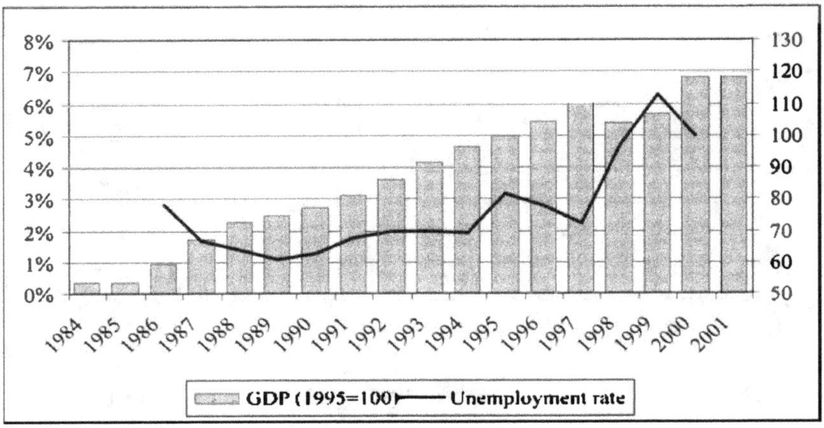

Source: IMF (2002c)

Figure 3.9: Unemployment rate and GDP, Hong Kong, 1984–2001.

term interest rates lead to higher interest rate risks for banks and great cost for short-borrowing/long-lending commercial banks. These problems can be transmitted to the real sector via credit contraction and fluctuation of interest rates. In the resulting economic recession, investment falls, unemployment increases, and budget deficits soar (Lu and Yu 1999, p. 125).

This general reasoning is reflected in Hong Kong's experience with speculative attacks 1997–1998. During a first wave in October 1997, the HKMA was forced to make huge US dollar sales. The resulting liquidity crunch and banks' panic rush for funds drove interbank rates up to 310%, although allegedly HKMA's initial handling of the crisis contributed to this high rate. Another wave of speculation in August 1998 allegedly involved, according to the Hong Kong government, hedge funds engaging in a double bet against the Hong Kong dollar and the Hang Seng stock index. Supposedly the hedge funds were betting that, with the monetary base contracting and interbank rates soaring, the stock market would slump. To fend off the attack the Hong Kong government resorted to unusual measures by engaging in direct intervention in the stock market, futures market, and exchange market. It defended the exchange rate in the exchange rate market, drew down the reserves in the Exchange Fund to finance a budget deficit to maintain liquidity in the money market, and to spend HK$ 118 billion to buy selected shares in the stock market, preventing the Hang Seng index from falling. Eventually, the massive intervention, under which 15% of Hong Kong's total foreign reserves were spent, proved successful, and the pressure on the peg was relieved. Yet, the late effects of these speculative attacks are still felt today (Fung 1999, pp. 3–4; Lu and Yu 1999, pp. 125–126).

3.3 Argentina (1991–2002)

Argentina is another example of a country that had had a currency board prior to the introduction of its recent currency board in 1991. Contrary to Hong Kong, though, these episodes, under which Argentina linked its currency to the value of gold 1902–1914 and 1927–1929, were completely unrelated to the renewed introduction of the currency board in the early 1990s. Additionally, Argentina is the country with the richest history in abandoning a currency board under duress. All three currency board episodes ended by suspension of currency board operation in order to avoid excessive cost of real adjustment.

3.3.1 Lead-Up to the Currency Board

The 1980s in Argentina, the so-called lost decade, have been characterized by chronic and even hyperinflation, huge fiscal deficits and average negative growth. As shown by figure 3.10, annual inflation was almost constantly above 100% in the period from 1981 to 1991, reaching its peak level in 1990, with a rise in the consumer price index (CPI) of more than 20,000%, compared to the previous year.

Consequently, devaluation of the domestic currency against the US dollar was enormous, as shown by figure 3.11. Between January 1981 and April 1991 the value of the domestic currency against the dollar declined by a factor of almost 50,000,000.

One of the reasons for abounding inflation and the rapid decline of the currency were huge government deficits, as shown in figure 3.12, financed through the printing press. On top of that, the quasi-fiscal deficit, generated at the central bank by interest rate subsidies, foreign exchange insurance, and interest payments required on reserves, is estimated to have amounted to another 4% of GDP in the mid-eighties. The results of such distorting and disruptive policies were negative average growth of -1.3% per year and rising unemployment in the 1980s (Kiguel 2002, pp. 86–87).

Repeated attempts were made to bring inflation under control, mostly using the exchange rate as a nominal anchor. The plan of Martínez de Hoz (1979–1981) used a *tablita cambiaria*, pre-anounced step-by-step devaluations of the currency. While initially effective, it resulted in an increasing over-valuation of the currency and allowed speculative gains. Furthermore,

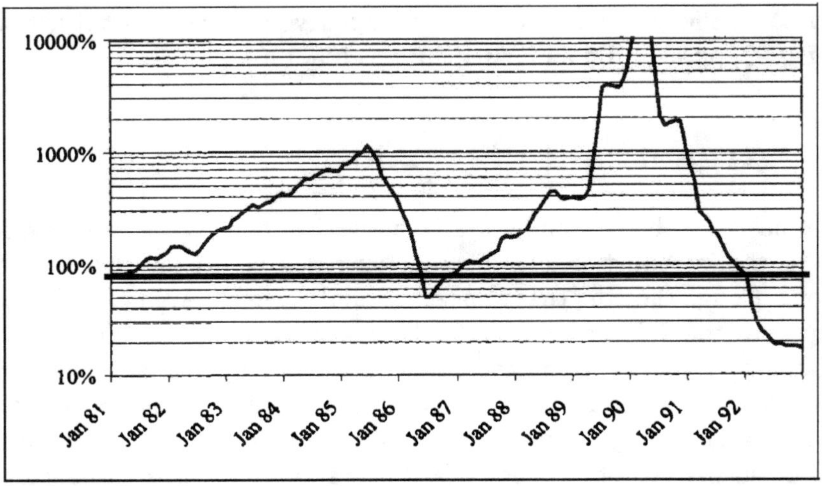

Source: IMF (2002c), own calculation

Figure 3.10: Inflation, change of CPI on previous year, Argentina, 1981–1992, logarithmic scale.

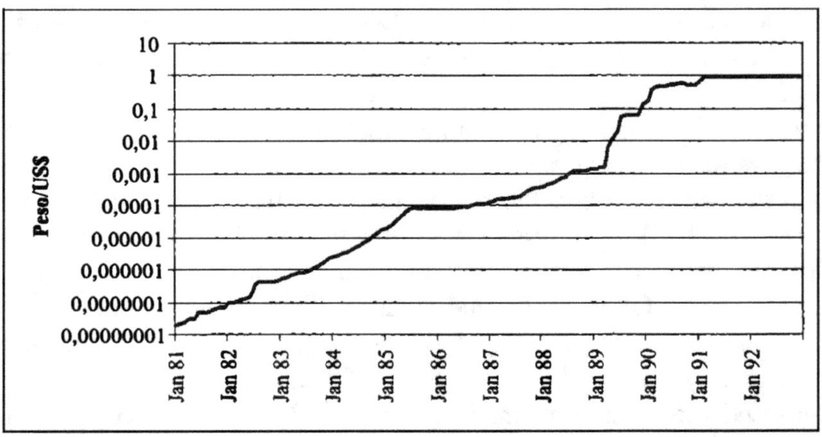

Source: IMF (2002c)

Figure 3.11: Exchange rate peso against US dollar, Argentina, 1981–1992, logarithmic scale.

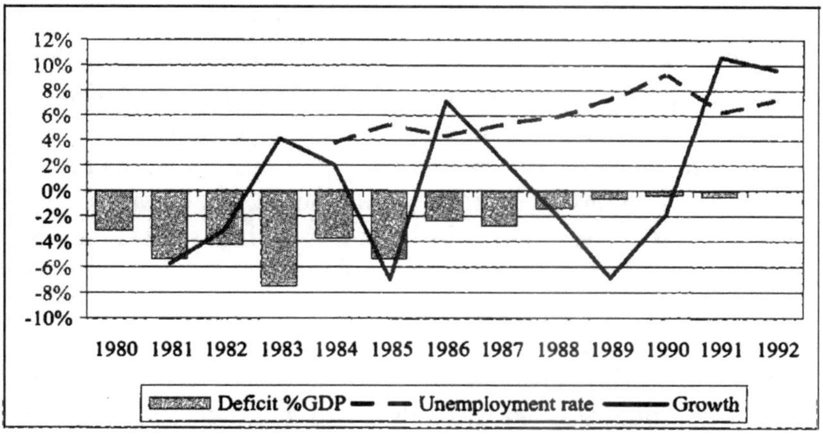

Source: IMF (2002c), own calculation

Figure 3.12: Government deficit, unemployment rate, and growth, Argentina, 1981–1992.

fiscal discipline was still weak, and increasing deficits aggravated the commencing banking crisis of the early eighties. Soon, inflation was on the rise again, reaching levels of more than 600% (Kiguel and Liviatan 1994, pp. 10–11; Purroy 1997, p. 14).

Another attempt at stabilization, the *Plan Austral*, was made in June 1985 under the new government of president Alfonsín. The plan combined a mixture of orthodox and heterodox measures to achieve its goal. Prices and wages were frozen at their current levels, and exchange rate and capital controls were introduced. The president publicly announced to refrain from using the central bank for financing the fiscal deficit. Again, the program was effective for some months, and inflation and interest rates were sinking. Yet, continuing lack of fiscal discipline, lax monetary policy, and combined unwillingness and inability to reform the public sector, for which the government thought macroeconomic stabilization to be a necessary precondition, led to a return of price instability in 1986. In an attempt to honor its promise not to resort to the printing press for financing the fiscal deficit, the government instead resorted to financing the deficit by raising domestic debt. Additionally, the government introduced a new tax on check transaction on checking accounts, and demanded a 40% pre-payment on capital gains and wealth taxes. The central bank, in turn, obliged to sterilize the spending excess of the public sector, increased and remunerated the reserve deposits of the banking system, laying the groundwork for an increasing quasi-fiscal deficit at the central bank (Artana 1993, p. 41; Purroy 1997, pp. 14–15).

With these measures still failing to put a stop to increasing inflation, 1987 and 1988 saw a broad mixture of new measures being implemented: repeated price and wage controls were enacted, which proved little effective and led to social unrest; the first steps toward liberalization of the exchange rate system were undertaken, leading to a grey market for financial transactions; non-tariff import restrictions were reduced; banks were coerced into exchanging their legal reserves at the central bank into special interest bearing government debt titles, to reduce the liquidity of the financial system. Yet, at that point new measures barely affected inflation at all anymore. The government had become completely incapable of reducing its expenditure, largely due to the increasing burden of domestic debt service. Most of the debt the government owed was indexed to inflation, and ever-increasing inflation expectations led to unsustainable real interest rates. On the income side, high inflation seriously eroded the real value of income from taxes. The complete loss of control over government finances translated into a complete loss of confidence in the domestic currency, speculative attacks against the currency, a run on the financial system and, eventually, hyperinflation (Purroy 1997, pp. 15–16).[23]

In 1989 a new president, Carlos Menem, was elected. The new government came up with a new catalogue of orthodox and heterodox measures to stabilize the economy, named *Plan Bunge y Born*, after the countries largest transnational firm whose advisors had helped to design it. The plan, which basically was based on the same instruments that had failed already under the Alfonsín administration, lasted five months, when the government was forced to carry out a large step devaluation (Pastor Jr. and Wise 1999, p. 479).

In January 1990 the government announced that all time deposits were to be converted into 10-year, dollar denominated treasury bonds, called BONEX. The central bank then used these bonds to pay off its debts with commercial banks and the banks used the bonds to pay their depositors. The mandatory swap was also extended to all then-outstanding domestic public debt. This measure had the double effect of dramatically reducing the supply of money in the economy, and recapitalizing the central bank, reducing the inflationary pressure. Furthermore, the government debt maturity structure was increased from one month to 10 years, and interest payments were dramatically reduced (Starr 1997, p. 91; Tanner and Sanguinetti 1997, p. 535).

[23]Unfortunately, this development of the budget deficit is not evident from official IMF or World Bank data, as shown in figure 3.12. Yet, other authors state significantly higher deficits: According to Kiguel (2002, p. 86), the average deficit 1981–1990 was 6.4%. Purroy (1997, pp. 16–17) estimates that in 1989 the budget deficit, including the quasi-fiscal deficit at the central bank, was 16.2% of GPD.

On the other hand, the factual confiscation of private deposits—the replacing government bond were traded at 30% face value in the grey market—led to a complete loss of confidence in the private sector and sent inflation rates sky-rocketing from 40% per month in December 1989 to 95% in March 1990 (Purroy 1997, p. 17).

The government tried to introduce additional orthodox measures and announced a contractionary monetary policy and a reduction of the budget deficit to 2% of GDP, and initiated a privatization program. The flexible exchange rate was maintained, though, but delayed devaluations were intended to serve as a nominal anchor. Inflation was reduced to an average of 13% per month in the second and third quarter of 1990, and to 6.2% in the fourth quarter. Yet, early 1991 inflation was gaining speed again, fuelled by renewed speculative attacks against the currency and a large devaluation. Eventually, in February 1991, Domingo Cavallo was named economics minister and introduced the *Plan de Convertibilidad*, whose centerpiece was a currency board fixing the value of the domestic currency against the US dollar (Purroy 1997, p. 17).

3.3.2 Currency Board Design

The Argentinean currency board was established in March 1991 through the *Ley de Convertibilidad*, which declared the peso to be fixed to the US dollar at a one to one rate. The newly independent central bank, the Banco Central de la República Argentina (BCRA), which was to maintain and operate the currency board, was required to hold reserves in gold or foreign currencies of at least 100% of the monetary base (República Argentina 1991a, artículos 1 and 4). The primary and essential mission of the BCRA was to preserve the value of the currency (República Argentina 1992, artículo 3).

The central bank was allowed to hold as reserves interest paying deposits or other investments with foreign banking institutions or low risk, high liquidity bonds payable in gold or foreign currency. Initially, no explicit limit was given for the amount of domestic public bonds denominated in dollars that could be held as reserves. In September 1991 the limit was set to 10% of the monetary base (República Argentina 1991b, artículo 37) and in September 1992 it was raised to a third of reserves, with the additional constraint of maximum annual growth of 10% (República Argentina 1992, artículos 20 and 33). Except for the first year, the coverage of the monetary base by foreign exchange reserves of the BCRA was slightly above 100% at most times, as shown by figure 3.13.

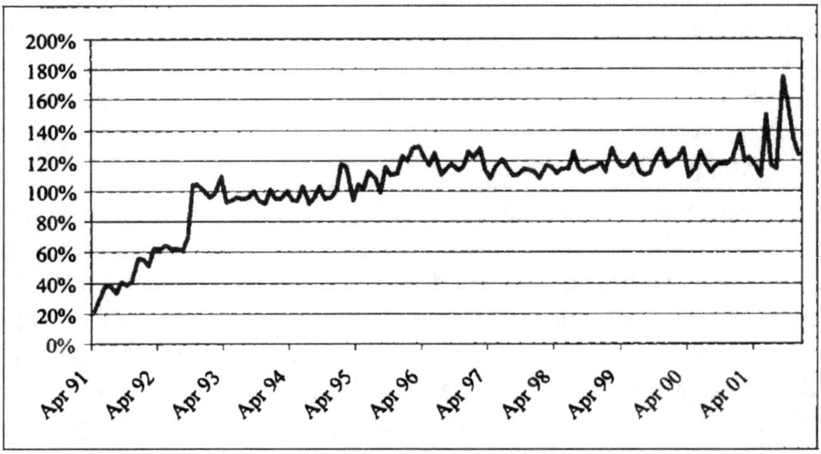

Source: Banco Central de la República Argentina (2002), own calculation

Figure 3.13: Cover of monetary base by foreign exchange reserves of BCRA, Argentina, 1991–2001.

The convertibility law required the central bank to sell dollars on demand at the fixed rate of US\$1 = 1 peso. It was allowed to buy dollars at the market exchange rate (República Argentina 1991a, Artículos 1–3).

To signal credibility of the exchange rate commitment, the US dollar, which had already been a wide-used unofficial currency during the years of high inflation, was given equal legal tender status with the peso. This bi-monetary system allowed for contracts and deposits to be made with equal freedom in either currency, and banks held required reserves exclusively in dollars (Chankova 1999, p. 5). A study by Baliño et al. (1999, p. 2) estimates the ratio of foreign currency deposits to broad money to have been 43.9% in 1995. Another recent study by Feige et al. (2002, p. 11) even estimates currency substitution to have been some 80% and asset substitution about 58% at the end of the 1990s. The extent of dollarization is also reflected in figure 3.14, which shows US\$ denominated long-term debt as a share of total long-term debt: during most of the period from 1991–2001 the share of US\$ debt relative to all long-term debt was around 60%.

As the currency board originated from a fully-fledged central bank, the BCRA retained considerable scope for discretionary monetary policy. Besides being able to issue domestic money against domestic government bonds, as discussed above, the bank could vary reserve requirements and carry out swap agreements to affect the liquidity of the financial sector (Hanson 1993, p. 43). It was allowed to engage in lender of last resort operations, though only on a very limited scale and as long as the backing requirement of the

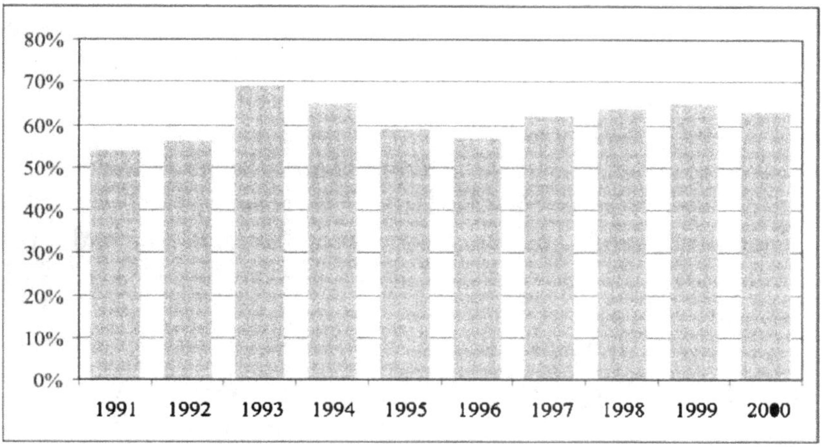

Source: World Bank (2002)

Figure 3.14: US$ denominated long-term debt as share of total long-term debt, Argentina, 1991–2000.

currency board was not violated (República Argentina 1992, artículo 17).[24] To compensate for the reduced ability of the BCRA to act as a lender of last resort, non-remunerated reserve requirements were replaced by remunerated liquidity requirements of 20%, for banks to have a liquidity cushion. Also, in 1996, the central bank negotiated a US$6.1 billion contingent repurchase facility with a group of international banks to provide the domestic banking system with liquidity in the event of a systemic liquidity crisis(Traa et al. 1998, p. 6). Another typical feature of a central bank, the deposit insurance system remained with the BCRA—though on very unfavorable terms for participating banks—until it was replaced by the Deposit Guaranty Fund in 1995 (República Argentina 1995).

While the currency board was the centerpiece of the convertibility plan, the plan consisted not of the board alone, but encompassed a broad package of reform measures to enhance and guarantee the sustainability of the currency board. The plan rested on four broad pillars. First, monetary reform, based on the convertibility law, to eliminate inflation and restore confidence in the peso, as has been discussed above.

Second, a reduction of the fiscal deficit, to ensure the government would not print money to finance it. The government had, even prior to the convertibility plan, begun to eliminate tax evasion, improve tax administration

[24]For a detailed account of lender of last resort functions in Argentina and general options to provide lender of last resort functions under a currency board, see Caprio Jr. et al. (1996a, 1996b).

and compliance, and curtail public spending. Income taxes and value added taxes were raised considerably (Pastor Jr. and Wise 1999, p. 479). Steps were taken to downsize and improve the efficiency of the national civil service, responsibilities for health and education were transferred to the provinces. Some 21 federal taxes and levies (including those on bank debits, and assets), exemptions (notably from the value added tax), and subsidies were eliminated. Employer payroll tax rates were reduced by 30%–80% and a pension reform—aimed at reducing future liabilities—was undertaken in 1994 (Traa et al. 1998, pp. 8–9).

Third, structural adjustment reforms, such as deregulation of key markets, the opening of the economy to international trade, and privatization of public enterprises. In the area of international trade export tariffs and nontariff import barriers were eliminated (except for automobiles, textiles, and shoes), and average import tariffs were reduced from over 40% to some 9% by the end of 1991. Tariffs for capital goods and and raw materials were eliminated completely. Deregulation comprehended abolishing all price controls, closing down a number of regulatory and marketing bodies, deregulating wholesale and retail trade (1992), and access to professional services (1993). Ports, public utilities, transport, and the oil and gas sectors were deregulated and privatized. More competition was introduced to the financial system and privatization of public banks begun. From 1991–1994 the government privatized some 90% of all state enterprises and used the receipts, more than US$20 billion, to clear arrears and reduce the debt burden. The only important area with some but little reforms was the labor market, where reforms were not as far-reaching as in other areas (Traa et al. 1998, pp. 5–7).

Fourth, strengthening the institutional framework by granting independence to the central bank, creating institutions to regulate the recently privatized utilities and strengthening the Securities and Exchange Commission (Kiguel 2002, p. 87).

In conclusion, the Argentinean currency board exhibited all the main features that are to be expected from a currency board, except that it permitted to hold domestic assets, such as domestic dollar denominated government securities. Also, the BCRA retained some atypical discretionary monetary policy powers. Contrary to Hong Kong, the currency board rules were explicitly set forth in law, stating the exchange rate, the anchor currency, the backing requirement, and the composition of reserves.

3.3.3 The Early Years of the Currency Board and the Tequila Crisis

The currency board had the desired effect in bringing down inflation. Within two years inflation was at single digit rates, as figure 3.15 shows, and towards the mid-nineties inflation was one of the lowest in the world. An exceptional achievement considering Argentina's inflation history: For the first time for more than 50 years inflation ceased to be an issue in Argentina (Kiguel 2002, p. 88). Not surprisingly, the peg of the peso to the dollar kept the exchange rate constantly around the one to one level (figure 3.16). Yet, the efficiency of the currency board in bringing down inflation was almost too good, as from 1999 on, paired with a severe recession, Argentina experienced almost continuous deflation until 2001. By December 2001 the CPI was at the level it had last had in August 1994.

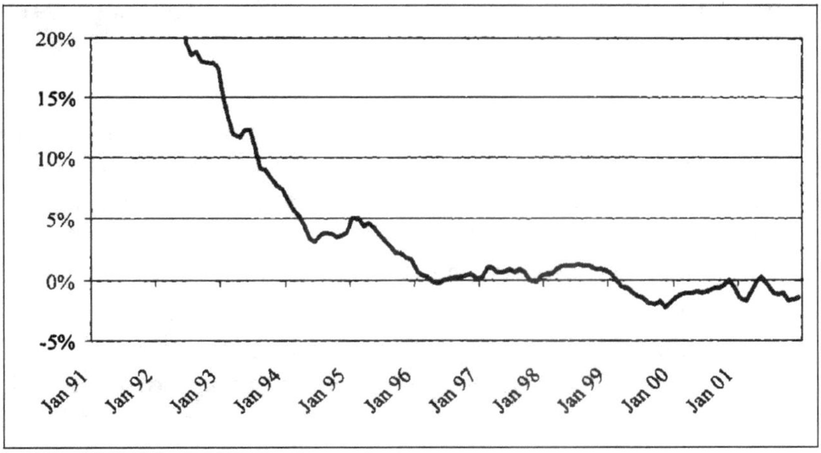

Source: IMF (2002c), own calculation

Figure 3.15: Inflation, change of CPI on previous year, Argentina, 1991–2001.

The first four years of the currency board proved to be a great success. With inflation reduced to single digit levels, a budget deficit strongly reduced by fiscal reforms[25] (see figure 3.17), and wide spread deregulation and liberalization, interest rates quickly converged to normal levels (see figure 3.18) and Argentina enjoyed a period of high growth, with an average growth of 8% between 1991 and 1994. In the same period, employment grew at an annual rate of 1,8%, creating 370,000 jobs per year, enough to compensate

[25]For a very detailed account of how fiscal reforms affected the government budget, see World Bank (1998).

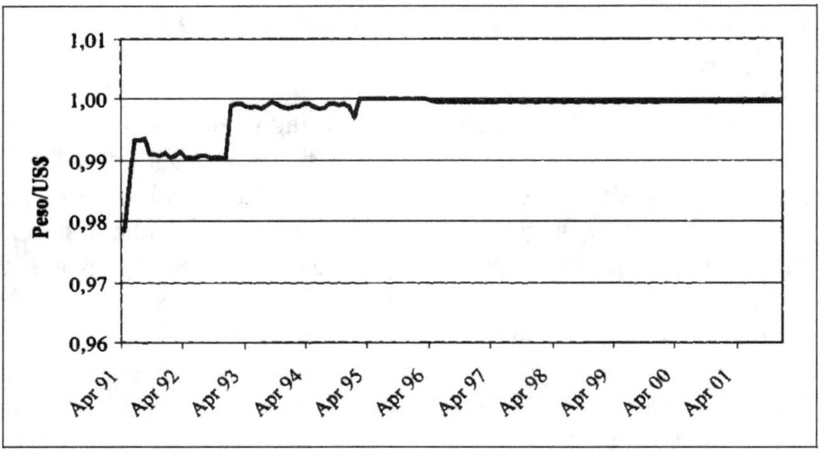

Source: IMF (2002c)

Figure 3.16: Exchange rate peso against US$, Argentina, 1991–2001.

for the losses from privatization of national enterprises and state reforms. Unemployment was not a major concern until 1994, when the repercussions of the tequila crisis hit the Argentinean economy (Kiguel 2002, p. 88). Yet, even during 1993 and the first half of 1994 there had already been a trend of growing unemployment, despite high economic growth (Purroy 1997, p. 54).

By 1994 some investors and financial analysts began to express concern that the peso might be overvalued. The peso had been fixed to the dollar since 1991, and despite the success in quickly bringing down the inflation rate, it had taken until 1994 before inflation fell in line with international levels. Consequently, the real value of the peso had increased over the period and by 1993 the real exchange rate had settled at approximately half the level it had had in the 1980s (Pastor Jr. and Wise 1999, p. 480). Whether this really represented an overvaluation of the peso against the dollar, is still subject to debate. A recent study by Hristov (2002, pp. 22–24), for example, concludes that the peso was actually undervalued until 1997, and then slightly overvalued between 1998 and 1999. Yet, a look at exports and imports, as in figure 3.19, clearly reveals that from 1991 to 1994 import growth by far outpaced export growth, resulting in the first trade balance deficit since 1980.

In 1995 Argentina was hit by the repercussions of the December 1994 Mexican currency crisis and the currency board came under attack. In the first few months of the crisis over US$8 billion, equivalent to about 18% of all deposits, exited the country (Pastor Jr. and Wise 1999, p. 484). The stock

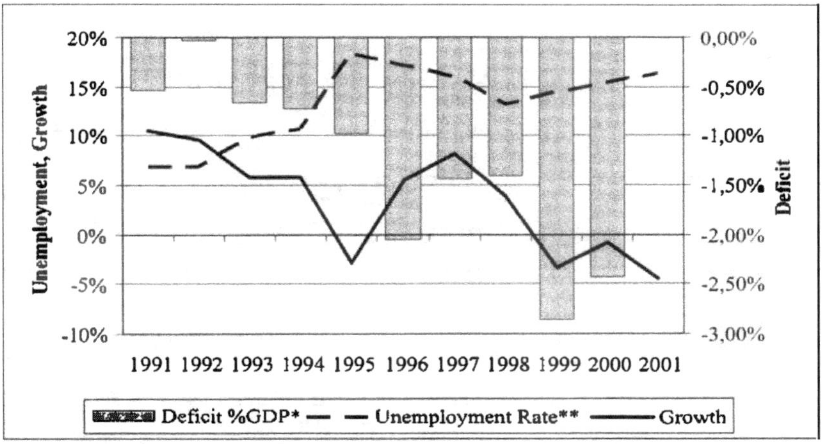

∗ net of lending 1991–1994, ∗∗ May value

Sources: IMF (2002c), Ministerio de Economía de la República Argentina (2002b), own calculation

Figure 3.17: Budget deficit, unemployment rate, and growth, Argentina, 1991–2001.

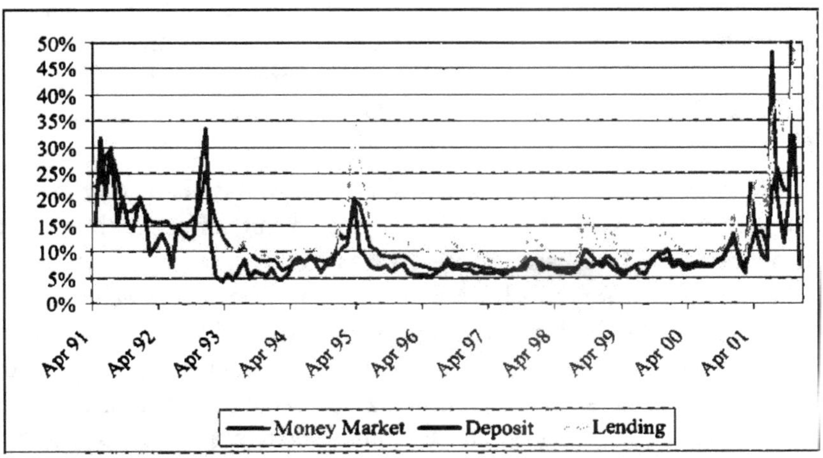

Source: IMF (2002c)

Figure 3.18: Selected interest rates (peso), Argentina, 1991–2001.

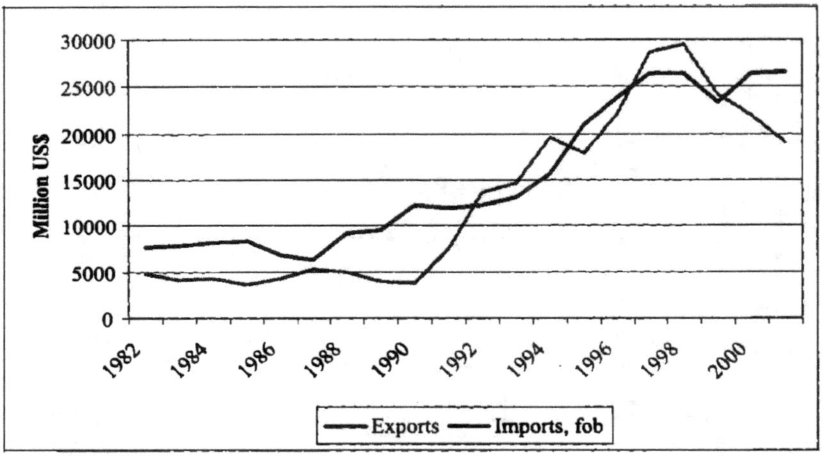

Source: IMF (2002c)

Figure 3.19: Exports and Imports (free on border), Argentina, 1982–2001.

market slumped, bond prices fell sharply and interest rates rose dramatically. To increase the liquidity of the financial system, the central bank directly injected liquidity into the financial system by entering into a set of repurchase agreements, reduced the reserve requirements on peso and dollar deposits in two steps from 43% to 30%, and dollarized bank deposits in the central bank, to increase confidence in the currency board. Further, the BCRA constituted a fund to help financial institution by purchasing their non-performing loans. The fund, which was administered by Banco Nación, was funded by the banking system and was to provide a safety net. Additionally, the BCRA charter was amended to give the central bank more powers to act as a lender of last resort (Fernandez 1996, pp. 135–136; Ganapolsky and Schmukler 1998, pp. 11–13).

The liquidity squeeze became a liquidity crisis in late February 1995 when international banks with branches in Argentina cut off credit lines to their branch operations. Interbank interest rates rose dramatically, to over 50% within hours after after credit lines had been cut. Fear of a freeze of deposits or a weakening of the fixed exchange rate commitment led to a run on banks and the currency. The fear of a devaluation prompted a steep increase of the peso-dollar interest rate spread, reflecting the exchange rate risk (see figure 3.20), which reached up to 1,647 basis points. To avert the crisis, the central bank used its excess reserves to make short-term loans exceeding 900 million pesos to solvent banks with liquidity problems, and relaxed reserve requirements further by allowing private banks to count up to 50% of their vault cash as part of the reserve requirement. The government announced emergency measures, such as reducing government spending by 2 billion pesos, including wage cuts of government employees, and increasing taxes, most notably the value added tax from 18% to 21%. It also announced to borrow up to US$7 billion from domestic and foreign private lenders, and from the IMF, the World Bank, and the Inter-American Development Bank (Fernandez 1996, pp. 136–137; Hanke 1999, pp. 349–353).

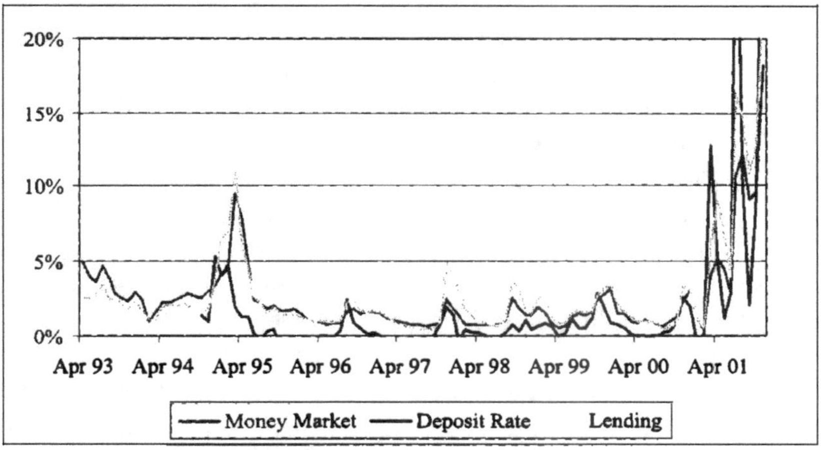

Source: IMF (2002c), own calculation

Figure 3.20: Interest rates differentials peso vs dollar, Argentina, 1991–2001.

The government's success in raising US$1 billion through an oversubscribed domestic bond, exhibiting the domestic credibility and creditworthiness of the government, led the IMF et al. to also grant their loans, which eventually put an end to the crisis. Interest rates and interest rate spreads declined and liquidity returned to the financial system. The re-election of president Menem in the first round of the presidential election in May, eventually removed any last doubts about the future of convertibility (Hanke 1999, p. 353).

While this ended the liquidity crisis, the economic consequences of the crisis were more persistent. The ensuing recession was short-lived; while the economy shrank by -2.9% in 1995, growth rebounded strongly in 1996 and 1997 with rates of 5.5% and 8.1%, respectively. Yet, the toll on unemployment was heavier: In 1995 unemployment stood at 18.4% and declined slowly only until 1998, despite strong economic growth, to reach 13.2%, a level still considerably higher than in pre-crisis years.

3.3.4 The Late Years and Currency Board Exit

Even though economic growth quickly resumed from 1996 on, Argentina emerged weakened from the Mexican crisis, with unemployment high and only slowly receding. In an economy with a tightly fixed exchange rate, markets need to be flexible, so adjustment can occur through changes in prices and wages in the absence of an exchange rate cushion. Yet, despite some reform, Argentina's labor markets remained rigid, especially in the public sector. Furthermore, the economy was very dependent on capital flows: Every time private capital was flowing into the country, as 1991–1994 and 1996–1997, the economy experienced an increase in growth, while during period of capital outflows or no private capital flows economic activity fell, as in 1995 and 1998–2001. Consequently, the economy remained vulnerable to shocks (Kiguel 2002, p. 92).

After the tequila crisis, a number of shocks affected the Argentinean economy: A booming economy in the US from 1995 to 2001 led to a strong appreciation of the dollar, increasing the real value of the peso against the currencies of main trading partners other than the US, and to relatively high US interest rates, thereby also increasing Argentinean interest rates, increasing the debt service burden for the government and reducing investment. In 1999 Brazil, Argentina's main trading partner, devalued its currency by some 30%, increasing the prices of exports to Brazil and reducing the prices of imports from Brazil. The Asian crisis 1997, the Russian debt default in 1998, and the Turkey crisis in 2000 led international investors to reconsider their investments in emerging markets. These crises led to peaks in domestic interest rates (figure 3.18), exchange rate risk (measured as the spread between interest rates on peso and dollar domestic deposits/loans, figure 3.20), and sovereign risk (expressed by J.P. Morgan's EMBI Argentina index, which measures the interest spread between Argentinean government bonds and US Treasury bills, figure 3.21). By the end of 2000 the sovereign risk stood at around 800 basis points, meaning the Argentinean government had to pay an 8% risk premium on (newly issued) government debt compared to the US.

All these factors led to a continuous worsening of fundamentals by the late 1990s (see figure 3.17). The economy entered into recession in the third quarter of 1998 and experienced negative growth for three consecutive years, from 1999–2001. Unemployment continued to rise again, approaching its previous peak level during the Mexican crisis. The budget deficit, which had not been erased during the years of high growth, increased to its highest levels since the introduction of the convertibility plan.

The government budget deficit, lack of growth, and high interest rates led to an increasing amount of government debt, which stood at 50% (provinces

Source: Ministerio de Economía de la República Argentina (2002a)

Figure 3.21: Sovereign risk (EMBI Argentina), interest spread of Argentinean government bonds over US T-bonds in basis points, Argentina, 1997–2000.

included) by the end of 2000. In turn, these same factors, which cast doubt on Argentina's ability to repay the debt, led to increasing interest rates, making it ever more difficult to refinance the debt.

The year 2001 saw a series of attempts to bring the budget deficit under control, to reduce the debt service burden and to rebuild trust in the currency board arrangement. Attempts to drastically curtail public spending, a precondition for further IMF loans, sparked social as well as political unrest within the government of president de la Rua, and led to the resignation of two economics ministers within two weeks in March 2001. The new minister, Domingo Cavallo, the initiator of the convertibility plan, sought to increase credibility of the currency board, and to alleviate the perceived over-valuation of the peso by pegging the peso to the US dollar *and* the euro, once the dollar/euro exchange rate reached unity (República Argentina 2001b, artículos 1 and 2). In June the government managed to convince creditors of a debt-swap of US$29.5 billion, which shifted repayment of debt into the future, yet at the price of higher interest rates (Buch and Stukenbrock 2002, p. 9; La Nación 2001).

Still, all these measures failed to reduce the sovereign risk, which stood at around 1000 basis points from mid-March to June (see figure 3.22). By end of June it became clear that the government had missed by far the budget deficit target for May agreed on with the IMF. This, and a complaint of the president that the government was not able to pay the high interest rates demanded by financial markets, pushed the sovereign risk further up to 1500 basis points. Early payment of a previously agreed upon loan, and the announcement of an additional US$8 billion payment by the IMF in August kept the sovereign risk at this level but did not manage to reduce it (La Nación 2001).

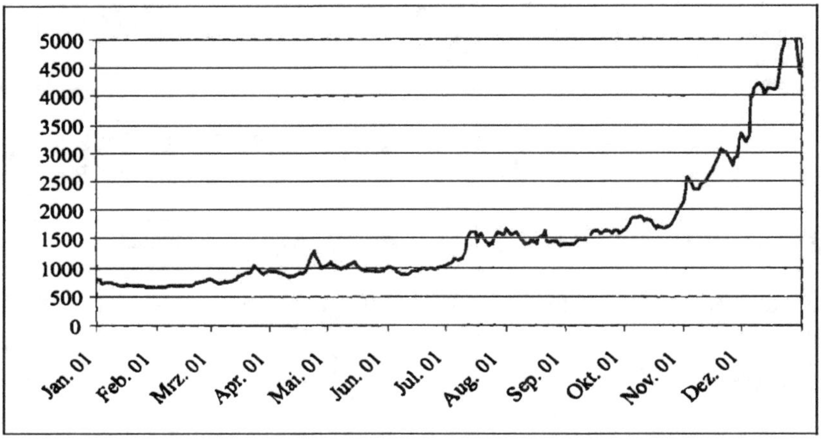

Source: Ministerio de Economía de la República Argentina (2002a)

Figure 3.22: Sovereign risk (EMBI Argentina), Argentina, 2001.

The end of the currency board started in late October, when the government started to have obvious problems to repay its debt, and when the province La Rioja defaulted on its debt a few days later. The run on the currency board's foreign exchange reserves, which were reduced by 50% from January to November, and on banks, where deposits had sunk by 20%, intensified. To put an end to the capital flight, the government enacted the "corralito" (República Argentina 2001a) on December 1, freezing all bank deposits and prohibiting the export of foreign currency, and thereby effectively freezing economic activity. Four days later the IMF announced it would not disburse any further payments to Argentina. At that point the sovereign risk reached 4000 basis points (Buch and Stukenbrock 2002, p. 9–10; La Nación 2001).

By the end of December Argentina defaulted on its debt. In early January 2002 it devalued the peso and ended the currency board (La Nación 2002). The devaluation of the peso, whose exchange rate had reached US$1 = 3.60 peso by September 2002, combined with the inability to raise foreign capital, threw Argentina into one of the worst recessions ever. The freeze of deposits paralyzed economic activity. On the other hand, devaluation and pesification of domestic dollar deposits and loans have rendered many banks and firms insolvent, and the government fears that loosening the freeze by too much might cause a run on the banking system. Since the beginning of the crisis until November 2002, real GDP is expected to have contracted by more than 20%, unemployment surged and reached a level of 21.5% in May 2002. Annual inflation reached 39% in October, fuelled by increasing prices of imports and government liquidity assistance to the financial sector (Boccara and Chambers 2002; Ministerio de Economía de la República Argentina 2002b, 2002a, 2002c). At the time of writing this subsection (December 2002), there was only slow progress being made on solving the complex economic problems the country is currently facing.[26] On top of economic turmoil, the country is also facing political chaos, as president Duhalde and the parliament fail to agree on coherent measures. Furthermore, the president is at feud with the supreme court, whom he tried but failed to impeach, and who has repeatedly ruled the freeze of deposits unconstitutional (The Economist 2002a). An agreement with the IMF on a comprehensive program, which would be an important first step toward reestablishing the country's credibility, is still not in sight, and it did not help that in November Argentina also defaulted on its outstanding loans with the world bank, now being one of only twenty countries that ever did so (Boccara and Chambers 2002; The Economist 2002b). On the positive side, the freeze of domestic currency deposits was lifted end of November 2002, without having a negative impact on banks, but restoring the domestic payment system. Still, the freeze of foreign currency deposits still remains in place (JPMorgan 2002, pp. 29–30).

It could be argued that the Argentinean currency board did not *collapse*, i.e. did not cease its operation due to internal factors such as the inability to honor its convertibility obligation, but was *exited*, i.e. was abolished due to external factors, in this case the governments decision to abandon it for fear of incurring even higher cost to the real economy. Such a distinction could be made to stress that per se currency boards are institutions that cannot fail as long they are set up and managed prudently, and to point out that the economic collapse of Argentina was not caused by its currency board but misguided economic policy. Yet, such a distinction does not made sense. A currency board can only be viable and feasible if the surrounding framework of economic policies is adequate, on its own it cannot accomplish successful stabilization over the medium-term. Therefore, separating the currency board from accompanying policies in analysis is futile and counterproductive, as it allows for exclusively blaming the currency board for Argentina's economic collapse on the one hand, as well as allowing for exclusively blaming misguided economic policies on the other hand.

[26]See IMF (2002a) for an end-of-July statement on Argentina's challenges ahead.

3.4 Estonia (1992) and Lithuania (1994)

3.4.1 Lead-Up to the Currency Boards

The three Baltic countries, Estonia, Latvia, and Lithuania, regained their independence from the Soviet Union in the latter half of 1991. Economic reforms had even begun in the late 1980s, and these reforms were implemented throughout the Baltics. At the time of independence the countries were still members of the ruble area. The abandonment of price controls in Russia at the start of 1992 led to high monthly inflation rates as prices rose to eliminate the monetary overhang (see figure 3.23). Along with high inflation, the external value of the ruble quickly eroded, prompting the Baltic countries to look for alternative monetary arrangements (Korhonen 1999, pp. 12–13).

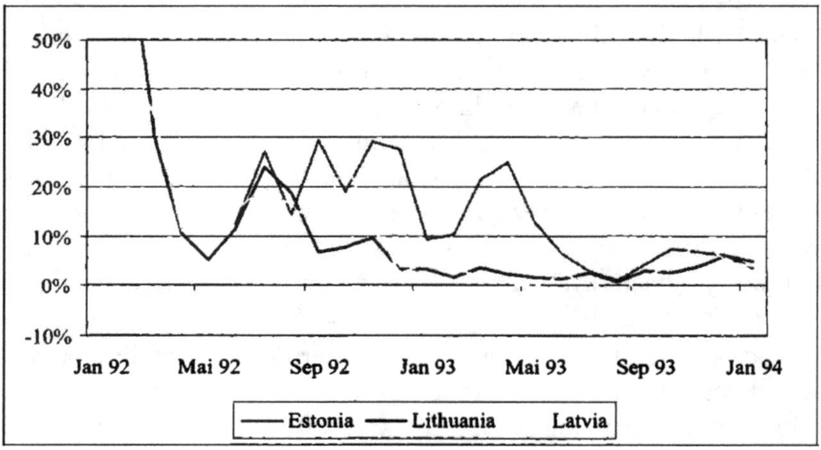

Source: IMF (2002c), own calculation

Figure 3.23: Monthly inflation rates, Baltic countries, 1992–1993.

Estonia acted swiftly. In March 1991 already it had created the Monetary Reform Committee of the Republic of Estonia, which was to decide the shape and framework for the monetary system of Estonia.[27] After some deliberation, it was decided to introduce a currency board with the domestic currency pegged to the Deutsche mark, a decision that enjoyed broad political support. On June 20, 1992 the new (and old) currency, the kroon, which had been phased out in 1939–1940, was introduced and the currency board

[27] Actually, preparations for the introduction of a sovereign currency had already begun in the mid-1980s. For a very detailed account on the recent history of the kroon and the early phase of currency board adoption, see Knöbl, Sutt, and Zavoico (2002).

started operating (Bank of Estonia 2002b; Korhonen 1999, p. 16; Republic of Estonia 1992a).

The first stage of monetary reform involved conversion of ruble balances, cash and deposits, into kroon. Persons wishing to convert had to register and proof their residency and were permitted to convert up to 1,500 rubles in cash (at that time some US$ 12) into kroon at a rate of 10 rubles = 1 kroon. Cash balances in excess of this amount could be converted at a less favorable rate of 1:50. Cash balances of firms, savings and deposit accounts of households, loans, etc. were converted at the 1:10 rate without a limit (Bennett 1993, pp. 461–462).

Lithuania opted for a more gradual approach to monetary reform. Although a law on the national currency board had been passed in December 1991, political debates delayed the exit from the ruble area. On May 1992 a new, temporary, currency was introduced, called talonas, the Lithuanian word for coupon. Until October 1992 the currency, at par value with the ruble, was in parallel circulation with the ruble, thereafter the ruble stopped being legal tender. With the domestic currency still tied to the ruble, Lithuania experienced markedly higher inflation than Estonia (see figure 3.23), and the external value of the domestic currency against the US$ was deteriorating rapidly, as demonstrated by figure 3.24 (Nenovsky, Hristov, and Mihaylov 2002, p. 18).

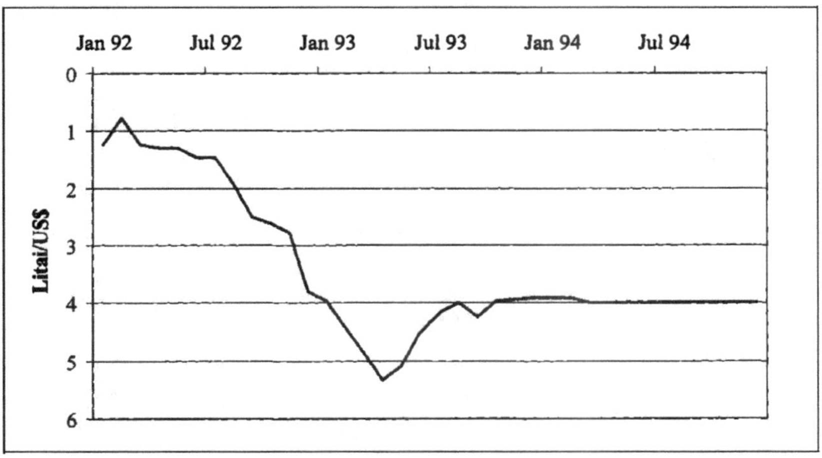

Source: IMF (2002c)

Figure 3.24: Exchange rate litas (talonas before July 1993) against US$, Lithuania, 1992–1994.

Tightening of monetary policy in April 1993 and the introduction of yet another domestic currency, eventually put an end to inflation and currency depreciation. In July 1993 the litas became legal tender, replacing the talonas. Inflation declined rapidly to levels similar to those in Estonia and Latvia, and the currency regained some of its external value (Nenovsky, Hristov, and Mihaylov 2002, pp. 18–19).

In October 1993 the prime minister, obviously motivated by Estonia's success in maintaining a fixed exchange rate, announced the intention to introduce a currency board in Lithuania, modelled on Estonia's example. Yet, while the introduction of the currency board in Estonia had been carried by broad political support, there was considerable opposition to a currency board in Lithuania. The central bank, the Bank of Lithuania, opposed it on the grounds that it had successfully managed to stabilize the exchange rate under a de facto peg. There was no need to curtail its rights for monetary policy, it said. The Governor of the bank continued to oppose the currency board up until the time of its implementation (Camard 1996, pp. 4–5).

The president of the influential Lithuanian Free Market Institute opposed the currency board for a different reason: A currency board modelled on Estonia's would still have too many discretionary powers. Instead, she demanded, the central bank should be dissolved and a truly orthodox currency board, holding all its assets abroad, should replace it. The Federation of Industrialist, concerned about Lithuania's competitiveness in international markets, desired for a highly depreciated exchange rate. The Association of Commercial Banks, earning profits from foreign exchange trade, opposed the proposal completely. The parliament, which began to consider the Litas Stability Law in January 1994, introduced its own concerns (Camard 1996, pp. 5–6).

Eventually, when the currency board started operating in April 1994, its design differed significantly from the design initially proposed.

3.4.2 Currency Boards Design

Estonia The currency board fixed the value of the Estonian kroon against the Deutsche mark at a rate of 1 DM = 8 kroon. The Bank of Estonia has the right to revalue, but not to devalue the exchange rate (Republic of Estonia 1992b). The latter right is reserved to the Estonian parliament, and only by a qualified majority (Nenovsky, Hristov, and Mihaylov 2002, p. 14). Initially there had been considerations to fix the kroon against the predecessor of the euro, the European currency unit (ECU), but this idea had been dismissed as it would have been less transparent, would have complicated the composition of the foreign exchange reserves, and would have posed the problem of how to set up the convertibility undertaking. Further, the Finish mark or Swedish krona had recommended themselves from the viewpoint of trade, but eventually the DM was chosen because of its strength and credibility. With the introduction of the euro in January 1999, the fix was converted according to the DM/euro exchange parity and the exchange rate is now 1 euro = 15.6466 kroon (Bennett 1993, p. 453; Ramon-Ballester 1999, p. 27).

In accordance with the Law on Security for Estonian Kroon (Republic of Estonia 1992b), the currency board has to fully back the monetary base, comprising of notes and coins in circulation, and accounts held with the central bank, by holding gold and foreign-currency denominated assets as reserves. As figure 3.25 shows, reserves have always exceeded the monetary base, leaving a good share of excess reserves available for discretionary monetary policy.

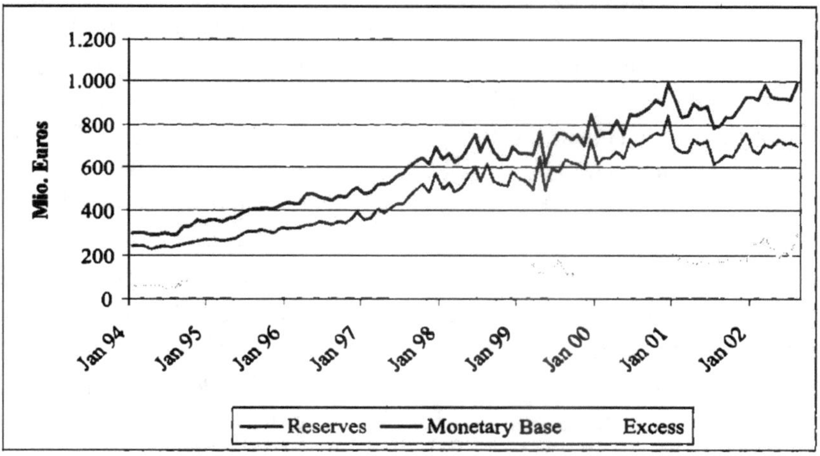

Source: Bank of Estonia (2002a), own calculation

Figure 3.25: Reserves (gold and convertible foreign currency assets) and monetary base, Estonia, 1994–2002.

The currency board is maintained and operated by the Bank of Estonia, which is independent and prohibited from granting loans to the government directly or indirectly by buying government securities (Republic of Estonia 1993). To increase the transparency of the operations of the Bank of Estonia, the bank was divided into an Issue Department and a Banking Department. The Issue Department, which is basically the currency board, concentrates all high-liquid assets and liabilities backing the monetary base, while the Banking Department, the arm of the bank conducting monetary policy, holds both less-liquid assets and liabilities, as well as the excess of foreign exchange reserves (Nenovsky, Hristov, and Mihaylov 2002, p. 15).

The Bank of Estonia is obliged to exchange with licensed banks US dollar, Japanese yen, Swedish krona, British pound and euro into kroons and vice versa, without limit. It buys and sells euro without a spread (Nenovsky, Hristov, and Mihaylov 2002, p. 14).

As with most modern-day currency board, the Bank of Estonia retained some scope for discretionary monetary policy action, but has sparingly engaged in active monetary policy. The instruments available to the Bank of Estonia are: reserve and liquidity requirements, a standing deposit facility, and issuing certificates of deposit (CD), which may be used to the extent as reserves of the Banking Department allow. Reserve requirements, which have been the most important monetary tool under the currency board, have been 10% for most of the time, but the base on which reserve requirements are calculated has been broadened between 1996 and 1998. An additional liquidity requirement of 3% has been introduced in 1997. Since 1999 reserve deposits have been remunerated with the European Central Bank's deposit interest rate, as have been excess reserves under the standing deposit facility introduced 1996. Certificates of deposit were introduced in 1993 to stimulate the development of the domestic interbank market. Volumes of CDs were kept small and over time CDs lost their initial importance. Auctions of CDs were terminated in May 2000 (Berensmann 2002, p. 110; Lepik 1999, annex 1; Nenovsky, Hristov, and Mihaylov 2002, pp. 15–16).

With a view on accession to the EU and EMU, Estonia launched a reform of the monetary policy operational framework in late 2000. The reform involves two stages: During the first stage the system of reserve requirements is to be revamped step-by-step, to attain the 2% EU level. Introduction of open market operations is planned for the second stage, after EMU integration (Bank of Estonia 2000).

Also, the Bank of Estonia is allowed to engage in lender of last resort actions, as excess reserves allow. Yet, there is no formal procedure for LOLR actions and liquidity support has been given on a case-to-case basis (Lepik 1999).

Along with the introduction of the currency board, Estonia liberalized and deregulated the economy. Major markets and basic prices were rapidly liberalized, and prices of non-tradeable goods are determined on a market basis. The capital account was liberalized in 1994. The labor market is very flexible. Transformation of ownership and economic restructuring were fast and radical. By 1999 75% of GDP was generated by the private sector, and the service sector contributed two-thirds of GDP (Nenovsky, Hristov, and Mihaylov 2002, p. 16).

With foreign currency deposits per broad money at 11.4% in 1995, Estonia would be considered a moderately dollarized economy (Baliño et al.

1999, p. 2). Another recent study by Feige and Dean (2002, pp. 14–16), which attempts to estimate the extent of dollarization in transition countries, suggests that some 12% of the total currency supply in Estonia was made up of foreign currencies in 1999. The extent of asset substitution is estimated to be some 19%. Compared to dollarization in Latvia (54%, 41%) or Lithuania (31%, 33%), this is relatively low.

In summary, the Estonian currency board design complies with the basic principles of a pure currency board, but also allows for some discretionary monetary policy measures, which are limited by excess reserves. The legal foundations of the currency board are firm, with convertibility, reserve currency, reserve requirement, and reserve composition set forth by law. Yet, the level of the exchange rate is not set in law, but devaluations require parliamentary approval, while the central bank has the discretion to revalue the currency. Furthermore, political and public commitment to the currency board is firm and broad.

Lithuania As has been mentioned before, the Lithuanian currency board was intended to mimic the Estonian currency board, yet opposition and discussion diluted much of the initial proposals.

The currency board pegged the litas to the US dollar at a rate of US$1 = 4 litas. The dollar was chosen instead of some European currency, because at the time of introduction of the currency board, 90% of trade were in dollars, most foreign-currency denominated assets and liabilities were in dollars, and, due to high inflation, most cash transactions were also conducted in dollars (Alonso-Gamo et al. 2002, p. 6). On February 2, 2002, with an eye to EU and euro area accession, the currency board switched from a peg to the dollar to a peg to the euro, based on the February 1 dollar/euro exchange rate. Since then the fixed exchange rate has been 1 euro = 3.4528 litas. Unlike in Estonia, the central bank has the power to re- and devalue the exchange rate, in consultation with the government. Changes in the exchange rate and/or a change of the anchor currency are to be undertaken only "in the case of extraordinary circumstances when further retaining of the exchange rate [...] would damage the stability of [the] national economy" (Republic of Lithuania 2001b, article 3).

According to the Law on the Credibility of the Litas (Republic of Lithuania 2001b, article 2), the currency board has to back the monetary base, consisting of notes and coins in circulation, accounts held with the Bank of Lithuania, and securities and promissory notes of the bank, with gold and foreign exchange reserves. Foreign exchange reserves are to consist of notes and coins of convertible foreign currency, convertible currency of the Bank of

Lithuania held with foreign banks and the IMF, and debt securities payable in convertible currency. As shown by figure 3.26, reserves have always exceeded the monetary base.[28]

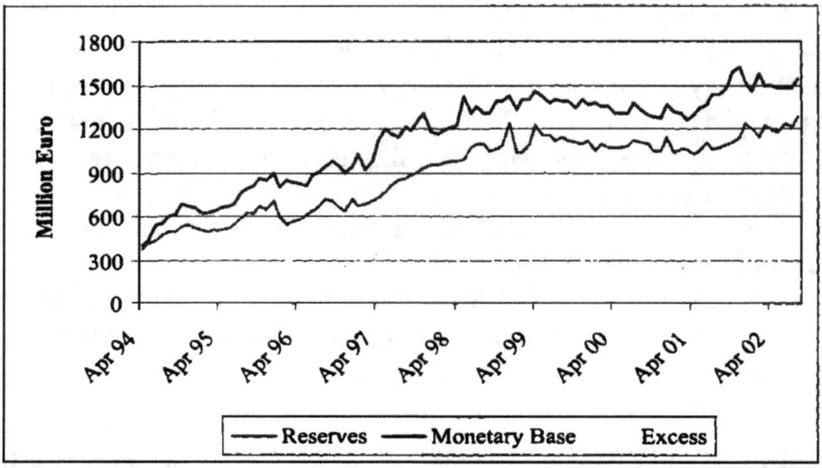

Source: Bank of Lithuania (2002b, 2002c, 2002d), own calculation

Figure 3.26: Reserves (gold and convertible foreign currency assets, net of government deposits in convertible currency) and monetary base, Lithuania, 1994–2002.

As in Estonia, the currency board is maintained by the independent Bank of Lithuania, which is also prohibited from granting loans to the government, directly or by buying securities in the primary market (Republic of Lithuania 2001a, articles 3, 37). But, the currency board is allowed to hold domestic government securities, which it may buy on the secondary market.

The institutional and organizational structure of the bank remained unchanged. Instead of setting up an Issue and a Banking Department with separate balance sheets, the Bank of Lithuania publishes only one balance sheet, making the currency board less transparent. Furthermore, despite ruling out lending to the government, the government nevertheless influences the money supply, whether intentionally or not, since the Bank of Lithuania keeps as a deposit the government's fiscal reserve. Changes in the fiscal reserve, therefore, result in changes in the money supply (Nenovsky, Hristov, and Mihaylov 2002, p. 20).

[28]To facilitate a comparison with the corresponding figure 3.25 for Estonia, only gold and convertible foreign currency assets of the Bank of Lithuania have been considered as reserves, net of government deposits in foreign currency.

The Bank of Lithuania is obliged to provide to banks and the government US$ (euros) for currency and all other liquid liabilities of the bank on demand at the specified fixed exchange rate (Camard 1996, p. 7).

As in Estonia, the Bank of Lithuania has retained some scope for discretionary monetary policy—yet, on such a scale that some authors even deny the existence of a currency board in Lithuania: "In essence the Lithuanian system is a normal system of a fixed exchange rate with certain limitations on money supply. [...] Lithuania is generally said to have a currency board while in fact this is not the case." (Äimä 1998, p. 23) The Bank of Lithuania is allowed to set reserve requirements, to engage in rediscount operations, to give loans to commercial banks as a lender of last resort, to conduct open market operations, and may establish and apply any other monetary policy instruments compatible with its primary objective, to seek price stability (Republic of Lithuania 2001a, articles 25–32). During its years of operation, the central bank has made ample use of those instruments. For example, during a banking crisis in 1995, the bank lowered required reserves from 12% to 10%, and then to 5% in May 1996. In addition, sanctions for the failure to fulfill reserve requirements were abolished in March 1996. Required reserves regained the 10% level in June 1996, when the banking crisis subsided (Nenovsky, Hristov, and Mihaylov 2002, p. 21). Although the broad scope for discretionary monetary policy represents a marked deviation from the currency board idea, the Lithuanian monetary arrangement still exhibits the central currency board characteristics, the fixed, exchange rate, the backing requirement, convertibility, and a legal commitment, and is therefore generally considered to be a currency board.

Accompanying the introduction of the currency board, Lithuania adopted far reaching first-generation market oriented reforms, such as price liberalization, liberalization of current and capital account transaction, the beginning of privatization, and trade policy reforms. However, second-generation reforms started to lag behind during 1994–1999, reducing potential productivity growth potential. In 2000-2001 structural reforms were accelerated again (Alonso-Gamo et al. 2002, p. 18).

Dollarization is widespread in Lithuania. The ratio of foreign currency deposits per domestic-currency denominated components of broad money (M2) was at 90% in 1993 and varied between 30% and 50% for most of the currency boards existence (Vetlov 2001, p. 35). Additionally, the re-pegging of the litas to the euro has left many small businesses and households exposed to exchange rate variations, as many assets and liabilities are still dollar denominated and the lack of access to financial services prevented the use of hedging instruments to cover those risks (Alonso-Gamo et al. 2002, p. 11)

Overall, compared to Estonia, the Lithuanian currency board exhibits much less commitment to the exchange rate peg. While the currency board operates in many respects along the lines of a pure currency board, it is allowed to hold domestic assets as reserves, and the scope for discretionary monetary policy is broader than in Estonia. Also, political and public commitment to the currency board have been weak. There have been repeated demands and official announcements of abolishing the currency board throughout the whole operation of the currency board, and government policy has in many cases undermined the credibility of the currency board. For example, the government pledged foreign exchange reserves of the Bank of Lithuania as collateral to obtain a loan from a German bank, and the largest bank in Lithuania has been partially exempt from reserve requirements in exchange for a loan to the state energy system (Camard 1996, pp. 9–10).

Furthermore, the legal commitment to the board is relatively weak, compared to Estonia. Neither the exchange rate nor the reserve currency are stated in the Credibility Law. The power to change the exchange rate as well as the anchor currency lies with the Bank of Lithuania and the government, instead of the parliament.

3.4.3 Currency Boards Performance

All Baltic countries managed to get inflation under control similarly well, regardless of whether they had a currency board or a fixed exchange rate, as in the case of Latvia (see figure 3.27). Yet, in all three countries inflation did not fall below 10% per year until 1997. During the last three years inflation has been lowest in Lithuania, even witnessing short periods of deflation, while Estonia has had above 4% inflation during the last two years.

The fact that inflation levels in the Baltic countries have and continue to exceed international levels has generally been attributed to four factors: First, structural change and price liberalization initiated a catch-up process, during which prices increased to international levels. Second, it is proposed that initial under-valuation of the currencies was made up by higher inflation. Third, high productivity growth in the tradeables sector led to increasing price levels, a phenomenon generally known as the Balassa-Samuelson effect. Finally, sustained high levels of capital inflows hampered efforts to reduce inflation, as currency boards rule out sterilized interventions, and capital inflows are largely translated into an expansion of the monetary base (Ramon-Ballester 1999, pp. 12–13).

Judging the macroeconomic performance of Estonia and Lithuania by GDP growth, Estonia has fared best. Not only did it experience the least marked drop of GDP after independence and during economic transforma-

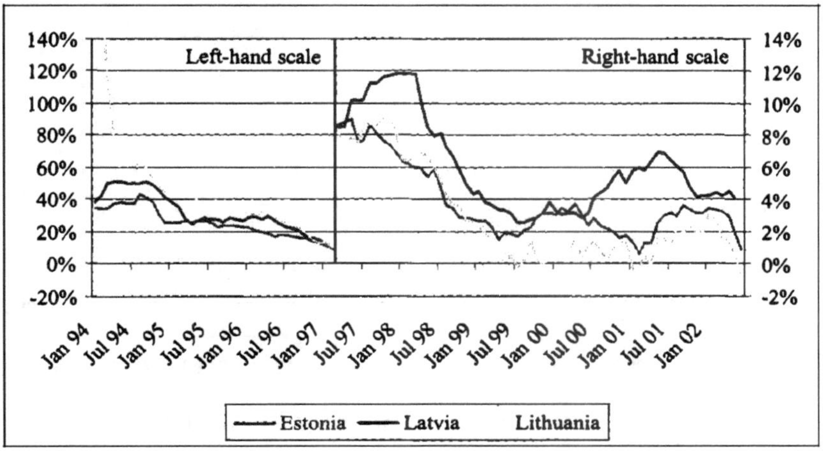

Source: IMF (2002c), own calculation

Figure 3.27: Annual Inflation, change of CPI on previous year, Baltic countries, 1994–2002.

tion, some 23% reduction of GDP between 1991 and 1994, but it also enjoyed higher growth rates afterwards, averaging 5.1% between 1995 and 2001 (see figure 3.28). By comparison, Lithuania's GDP fell by approximately 40% between 1991 and 1994 and has grown at a slower pace since then, at an average of 3.7% between 1995 and 2001 (see figure 3.29). Yet, Lithuania still outperformed Latvia, whose GDP fell by an initial 55% and has since then enjoyed even slower growth (Korhonen 1999, p. 23).

In Estonia, where the currency board was the centerpiece of economic reform, macroeconomic performance of the economy was impressive. Driven by far reaching structural reforms, privatization, a very liberal trade regime, tight fiscal policy, which even produced surpluses in 1993 and 1997, Estonia experienced strong growth, reaching a peak of more than 10% in 1997. The discipline effect of the currency board helped in quickly bringing down interest rates close to German levels, and from mid-1994 to end of 1997 and since the end of 1999 the spread between money market interest rates has generally not exceeded 0.5% (see figure 3.30).

The Estonian economy and the currency board came under pressure from late 1997 until early 1999, when the Asian crisis in 1997 and the Russian debt default in 1998 led to reduction in capital inflows. The resulting liquidity shock led to a steep increase of interest rates, reaching levels of up to 17% in the money market. The financial system came under strain, revealing some excessive risk-taking positions and poor management by certain banks. Yet, the central bank did not intervene to inject liquidity into the market. Instead,

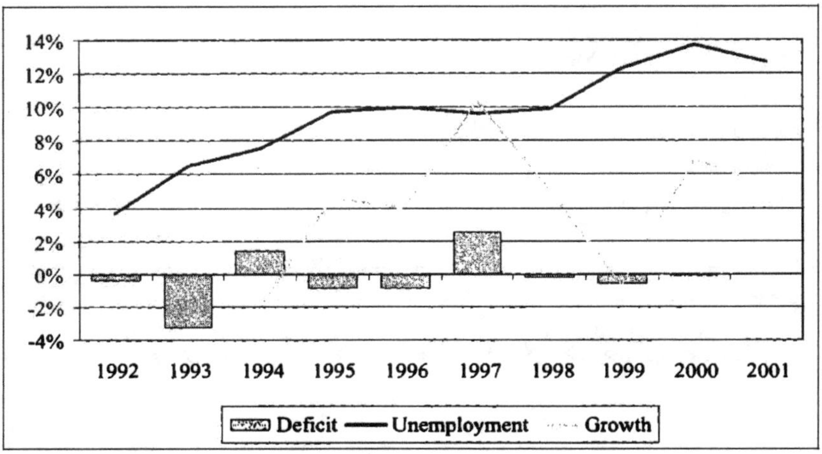

Source: IMF (2002c), own calculation

Figure 3.28: Budget deficit (net of lending and grants), unemployment rate, and growth, Estonia, 1992–2001.

two small banks were allowed to go bankrupt while one medium-sized bank was saved from bankruptcy by acquiring a majority stake (Ramon-Ballester 1999, p. 14; Bank of Estonia 1999, June 28, October 1).

The speculative pressure against the Estonian economy ebbed away by early 1999, but resulted in a reduction of growth in 1998 and negative growth in 1999. Since then, though, the economy has made a strong recovery.

One accompaniment of economic transformation in both Estonia and Lithuania (though to a lesser extent) has been the steep increase in unemployment (see figures 3.28 and 3.29). After the initial phase of transformation from 1991 to 1994, unemployment reached approximately 9.9% in Estonia and 7.3% in Lithuania. Yet, the ensuing boom from 1995 to 1998 failed to yield a reduction in unemployment, while the recession in 1999 drove unemployment up even further, to reach a high of 13.6% in Estonia and of 12.6% in Lithuania in 2000. A recent study by the IMF on the labor markets in the Baltic countries and in Bulgaria (Schiff et al. 2001, p. 7) found that this cannot be explained by labor market constraints, as labor laws allow for easy hiring and firing of employees, unions have relatively minor roles, labor mobility is high, and minimum wages and unemployment benefits are relatively low. Instead, the authors conclude, high unemployment can partially be explained by a mismatch between skills of the unemployed and the needs of new enterprises.

Compared to Estonia, the performance of the Lithuanian economy has not been as good. The initial loss in GDP during the early phase of trans-

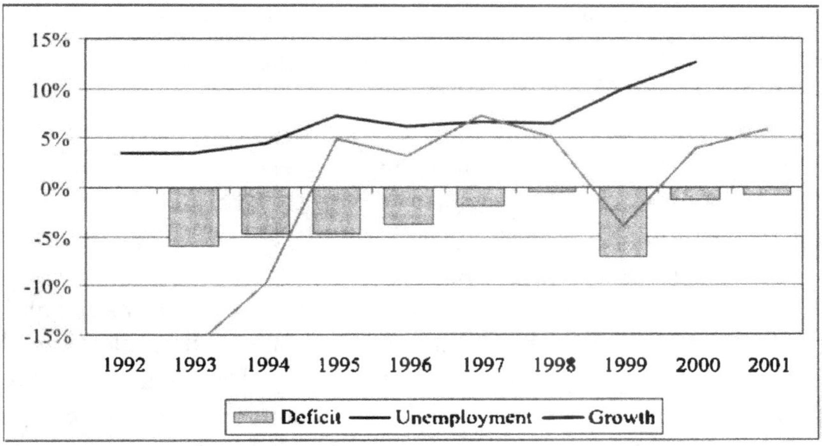

Source: IMF (2002c), own calculation

Figure 3.29: Budget deficit (net of lending and grants), unemployment rate, and growth, Lithuania, 1992–2001.

formation has been higher and growth has been lower afterwards, with the recession in 1999 leading to negative growth of -3.9%. Also, while inflation in Lithuania has in general been lower since 1997, the country even experienced short periods of deflation. Part of this can be attributed to less far reaching reforms in Lithuania and less disciplined fiscal policy, with the budget deficit averaging -3.4% from 1993 to 2001, reaching a high of -7.1% in 1999.

Furthermore, the potential credibility and stability effects of the currency board were undermined by constant uncertainty about the commitment to and the future of the currency board. As early as November 1994 the bounds of the currency board were stretched by authorities by partially exempting a bank from reserve requirements in exchange for a loan to a state enterprise, and by pledging as collateral foreign exchange reserves of the Bank of Lithuania to a German bank in order for the government to receive a loan. At the same time, rumors of an impending devaluation led to an outflow of foreign exchange from the Bank of Lithuania. The rumor was sustained by disquieting statements by central bank officials, questioning the governments commitment to the exchange rate parity, and an open letter signed by 32 of the 114 members of parliament, calling for a devaluation. Yet, only when foreign exchange outflows became substantial in February 1995 did authorities issue a strong and categorical denial of devaluation and spoke out in support of the currency board (Camard 1996, pp. 10–11).

At the end of 1996, an new proposal for abandoning the currency board and replacing it with a fixed exchange rate was launched, justified with the need to regulate and offset money market volatility and to extend the use of the lender of last resort function. The proposal found formal expression in January 1997, when the Bank of Lithuania announced its 1997–1999 monetary policy program. The bank envisaged a three stage exit from the currency board, developing and applying a wider range of monetary policy instruments, and eventually pegging the litas to a basket of currencies, including the dollar and the euro, by 2000 (Nenovsky, Hristov, and Mihaylov 2002, pp. 21–23). Yet, in 1999, and in the wake of the Russian crisis and subsequent pressures, the plan to exit the currency board was abandoned and in October 1999 the Bank of Lithuania announced it would instead aim at directly re-pegging the litas to the euro in 2001. Eventually, in June 2001 the bank announced the exact schedule and modalities of the re-pegging: it was going to peg the litas to the euro starting February 2, 2002, based on the dollar/euro exchange rate prevailing on February 1 (Alonso-Gamo et al. 2002, pp. 8–9).

On top of discussion about the future of the currency board, Lithuania faced a severe banking crisis from 1994–1996. In 1994 a number of banks failed to make progress towards compliance with prudential norms established in 1994, most notably capital requirements. Yet, the continued violations remained unsanctioned. Eventually, a total of 14 smaller banks were forced into bankruptcy, accounting for 5% of banking system assets. Signals of banking system stress intensified in mid-1995, when Aura Bank, a medium-sized bank, faced liquidity problems after deposit withdrawals, initiated by rumors questioning the banks solvency. The government and the Bank of Lithuania gave support to Aura Bank, but public confidence in the system continued to erode and withdrawals continued. In fall 1995 another mid-sized bank, Vakura Bank, needed liquidity support. (Enoch, Gulde, and Hardy 2002, p. 26).

By late December banking sector fragility had evolved into a crisis. The largest private bank, Innovation Bank, and its would-be merger partner, Litimpex Bank, were discovered to be insolvent and were put under moratoria, suspending their commercial operations. Additionally, Vakura Bank again experienced liquidity problems and was put under conservatorship of the Bank of Lithuania. At that point, 30% of deposits in the system were affected by the crisis. Depositors reacted by shifting their deposits to state-controlled banks, where deposits were fully guaranteed by the Civil Codes. Consequently, even solid private banks began to face liquidity problems. Also, an audit revealed that two of the three state banks would need to be recapitalized to meet the capital adequacy ratio, pushing the financial system to the verge of a systemic crisis, and money market rates up to 25% in April 1996 (Enoch, Gulde, and Hardy 2002, pp. 26–27).

By mid-1996, banks holding more than three quarters of the system's asset and liabilities were insolvent or undercapitalized. The government decided that a strategic plan was needed to resolve the banking crisis. In September 1996 the government adopted a plan based on three principles: First, no bank would be allowed to operate until it met the capital adequacy requirement by the end of 1996. Second, any capital support from the government had to give the government adequate share capital and voting rights, so existing shareholders would not benefit unduly from government support. Third, any government support would be conditional on change of the management of the bank. Eventually, the government paid all depositors in banks that had failed before 1997 in full. Overall, the restructuring plan was estimated to have cost roughly US$261 million, or 3.5% of GDP (Enoch, Gulde, and Hardy 2002, pp. 28–31).

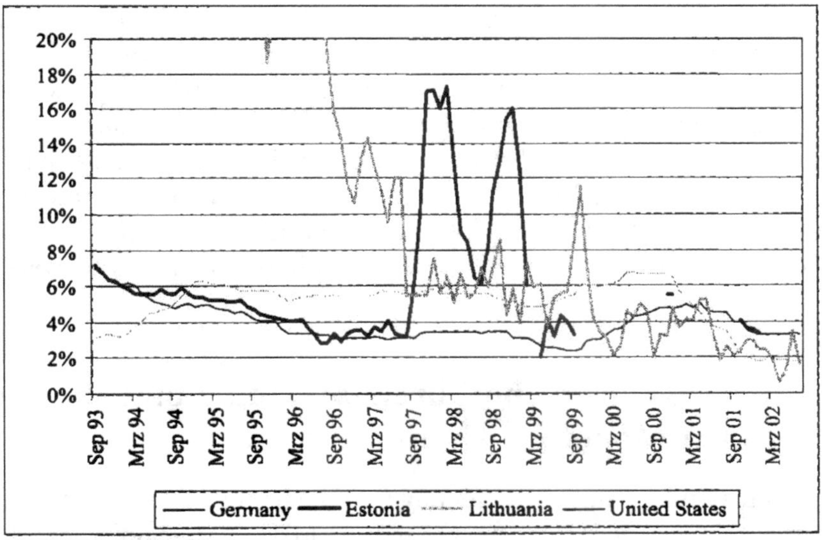

Source: IMF (2002c)

Figure 3.30: Money market interest rates, Estonia, Germany, Lithuania, and USA, 1993–2002.

The stability of the financial system was tested again in 1997 and 1998 during the Asian and Russian crises, respectively. While the Russian crisis caused a deep recession, the banking system remained largely unaffected, except for the—orderly—failure of one bank, which did not lead to a renewed loss of confidence (Enoch, Gulde, and Hardy 2002, p. 32). Yet, the recession brought the currency board to the verge of collapse in late 1999, due to an unsustainable fiscal position, intensified currency substitution, and political instability as two successive governments resigned, nourishing fears of an impending devaluation. The large deficit was largely due to the costs of bank restructuring and lending to a distressed oil company, and as interest rates soared, the government had difficulties financing the deficit. Temporary trade restrictions and price controls increased currency substitution as agents shifted out of litas and into dollar deposits. Eventually, corrective measures of the newly sworn in government in November 1999, such as massive fiscal adjustment and a package of comprehensive structural reforms in 2000, managed to reduce the pressure, and to avert another banking crisis (Alonso-Gamo et al. 2002, p. 7).

The combination of the events described above, the ongoing insecurity about the currency board, the banking crisis 1994–1996, and the deep recession in 1999, is reflected in the evolution of interest rates in Lithuania, as shown in figure 3.30. Contrary to Estonian interest rates, money market rates in Lithuania have been high and volatile, and did not converge close to US levels until mid-1997. On the other hand, during the Asian and Russian crises 1997–1998, interest rates in Lithuania remained relatively low, partly due to the newly stabilized banking system and to the returned confidence in it, while interest rates in Estonia shot up, mainly since the banking system had not been tested before and the government largely refrained from intervention. The recession in 1999 led to another peak in interest rates in Lithuania, but since then money market rates have remained relatively low, yet still volatile.

3.4.4 Accession to the European Union and the European Monetary Union

Both Estonia and Lithuania are aiming for accession to the European Union (EU) and the European Monetary Union (EMU). Accession to the EU is scheduled for 2004, but accession to EMU requires prior successful participation in the European Exchange Rate Mechanism (ERM II), starting after becoming an EU member.

Participation in EMU and the adoption of the euro as domestic currency is conditional on fulfilment of the Maastricht convergence criteria, which are to assure stable and sustainable economic development prior to joining the monetary union. The criteria put limits on the budget deficit (3% of GDP) and government debt (60% of GDP)[29], on the inflation rate (no to exceed

[29]In both cases, though, exceptions to these rules exist, when a country is rapidly converging toward these levels from a higher level, or when a deficit is only exceptionally and temporarily above the 3% level (Kutan and Pautola-Mol 2002, p. 9).

inflation in the euro area by more than 1.5 percentage points), on interest rates (average long-term interest rates are not to exceed the interest rate(s) of the euro area member state(s) with the best price stability performance by more than two percentage points over the course of the year prior to accession to the euro area), and on changes of the exchange rate (under ERM II the exchange rate of the domestic currency vis a vis the central euro rate must remain within a maximum band of ±15% for two years prior to joining the euro area) (Rohde and Janssen 2000, p. 177).

Estonia and Lithuania have both, in recent years, started comprehensive reforms to prepare for EU, ERM II and ensuing EMU membership. The Bank of Estonia launched a monetary reform project in 2000, to bring the monetary policy operational framework, liquidity management, financial supervision, and safety regulations for the financial sector in line with EU regulations (Ross 1999; Bank of Estonia 2000; Kraft 2001). The Bank of Lithuania has started similar reforms, most notably switching the anchor currency of the currency board in February 2002, but also measures on the development of monetary policy instruments, improving the payment system and ensuring prudential banking (Bank of Lithuania 2002a, pp. 103–106).

From the current point of view, both countries look more or less set to fulfill the Maastricht criteria: They easily fulfill the debt criterion (Estonia: 3.2% of GDP in 2000, Lithuania: 26.9% of GDP in 2001) and at present interest rates conform to the Masstricht criteria as well, though prior to 2000 they have at times exceeded European levels by far. Budget discipline has been stronger in Estonia, with an average budget surplus of 0.15% 1996–2000, while Lithuania had an average deficit of -2.54% 1996–2001, yet, still complying with the respective Maastricht criterion, and largely due to the excessive deficit during the recession in 1999.[30] Inflation has been greatly reduced since the introduction of the currency boards, but has recently been on the rise again in Estonia, with average annual inflation of 4.4% since 1999, not fulfilling the respective Maastricht criterion, while Lithuania's inflation has been very low since 1999, averaging 1.1%.

Estonia has repeatedly announced the intention to maintain its currency board during participation in ERM II, and Lithuania is considered to intend to do the same. Therefore, judging from past experience and success in maintaining the currency boards, one would expect the likeliness of both countries fulfilling the fifth, the exchange rate criterion, to be relatively good, at least the same as during the years prior to a potential EU and ERM II

[30]See Kutan and Pautola-Mol (2002) for an overview of the appropriateness of the Maastricht fiscal criteria for the Baltic countries, and fulfilment of these criteria by Estonia, Lithuania, and Latvia.

membership. Yet, the appropriateness of having a currency board during ERM II is not acknowledged unanimously (Gulde, Kähkönen, and Keller 2000; Rohde and Janssen 2000, 2001).

Generally, there are no formal obstacles to participating in ERM II with a currency board using the euro as an anchor currency. The compatibility of currency boards with ERM II has been acknowledged by both the Ecofin Council and the Council of Europe (Rohde and Janssen 2001, pp. 356–357). Currency board countries could apply to have the fluctuation band narrowed from ±15% to ±0%, as in the case of Denmark, where the domestic currency is allowed to fluctuate by ±2.5% around the central euro rate. Yet, in this case problems could arise from intervention requirements. Once the margins of the agreed band are reached, the European Central Bank (ECB) and the domestic central bank are required to engage in compulsory intervention to support the exchange rate, which would be necessary whenever the fixed exchange rate gets under pressure. In theory, such support could be unlimited. In practice, though, both, the ECB and the domestic central bank can stop intervention whenever price stability is endangered. Further, it is assumed, the ECB would shy away from unlimited support, even for small countries like the Baltic countries, for fear of creating a precedence that would oblige the ECB to grant unlimited support to large countries exchange rates, as well. Yet, a stop of support from the ECB might be interpreted as a bad signal about the sustainability of the respective exchange rate, increasing the pressure even further (Rohde and Janssen 2000, pp. 178–179; Rohde and Janssen 2001, pp. 357–358).

Therefore, the ECB announced that generally currency boards may be suitable for participation in ERM II—which is to be decided on a case-to-case basis—but with the fluctuation band narrowed to ±0% only by unilateral commitment of the accession country (Bank of Estonia 2000, paragraph 9). Such an unilateral commitment relieves the ECB from the duty of compulsory intervention and leaves the burden of defending the exchange rate with the domestic central bank. Prima facie, this resembles the situation currency board countries faced prior to entry in ERM II.

Yet, as Rohde and Janssen (2000, pp. 179–180, 2001, pp. 358–359) point out, the economic environment in which the currency boards operate, might differ, undermining their stability. While the history of the currency boards in Estonia and Lithuania has proven the authorities' willingness to accept the cost of adjustment during times of exchange rate pressure, the European Union might not be willing to accept these cost, once Estonia and Lithuania are members of the EU. The resolution of the Council of Europe on the introduction of ERM II states in its principles that a stable economic environment is necessary for both the functioning of the single market, and for investment, growth, and employment. Consequently, the process of real adjustment in a currency board economy under speculative pressure might be considered incompatible with these principles and the EU or ECB might have an interest in a rapid realignment of the respective exchange rate.

Eventually, just the awareness of financial markets of this possibility might lead to speculative attacks on the currency boards, testing the willingness of both the currency board country and the EU and ECB to accept the resulting adjustment cost.

Therefore, the authors conclude, currency boards might not be as suitable for ERM II participation as initially assumed. If currency board countries are forced to devalue, even by a little, this would constitute a violation of the exchange rate criterion, stating that a stable exchange rate has to be maintained for at least two years prior to accession to EMU, and eventually delay entry into the euro area.

On the other hand, the alternative of instituting an interim exchange rate arrangement for ERM II also poses a lot of problems. First of all, a host of legal, institutional, and practical problems would have to be overcome. Second, both Estonia and Lithuania lack deep foreign exchange markets, which is one of the reasons they chose a fixed exchange rate in the first place. It is, therefore, likely that an interim exchange rate arrangement would be characterized by wide swings in the exchange rate as market participants speculate about the entry rate. Third, abandoning a well-established, well-functioning, and transparent currency board could bring about an adverse market reaction, as markets might see it motivated by some hidden, underlying weakness. Furthermore, the loss of discipline and credibility entailed in a currency board might even worsen the reaction of markets (Gulde, Kähkönen, and Keller 2000, pp. 18–20).

Ultimately, the decision on an exchange rate mechanism for ERM II involves a tradeoff between potential benefits and drawbacks of the available exchange rate mechanisms. Both Estonia and Lithuania appear determined to join ERM II with their present currency boards and have, therefore, opted for sticking with the exchange rate system they have gotten to know and have learned to handle for almost a decade now, instead of switching to a more flexible arrangement they are not—or barely not, in the case of Lithuania—experienced in.

3.5 Bulgaria (1997)

The most recent currency board to be installed, along with the currency board in Bosnia, was the Bulgarian currency board. While transition in

Bulgaria started at the same time as in Estonia and Lithuania, Bulgaria adopted a more hesitant approach to reform and instead adopted a managed exchange rate, supported by a full-fledged central bank. Lack of economic reforms, unsustainable economic policy and bad management led to a combined fiscal, banking, and currency crisis, which eventually required drastic reform measures, including the introduction of a currency board.

3.5.1 Lead-Up to the Currency Board

Unlike Estonia and Lithuania, Bulgaria had not been part of the Soviet Union, but of all Comecon members (Council for Mutual Economic Assistance), it had been the country most closely attached to the Soviet Union, and the structure of its economy had probably been more similar to that of some ex-Soviet republics than to the economies of other Comecon countries (Dobrinsky 2000, pp. 582–583).

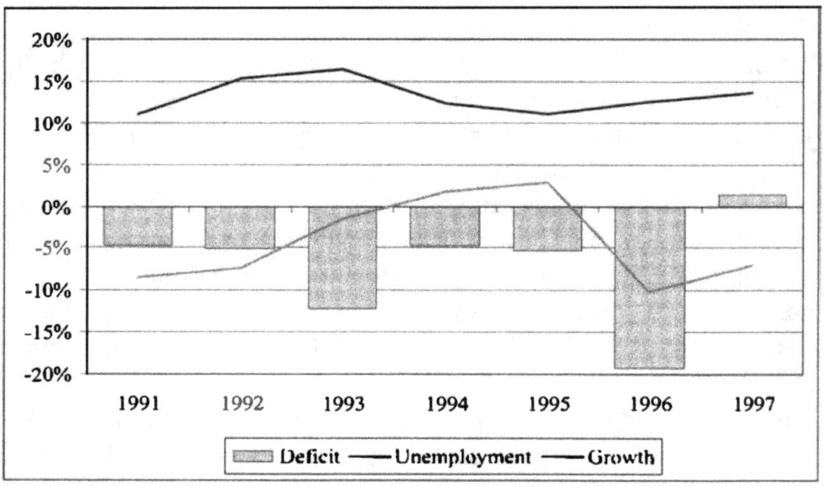

Source: IMF (2002c), own calculation

Figure 3.31: Budget deficit (net of lending and grants), unemployment rate, and growth, Bulgaria, 1992–1997.

The economic performance of Bulgaria during the first years of transition has been dismal, even after taking into account the economic cost of structural adjustment experienced by all transition countries. From 1991 to 1997 the economy shrank at an average annual rate of -4.2%. Only in 1994 and 1995 did Bulgaria experience some, though little, growth (see figure 3.31). Fiscal discipline was barely non-existent, with the government running an average deficit of 7.1% of GDP between 1991 and 1997. The budget deficit amounted to a staggering 19.3% in 1996, at the height of the financial and economic crisis.

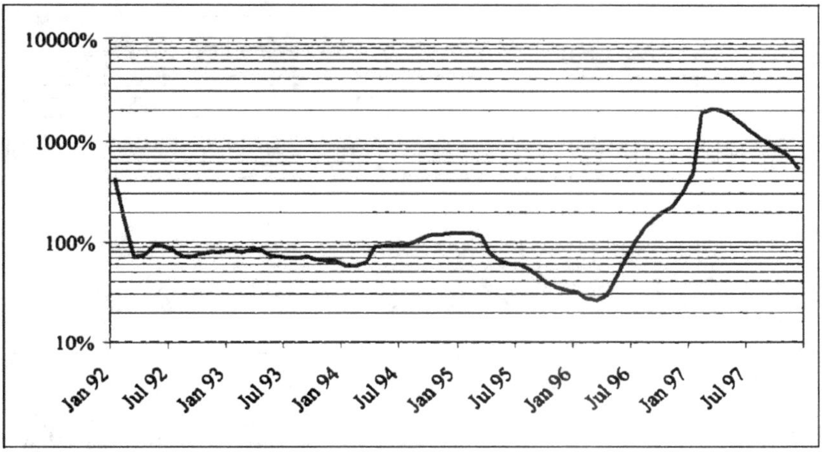

Source: IMF (2002c), own calculation

Figure 3.32: Inflation, change of CPI on previous year, Bulgaria, 1992–1997, logarithmic scale.

As a consequence of bad economic management and monetization of the budget deficit, inflation has been high and chronic, eventually resulting in hyperinflation in late 1996, when annual inflation rates reached more than 2000% (see figure 3.32). Not surprisingly, the domestic currency, the lev, lost more than 99% of its value relative to the US dollar between January 1992 and February 1997, when the exchange rate reached its peak (see figure 3.33).

Economic transition in Bulgaria was preceded by default on foreign debt in early 1990, which had been accrued in the second half of the 1980s. In 1991 a transformation program was launched, which envisaged wide-ranging price liberalization, the opening of the economy, abolition of central planning and the free entry of private economic agents to the markets. Because of low foreign exchange reserves due to the debt default, Bulgaria opted for a managed floating exchange rate and money-based stabilization. However, the first period of of transformation was characterized by slow reforms, inconsistent policies, a lax fiscal stance, and weak regulation of banks and firms, especially state enterprises (Dobrinsky 2000, pp. 583–585).

The economic crisis that would eventually lead to the introduction of the currency board evolved in three areas. The fiscal crisis was mainly related to the financial rescue of state-owned firms and banks. Until 1996 no effort had been made to impose hard budget constraints on the operation of state-

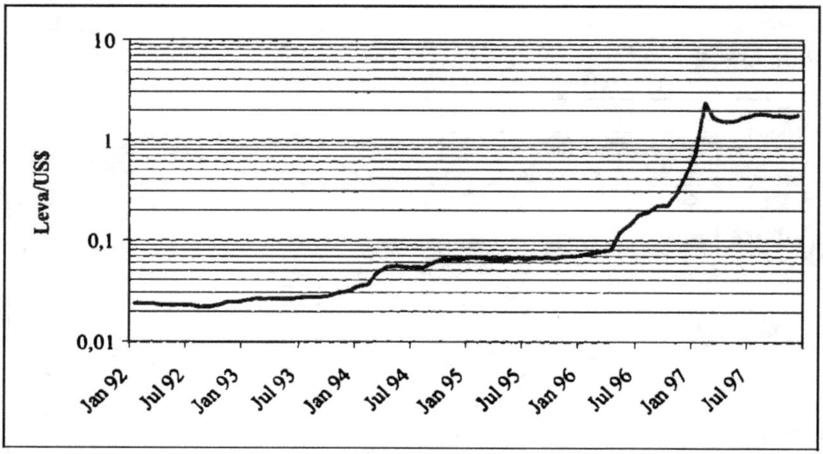

Source: IMF (2002c)

Figure 3.33: Exchange rate, lev against US dollar, Bulgaria, 1992–1997, logarithmic scale.

owned firms, of which many had become unviable after the start of economic transformation. Instead, a series of unconditional financial bailouts of state banks and enterprises had been performed 1991–1996, resulting in the fiscalization of quasi-fiscal deficits and skyrocketing public debt. Together with the resumption of external debt service in 1994, after a debt-restructuring-and-rescheduling agreement with the London Club creditor banks, the service on domestic debt led to the crowding out of non-interest budget expenditure and still increasing budget deficits. The authorities attempted a variety of approaches to finance the deficit, all of them leading to the eventual monetization of the deficit, though (Dobrinsky 2000, pp. 587–590).

The banking crisis, commencing in 1995, was the consequence of the policy of soft budget constraints, leading to an amassment of bad loans, and of weak banking supervision and improper banking practices. In late 1995 some banks began to experience liquidity problems, caused by the unsustainable number of bad loans, leading to a run on the banks concerned. When in May 1996 several of the affected banks were closed, the situation gradually escalated into a full-fledged run on the banking system. In September 1996 the Bulgarian National Bank (BNB) placed another nine banks under conservatorship, amounting to the closure of one-third of the banking sector, including the banks closed in May. To further support the banking system, the BNB injected liquidity into the system through its Lombard window and by repurchasing government bonds, thereby fuelling already rampant inflation even further (Gulde 1999, p. 4).

The collapse of the banking system aggravated the fiscal crisis, as by mid-1996 most new government security issues were under-subscribed and remained partly unsold. In turn, the government started to pay the interest on outstanding securities through newly issued ones, thereby further reducing the liquidity of the banking sector (Dobrinsky 2000, p. 592).

The third crisis, the currency crisis, was a direct consequence of the other two. For most of the time since 1991 the BNB had pursued a policy of nominal exchange rate stability, implicitly using the exchange rate as a nominal anchor. To support the exchange rate, the bank had kept interest rates relatively high. Starting in 1995, when debt service started to become an unsustainable burden on the government budget, the BNB began lowering interest rates, pressured by fiscal authorities. Yet, lower interest rates, in combination with the ongoing banking crisis, led to destabilization of money demand, demonetization and capital flight. Up to a point, the central bank defended the lev by intervening in the foreign exchange market, but the main outcome was a depletion of reserves. By mid-1996 the exchange rate was in free fall and any further attempts of BNB at stabilizing it, such as repeatedly raising interest rates, failed (Stefanov 1999, p. 139; Dobrinsky 2000, pp. 592–596).

In November 1996 the IMF initiated discussions concerning the adoption of a currency board. While opponents stressed that Bulgaria did not fulfill the necessary preconditions, troubled by a weak banking sector that might require lender of last resort assistance, and very low currency reserves, which might require a large up-front devaluation, the newly-elected government eventually adopted the plan and initiated a drastic change in the course of economic policy. Furthermore, as noted by (Gulde 1999, p. 8), "the near-hyperinflation[...]—while being difficult and costly from a distributional point of view—was crucial for the eventual viability of the currency board. It reduced the real value of the domestic debt overhang, which initially had been a threat to a balanced budget[, and] allowed banks some breathing space by rapidly devaluing the size of their domestic currency liabilities [...]".

Eventually, the Bulgarian currency board started operating on July 1, 1997.

3.5.2 Currency Board Design

Under the currency board, the value of the lev was pegged to the Deutsche mark at a rate of 1 DM = 1000 lev, as specified by the Law on the Bulgarian National Bank (LoBNB) (Republic of Bulgaria 2002, article 29). There had been some debate of whether a peg to the US dollar would be preferable due to its widespread use in informal transaction and as a store of value, and since oil imports, which are important for the Bulgarian economy, are priced in dollars. Yet, eventually the Deutsche mark was chosen, being more consistent with the country's trade structure, and with an eye on integration into the EU (Miller 2001, p. 56; Gulde 1999, p. 9). From the beginning on, the LoBNB had contained a provision for switching from a peg to the Deutsche mark to a peg to the euro, which became effective on January 1, 1999 (Republic of Bulgaria 2002, article 29, paragraph 2). Furthermore, the lev was re-denominated in mid-1999, effectively stripping the last three zeros from notes and coins (Republic of Bulgaria 1999), so the current fixed exchange rate stands at 1 euro = 1.95583 lev. Consequently, as the exchange rate is specified by law, neither the central bank nor the government have the power to change it, and re- or devaluations of the currency can only be decided by parliament.

The LoBNB specifies that the BNB has to fully back the monetary base with its gross international foreign exchange reserves. The monetary base is defined as notes and coins in circulation and accounts held by other parties with the BNB. Gross international foreign exchange reserves comprise of banknotes and coins in freely convertible currency, funds in convertible currency held by the BNB with other central banks or highly rated[31] financial institutions, special drawing rights of the IMF held by the BNB, highly rated foreign issued debt instruments, payable in convertible foreign currency, and gold (Republic of Bulgaria 2002, article 28).

The currency board is operated by the BNB, which is an independent legal entity (Republic of Bulgaria 2002, articles 1, 44). The BNB is prohibited from extending credit to the government, except for onlending of proceeds of purchases from the IMF under clear procedures (Republic of Bulgaria 2002, article 45; Gulde 1999, p. 14). As in Estonia, two separate departments of the BNB have been established: An Issue Department, which is effectively the currency board, and a Banking Department, which may use the excess reserves of the currency board for limited monetary policy and lender of last resort actions. Additionally, a Supervision Department has been established, responsible for banking system regulation (Avramov 1999, p. 8; Republic of Bulgaria 2002, article 20).

The LoBNB requires the BNB to sell or purchase on demand Deutsche mark / euro against lev without limit on the basis of spot exchange rates, which must not depart by more than 0.5% (including fees and commissions) from the official exchange rate (Republic of Bulgaria 2002, article 30).

[31] The term "highly rated" refers to the credit rating of such financial instruments. Specifically, the law requires that "obligations are assigned one of the two highest credit ratings by two internationally recognized credit rating agencies" (Republic of Bulgaria 2002, article 29, paragraph 3).

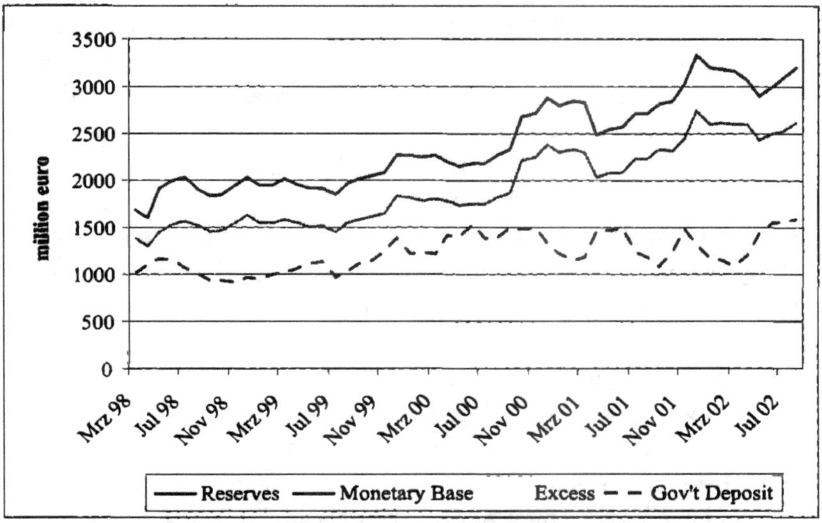

Sources: Bulgarian National Bank (2002a, 2002b), own calculation

Figure 3.34: BNB Issue Department: Reserves (excluding government deposits), monetary base (excluding government deposits), government deposits, excess reserves, Bulgaria, 1998–2002.

Of all present currency boards discussed in this chapter, the Bulgarian currency board has the most narrow scope for discretionary monetary policy. The BNB is allowed to change reserve requirements, which were initially at 11% and have been lowered to 8% in 2000. Reserve requirements were lowered not to affect the money supply, but rather reflecting a policy of step-by-step reduction towards the level established in the euro zone (Bulgarian National Bank 2002c; Nenovsky, Hristov, and Mihaylov 2002, p. 27). Furthermore, the BNB may, as excess reserves permit, extend short-term (up to three months), collateralized loans to solvent banks as lender of last resort support in the event of a liquidity risk affecting the stability of the banking system (Republic of Bulgaria 2002, articles 19, 33; Bulgarian National Bank 1998; Dobrev 1999, pp. 12–13). Yet, besides these two measures of discretionary monetary policy through the BNB, a third channel exists affecting money supply: As the BNB is obliged to maintain the fiscal reserve of the government (Republic of Bulgaria 2002, article 43), any changes in the fiscal reserve affect the money supply in the Bulgarian economy, allowing the government, whether intentionally or not, to pursue discretionary policy. This effect is clearly highlighted by figure 3.34, which shows that marked reductions of the government deposit at the central bank tend to lead to marked increases in the monetary base (excluding the government deposit), as the withdrawn fiscal reserve is monetarized. This design feature, which distorts the inherent stabilization through the link between balance of payments dynamics and monetary base dynamics, has often been criticized and has been found to be a destabilizing element of the Bulgarian currency board design (Nenovsky and Hristov 1998, pp. 39–41, 1999, p. 20). On the other hand, the alternative, keeping the government fiscal reserves with commercial banks, had been discarded, first, because at the time of currency board introduction the banking system had been considered too weak, and, second, such a design would create money supply volatility through IMF tranches and debt service payments (Miller 1999, p. 8).

Accompanying the introduction of the currency board, wide-ranging economic reforms were initiated. Almost all non-infrastructure enterprise assets and 80% of bank assets have been privatized, and loss-making state enterprises have been made subject to a strict income policy. Trade and price liberalization have been achieved, and the overhaul of the pension and health care system is on its way. However, as noted by the IMF, progress has been limited in improving the efficiency of the public administration, reforms in the energy and transport sectors has been slow, and key enterprises have yet to be privatized (IMF 2000, 2002b).

Due to the hyperinflation late 1996, the extent of currency substitution is relatively high in Bulgaria. While in 1995 the ratio of foreign currency deposits per broad money was estimated to be 28.4% (Baliño et al. 1999, p. 2), a more recent study estimates currency substitution to be some 53% and asset substitution roughly 57% (Feige and Dean 2002, p. 16).

Like Estonia and Lithuania, Bulgaria is aiming at joining the EU and the EMU; one reason why the Deutsche mark was chosen as anchor currency on establishing the currency board in 1997. While Bulgaria will most likely not belong to the first wave of accession countries scheduled to join the EU in 2004, it has already expressed its intention to maintain the currency board during a prospective ERM II membership (Kabakchiev 2000; Gavriiski 2000). Therefore, the deliberations made in subsection 3.4.4 also apply to Bulgaria.

3.5.3 Currency Board Performance

The currency board succeeded in rapidly reducing inflation to single-digit levels. After a short period of deflation in 1999, inflation has been ranging between 5% and 10% (see figure 3.35).

The economy has recovered from economic and political turmoil in 1996 and 1997, and growth has resumed under adverse external economic conditions, yet at relatively modest levels, averaging 3.9% 1998–2001 (see figure 3.36). By the end of 2001 real GDP was still below its 1995 level. The

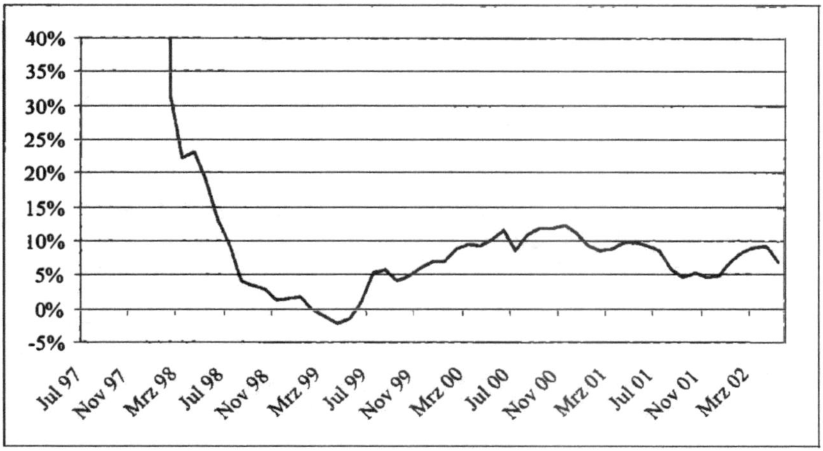

Source: IMF (2002c), own calculation

Figure 3.35: Inflation, change of CPI on previous year, Bulgaria, 1997–2002.

government has kept a tight fiscal stance with an average surplus of 1% of GDP (excluding grants to the government and net lending) 1997–2000, only in 2000 experiencing a slight budget deficit.

Only unemployment, already at high levels when the currency board was instituted, has risen to worrisome levels, reaching a peak level of 18.1% in 2000, the year after the most intensive stage of privatization. Three main forces contributed to high unemployment in Bulgaria: First, wide-ranging privatization of state enterprises led to a conversion of hidden underemployment into official unemployment. This effect is evident from the steep rise of unemployment after privatization reached its peak in 1999. Second, relatively weak job creation in the private sector failed to provide new employment opportunities. And finally, as has already been noted for Estonia and Lithuania, a mismatch between the skills of many unemployed and the needs of the private sector further prevented employment of many unemployed (Schiff et al. 2001, p. 47).

External shocks, such as the Russian debt default, that have severely affected all other four currency board countries discussed in this chapter, did not have such a marked impact on Bulgaria. This is evident from the movement of interest rates (see figure 3.37), which quickly converged to and below German levels and have since then been lower than in Germany for most of the time. Yet, contrary to Hong Kong, Argentina, Estonia, and Lithuania, which had all experienced an economic boom prior to being hit by these external shocks, Bulgaria was just recovering from a severe economic crisis

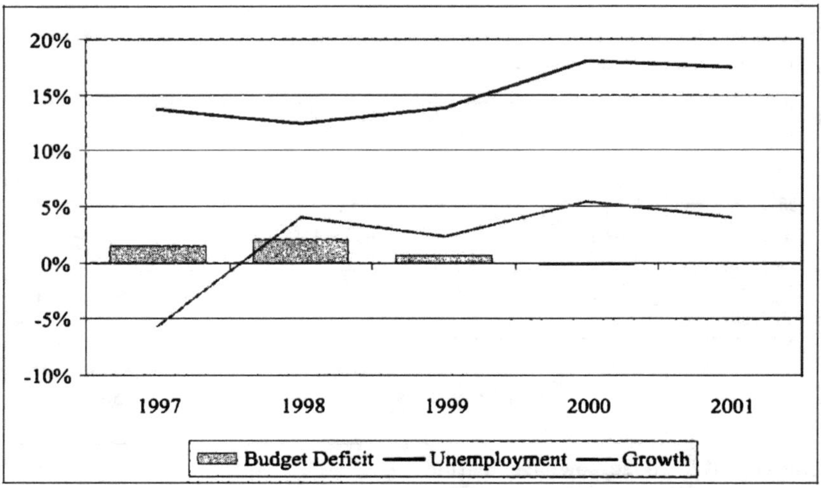

Sources: IMF (2002b, 2002c), Bulgarian National Statistical Institute (2002), own calculation

Figure 3.36: Budget deficit (net of lending and grants), unemployment rate, and growth, Bulgaria, 1997–2001.

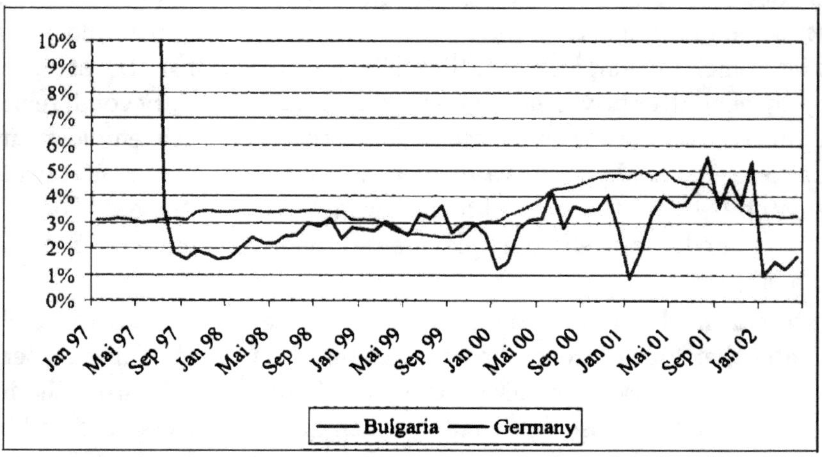

Source: IMF (2002c)

Figure 3.37: Money market interest rates, Bulgaria and Germany, 1997–2002.

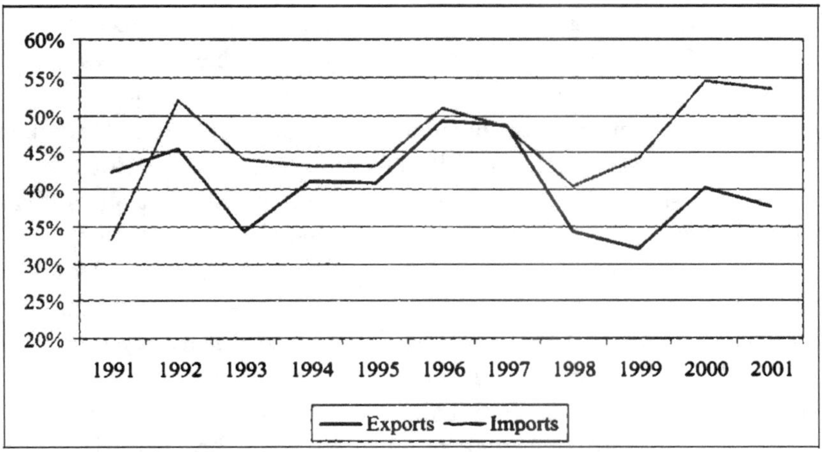

Sources: IMF (2002c), own calculation

Figure 3.38: Imports (cif) and exports, Bulgaria, 1991–2001.

and the banking system had already been shaken out. Yet, some impact of these shocks was still felt in Bulgaria: Starting in 1998, exports and economic activity suffered from an economic slowdown in partner countries and lower export prices. In 1999, the Kosovo conflict blocked transit routes to western Europe, raising transport costs and causing further losses in exports. The consequence was a sizeable trade deficit (see figure 3.38). While exports have recovered somewhat since 1999, imports have been rising even faster, increasing the trade deficit even further (IMF 2000, 2002b).

3.6 Summary

Table 3.1 summarizes to what extent the currency boards discussed in the previous sections comply with the currency board definition given in subsection 2.1.1 (see also table B.1 for a very detailed overview over the design features of theses currency boards). As has already been discussed in 2.1.3, none of the currency boards fulfills the currency board definition to the fullest extent, and all of them have introduced some deviations from pure currency board design, resulting either from the historical background of the currency board (Hong Kong), or from the desire to introduce some flexibility for restricted LoLR support and monetary policy options (all five CBs). In fact, the five present-day currency boards share only two common aspects: They all require full backing of the monetary base (or, in the case of Hong Kong, of notes in circulation), and they all lack a marginal backing rule, i.e. a provision that any change in the monetary base has to be accompanied by an equivalent change in foreign exchange reserves, which endows them with some scope for discretionary monetary policy and LoLR support.

Apparently, two of the three currency currency boards with the firmest legal commitment are those that resulted from an acute crisis: Both Argentina and Bulgaria instituted currency boards to end hyperinflation. Obviously, if the introduction of a currency board is intended to restore lost credibility and trust in the domestic currency, this can only be achieved by signalling the government's unconditional willingness to subject economic policy and government spending to the necessities for price stability. By introducing a currency board a government can send such signals, but to achieve credibility, especially under adverse circumstances, the commitment has to be firm. Therefore, it is advisable to stick to pure currency board design as far as possible, and to make the legal framework for the currency board as rigid and transparent as possible.

It is tempting to attempt inference of currency board performance based on currency board design and legal and public commitment. Take for example Estonia and Lithuania. These two countries are very similar to each other, both faced the same economic challenges in the early 1990s, and both opted for a currency board. Estonia's currency board design is much closer to a pure currency board, leaving less room for discretion, and legal, political, as well as public commitment to the currency board are firm. On the other hand, Lithuania's currency board faced stiff opposition, even by the central bank, allows for almost as much discretion as a central bank, and legal, political, and public commitment to the currency board have been rather weak. Consequently, one might be tempted to attribute the far better growth performance of Estonia over Lithuania to the stricter design and the higher credibility of the Estonian currency board. Yet, such a conclusion would be an oversimplification, as economic performance is not exclusively determined by choice and design of a monetary arrangement. The more consistent design of the Estonian currency board may just as well be the manifestation of a generally more consistent and disciplined economic policy, that might have led to better economic performance even without a currency board.

Another fact well worth noting is that the economies with the strictest currency board design have also been those plagued by the highest unemployment. In Argentina, Estonia, as well Bulgaria, unemployment has reached record-high levels during the operation of the currency board. Employment in all three economies seems to have been very sensitive with respect to low or negative growth. In all cases unemployment has increased markedly during economic crises (the tequila crisis for Argentina, the Asian and Russian crises for Estonia) or during times of slowing growth (Bulgaria 1999). Yet, during times of high economic growth, at times even exceeding 10%, unemployment declined only slowly, if at all (Argentina 1991–1994 and 1996–1998, Estonia 1995–1998 and 2000–2001, Bulgaria 1998 and 2000). In contrast, unemployment in Lithuania has been considerably lower than Estonia's prior to the 1999 crisis, even though growth has been weaker. After the 1999 crises both countries experienced a marked increase in unemployment, after which unemployment in Lithuania remained only slightly below Estonia's, yet the rise in unemployment in Estonia resulted from negative growth of -0.7%, while in Lithuania it resulted from -3.9% growth in 1999. Hong Kong also experienced a marked increase of unemployment during the Asian crisis, yet from a significantly lower level. Also, unemployment started to decrease again soon after the crisis was over.

The importance of flexible labor and goods markets for currency board economies, in order to facilitate smooth adjustment in times of external pressure, has already been stressed in subsection 2.2.2. If markets are not sufficiently flexible to allow for downward-flexibility or prices and wages, adjustment will have a deeper impact on incomes and unemployment. Yet, the previous sections have shown that lack of labor market flexibility has apparently only been a problem in Argentina, while labor markets in Estonia, for example, are very flexible. High unemployment in the transition countries has generally been attributed to reforms and privatization of public enterprises, whereby hidden unemployment was transferred to official unemployment, insufficient creation of employment by newly established private enterprises, and a mismatch between the skill of the unemployed and the skills wanted by private enterprises. Yet, especially the superior unemployment performance of Lithuania prior to the 1999 crisis hints that perhaps the rigidity of currency board design might also play a role in unemployment figures, for example through the wider scope for discretionary monetary policy that less rigid currency boards posses. While further researching the connection between monetary policy discretion and unemployment levels under a currency board might yield interesting results, it is beyond the scope of this thesis to follow this potential connection further. Yet, we will again raise the question of how rigid currency board design and high unemployment levels might be related in the following chapter, where we analyze an economy under a currency board by using a model.

Table 3.1: Basic design of present-day currency boards

	Hong Kong	**Argentina**	**Estonia**	**Lithuania**	**Bulgaria**
Fixed exchange rate	US$1 = HK$7.8	US$1 = 1 peso	1 euro = 15.6466 kroon	1 euro = 3.4528 litas	1 euro = 1.95583 lev
Backing requirements	100% backing of notes issued. In practice, monetary base is covered more than threefold. No marginal backing requirement, to allow discretionary monetary policy and LoLR support. Reserves may include domestic assets.	100% backing of monetary base. No marginal backing requirement, to allow discretionary monetary policy and LoLR support. Reserves may include domestic government securities.	100% backing of monetary base. No marginal backing requirement, to allow discretionary monetary policy and LoLR support.	100% backing of monetary base. No marginal backing requirement, to allow discretionary monetary policy and LoLR support. Reserves may include domestic government securities.	100% backing of monetary base. No marginal backing requirement, to allow LoLR support.
Convertibility	HKMA has to buy and sell Certificates of Indebtedness at official rate. Otherwise, one-way convertibility, as banks can convert their HK$ balance in clearing accounts at HKMA into US$ at official rate.	One-way convertibility. BCRA was required to sell US$ for pesos at official rate.	Two-way convertibility. BOE has to buy and sell euro at official rate.	One-way convertibility. BOL has to sell euro at official rate. Is also required to buy euro, but no exchange rate specified.	Two-way convertibility. BNB is required to sell and buy euro at spot exchange rate, which must not deviate from official rate by more than 0.5%.

Table 3.1: (continued)

	Hong Kong	Argentina	Estonia	Lithuania	Bulgaria
Legal and political commitment to currency board	Weak legal commitment. Only total backing requirement specified by law. Otherwise, no legal obligation to operate currency board. No exchange rate, no anchor currency, no convertibility set forth by law. Strong political commitment, as is obvious from determined defense of currency board during speculative attacks following Asian crisis.	Strong legal commitment. Anchor currency, exchange rate, backing requirement, and convertibility specified by law. Change of exchange rate only through act of parliament. Strong political commitment to currency board.	Relatively strong legal commitment. Anchor currency, backing requirement, and convertibility specified by law, but not exchange rate. Revaluation through BOE, devaluation through parliament only. Very strong political and public support for currency board.	Relatively weak legal commitment. Backing requirement and convertibility specified by law, but neither anchor currency nor exchange rate. Change of exchange rate through BOL after consultation with government. Weak political commitment. Strong opposition to introduction by BOL, and repeated announcements of abandonment.	Strong legal commitment. Anchor currency, exchange rate, backing requirement, and convertibility specified by law. Change of exchange rate only through act of parliament.

4

A Theoretical Study of Currency Boards

This chapter develops a model of currency crises in a currency board based on second generation currency crises models. The model is used to examine the dynamics of a simple currency board economy, taking into consideration the legal and political commitment to the currency board, and, at a later stage, the extent of liabilities dollarization of the economy. Section 4.1 gives a general overview over features and implications of first and second generation currency crises models, and explains how the model used in this chapter relates to them. Section 4.2 introduces the basic currency board model, explores the general model dynamics, and examines the stability of a currency board under different circumstances. Section 4.3 then introduces potential effects from liability dollarization, and examines how the presence of foreign-currency denominated debt alters the model behavior.

4.1 Models of Currency Crises

4.1.1 First and Second Generation Currency Crises Models

The general objective of currency crises models, whether first or second generation, is to explain how and why fixed exchange rate regimes come under attack, and how and why they are abandoned, as has frequently been the case since the second half of the twentieth century.

First generation currency crises models, as exemplified by Krugman (1979) and Flood and Garber (1984), attribute the speculative pressure and eventual breakdown of the exchange rate parity to unfavorable developments in some of the fundamental macroeconomic variables, such as growth rates, price or wage inflation, budget or trade deficits (Weber 1998, p. 5), which make it impossible to maintain the exchange rate parity, as, for example, foreign exchange reserves become insufficient to defend the exchange rate. It follows from these models that currency crises should, therefore, be predictable from observing the movements of the fundamentals in question.[1]

First generation currency crises models were the predominant for explaining and predicting currency crises in the 1980s and early 1990s. Yet, crises in the 1990s, such as the crisis of the European Exchange Rate Mechanism (ERM) 1992/93, during which speculative attacks on the British pound, the Italian lira, the Swedish krona and the Finish markka occurred, the Mexican, so-called tequila crisis 1994/95, and the Asian crisis 1997, challenged this predominance: All these crises had not been preceded by a worsening of fundamentals that would have allowed to predict these crises, as should have been possible according to first generation models (Wu 2000, p. 2).

The perceived failure of first generation models in predicting currency crises furthered the evolution of second generation currency crises models, to which the model employed in the following sections of this chapter belongs. Second generation models, as exemplified by Obstfeld (1994, 1996b), do not focus exclusively on fundamentals, but also stress the importance of expectations. Fundamentals still play an important role, but negative expectations can lead to the collapse of an exchange rate regime, even if fundamentals alone would allow for indefinite maintenance of the exchange rate commitment (Weber 1998, p. 6). If economic agents just expect the exchange rate to collapse, such expectations alone may be sufficient to initiate a currency crisis, ex-post validating negative expectations.

Second generation models generally presume the existence of multiple equilibria. For example, one possible equilibrium may allow for the first-best continuation of the fixed exchange rate, while a likewise possible equilibrium implies the collapse of the currency. Which of these two is realized depends entirely on expectations. Expectations "[...] are among the forces that determine the economic reality, rather than the passive reflections of the latter" (Wu 2000, p. 2).

Facing multiple equilibria, a policymaker is powerless to enforce the realization of the desired equilibrium. Any seemingly unimportant event might trigger an abrupt change in expectations, shifting the economic outcome from

[1]For a detailed survey of first generation currency crises models see Willman (1992).

a good to a bad equilibrium. Still, while expectations play an important role in second generation models, it is important to note that for a wide range of these models an economy with strong fundamentals is less vulnerable to such speculative attacks than an economy with weak fundamentals. Speculative attacks are not entirely divorced from fundamentals (Obstfeld and Rogoff 1996, pp. 652–653).

Second generation models generally assume three channels through which currency crises may occur: self-fulfilling expectations, herding, and contagion. *Self-fulfilling expectations* refer to the phenomenon that any possibly minor event, a political scandal, or negative official statistical reports, may trigger a shift of market sentiment towards negative expectations, and these expectations, or the resulting actions, such as a capital flight, will lead to devaluation, ex-post validating the negative expectations (Babić and Žigman 2001, p. 4).

Herding refers to a problem that might arise, when gathering information is costly for small investors: the majority of the market, supposedly small investors, follows big participants in their investment, whom they consider to be well informed. Investors buy because prices are rising and sell because prices are dropping, as was the case in the 1987 stock market crash. Consequently, a wave of selling, whatever its initial cause, might turn into a run out of the currency and lead to a collapse of the exchange rate (Krugman 1997, pp. 6–7).

Contagion explains the perception that in many currency crises, such as the ERM crises in Europe, the tequila crisis in Latin America, and the Asian crisis, a crisis in one country tends to spread to other countries in the same region. One explanation put forward for this phenomenon is the existence of regional trade and financial linkages. A currency crisis and worsening fundamentals in one country have an adverse effect on economic conditions in a linked country, raising the probability of a second currency crisis in that country (Babić and Žigman 2001, p. 4). Yet, the importance of these linkages is questioned by some authors. Instead, they suggest, investors may perceive countries as members of a group of countries with some common, but imperfectly observed characteristics. As one country of the group devalues, investors may revise downward their estimate of the willingness of the other countries of the group to defend their exchange rate parity (Krugman 1997, p. 8).

4.1.2 Critique of Second Generation Crises Models

While second generation models can explain the occurrence of currency crises that are not preceded by a worsening of fundamentals, they have also provoked a lot of criticism, which is either based on the methodology, their policy implications, or empirical evidence. One main objection on the grounds of *methodology* is the indeterminacy of these models, as described by Obstfeld (1986, p. 79). A second generation model cannot predict whether or when a crisis may occur. The outcome of the models is indeterminate and currency crises cannot be predicted. As Morris and Shin (1999, p. 232) point out "the multiple equilibrium approach is vulnerable to the charge that it does not fully explain a currency attack, since the shift in beliefs, which leads to the shift from one equilibrium to another, is left unexplained. In short, there is indeterminacy in the theory". Yet, as both Wu (2000, pp. 13–14) and Irwin and Vines (1999, pp. 5–6) reply, the multi equilibrium approach highlights the inherent unpredictability of currency crises. Although a definite, clear prediction is always the ideal of economics, unpredictability is usually a reality we have to live with. Secondly, they argue, second generation models give expectations a proper role to play. In models with rational expectations and unique equilibria, expectations are completely endogenous, a passive reflection of reality, whereas in multiple-equilibrium models expectations are still consistent with the model, yet also have strong powers to influence economic outcomes.

Another objection to second generation models stems from their *policy implications*. Since these models highlight the role of capricious market sentiments, critics are concerned this might deviate attention from flawed policies and institutions in the attacked countries, giving policymakers an easy scapegoat to blame. Some even suspect political motivation behind the existence of second generation models: "Obviously, it is a political rather than a scientific motivation that has led to this ascendancy, through officially supported conferences, of one class of models. As usual, it is expedient for the official sector to put the blame on the destabilizing speculators rather than on destabilizing policies." (Garber 1996, pp. 403–404). Yet, as has been stated previously, the existence of multiple equilibria is not divorced from fundamentals. Worse fundamentals are more likely to lead to the existence of multiple equilibria. Second generation models do not ask the question of whether a crisis was justified by fundamentals or not, but help shed light on the question of whether fundamentals were such as to make the crisis an inevitable and unique outcome (Obstfeld 1996a, p. 395). Additionally, the multiple equilibria approach highlights the instability of the international financial markets. Ignoring this might well lead to wrong prescriptions on the management of crises. The IMF's initial response to the Asian crisis is an often cited example (Wu 2000, pp. 14–15).

Another challenge to second generation models comes from *empirical evidence*. Krugman (1996, pp. 367–375) analyzes the 1992/93 ERM crises and concludes that these were all the inevitable result of a continuous deterioration of the fundamentals. "It is puzzling that markets did not seem concerned about the possibility of such attacks until very late, especially since many economic analysts had warned about them well in advance; but this lack of early warning can be made into evidence for self-fulfilling-crisis models only through a fairly convoluted and indirect argument". (Krugman 1996, p. 375)

Another study by Bordo and Schwarz (1996) examines all major currency crises from 1797 to 1994 and concludes that all these crises can be explained by economic fundamentals. The authors conclude that while currency crises may be logically possible, it does not mean that they have actually occurred, and that the theory of self-fulfilling speculative attacks contributes nothing to understanding real-world events (Bordo and Schwarz 1996, pp. 45–48).

Yet, there are other studies, covering the Mexican crisis, the Asian crisis and crises between the 1950s and 1990s, which suggest that second generation currency crises models may be valid: No significant increase of domestic interest rates in the crisis countries relative to the world interest rate was observable prior to the crises, implying that these crises were indeed unanticipated (Wu 2000, pp. 16–17).

Eventually, even Krugman, one of the strongest critics of multiple equilibria models, accepted the explanatory validity of these models. In an attempt to account for the events leading to the Asian crisis 1997 he conceded: "I hereby capitulate. I cannot see any way to make sense of the contagion of 1997–8 without supposing the existence of multiple equilibria, with countries vulnerable to self-validating collapses in confidence, collapses that could be set off by events in faraway economies that somehow served as a trigger for self-fulfilling pessimism." (Krugman 1999, p. 35)

4.1.3 Classification of the Currency Board Crises Model

The basic model introduced in the following section is borrowed from Irwin (2001), who in turn bases his model on Obstfeld (1997). It is a typical second generation currency crises model with self-fulfilling expectations, based on the Kydland and Prescott (1977) and Barro and Gordon (1983a, 1983b) framework of monetary policy. In this framework a policymaker is trying to achieve two rivaling policy goals, the minimization of inflation and the minimization of unemployment, which is affected by unanticipated inflation. Under discrete monetary policy, given inflation expectations, the policymaker would under most circumstances decide to generate some surprise inflation, to lower unemployment, and to minimize his loss function, which depends on both inflation and unemployment. But, assuming rational expectations of economic agents, the public is aware of the inflation-unemployment tradeoff faced by the policymaker and inflation expectations are increased to preclude the generation of surprise inflation. In equilibrium inflation expectations are such that the policymaker, to minimize his loss function, will have to generate exactly as much inflation as expected. The result is high inflation without a reduction in unemployment. The economy would be better off if expected and actual inflation were both zero, but the public's knowledge about the incentives facing the policymaker precludes this result under discrete monetary policy. This result exhibits the inflation bias of discrete monetary policy: The ability to generate inflation will lead to inflation without having an impact on the real economy.

Instead of pursuing a discretionary monetary policy, a credible rules-based monetary policy, for example prescribing zero inflation, could improve social welfare. Yet, such a policy is not feasible due to the problem of time inconsistency. If the public set its inflation expectations according to the policy rule, the policymaker could further reduce his loss function by cheating on the exchange rate commitment and generating surprise inflation. Due to rational expectations the public is aware of this incentive to cheat and will have positive devaluation expectations, rendering a rules-based policy infeasible.

In our model the policy variable is the exchange rate instead of inflation, since in a small open economy, given purchasing power parity (PPP) and assuming foreign prices to be constant, the domestic price level can be identified with the the exchange rate.[2]

To circumvent the problem of time-inconsistency, the model assumes a fixed exchange rate rule with a discretionary escape clause, as described in Obstfeld (1991, p. 14) and Obstfeld (1997, p. 68). The policymaker can decide to abandon the exchange rate commitment, but only at a personal cost, which is exogenously given. This keeps the policymaker from devaluing the currency under most circumstances, thereby also lowering devaluation expectations, allowing for the socially optimal fixed exchange rate solution.

Additionally, the Irwin (2001)-model adds unemployment persistence to the unemployment equation and omits stochastic shocks to unemployment. Instead, the uncertainty shaping the public's devaluation expectations stems from incomplete information about the political cost of devaluation. Also, the policymaker is only concerned about the current-period outcome of his

[2]The validity of the PPP is a debated subject in economics, see for example Rogoff (1996), and Goldberg and Knetter (1997). Yet, it is a standard approach in these models (Obstfeld 1997, p. 63).

policy actions and not about possible future outcomes, as is consistent with Masson (1995, p. 574).

Few other currency board crises models exist. Rivera Batiz and Sy (2000) and Oliva, Rivera Batiz, and Sy (2001) also use a second generation crises model approach. Instead of assuming a personal cost from devaluation, the policymaker's incentive to maintain the fixed exchange rate stems from the assumption that any devaluation must be of an arbitrarily fixed size, as in Drazen and Masson (1994, p. 738). The authors examine the exchange rate selection (currency board vs. standard peg) of different types of policymakers (a weak policymaker with relatively low inflation aversion, and a tough policymaker with relatively high inflation aversion). They conclude that in the case of a separating equilibrium, in which the currency regime choice sends a signal allowing the public to identify the government type, the weak government tends to select the currency board, which entails a strong discipline effect, while the tough government tends to chose the standard peg, which offers greater flexibility for devaluation in case of a very unfavorable unemployment shock. A low standard deviation of unemployment shocks can favor the adjustable peg while a high standard deviation can favor the currency board. Also, high unemployment persistence and a high responsiveness of unemployment to unexpected devaluation favor the choice of a currency board.

Chang and Velasco (2000) use a Diamond and Dybvig (1983) class model to study financial fragility, exchange rate crises, and monetary policy under different exchange rate regimes. They conclude that a currency board is prone to self-fulfilling bank-runs, but not to currency crises (which is due to the modelling of the currency board). Notably, a run on the financial system is not incompatible with defending the exchange rate parity. Also, they conclude, a currency board cannot yield a socially optimal outcome (Chang and Velasco 2000, pp. 2, 12).

4.2 The Standard Model

4.2.1 Model Outline

Each period t the policymaker sets the (log) exchange rate e_t and at the same time the labor market determines an economy-wide nominal wage w_{t+1} (log), at which workers agree to supply all the labor that firms demand in period $t+1$.

There is only one consumption good whose foreign-currency price is fixed at one foreign currency unit. Therefore the exchange rate (the price of foreign money in terms of domestic money) equals the domestic price level. Assume that labor market equilibrium requires a constant expected real wage of 1. With Ee_t denoting the date $t-1$ conditional expectation of the period t exchange rate, the wage negotiated in period $t-1$ for period t is:

$$w_t = Ee_t \tag{4.1}$$

Labor demand in period t is inversely related to the real wage $w_t - e_t$. The equation for date t employment, n_t, is:

$$n_t = n^* + \sqrt{\alpha}[(e_t - Ee_t) - k] \tag{4.2}$$

In (4.2), n^* is the employment level targeted by the policymaker, while $k > 0$ represents a fixed distortion in the economy that causes employment to systematically fall short of n^*. $\sqrt{\alpha}$ determines the responsiveness of employment to unanticipated changes in the exchange rate.

Subtracting both sides of (4.2) from the labor force, $\bar{n}$, yields unemployment terms, $u_t = \bar{n} - n_t$ and $u^* = \bar{n} - n^*$, and adding $+e_{t-1} - e_{t-1}$ to the inner bracket on the right side gives (expected) rate of change of the exchange rate, $\Delta e_t = e_t - e_{t-1}$ and $E\Delta e_t = Ee_t - e_{t-1}$:

$$u_t = u^* + \sqrt{\alpha}[(E\Delta e_t - \Delta e_t) + k] \tag{4.3}$$

Eventually, adding a persistence term and defining $ur_t = u_t - u^*$ to be the deviation of unemployment from the target rate, results in the unemployment equation used by Irwin (2001, p. 5):

$$ur_t = \sqrt{\alpha}\,[(E\Delta e_t - \Delta e_t) + k + \delta ur_{t-1}] \tag{4.4}$$

where δ measures unemployment persistence. Unemployment above the target rate will be carried on to the next period, by a magnitude determined by the autoregressive coefficient $\sqrt{\alpha}\,\delta$.

Given the behavior of unemployment, the policymaker minimizes the following one-period quadratic loss function:[3]

$$L_t = (ur_t)^2 + \theta\,(\Delta e_t)^2, \qquad \theta > 0 \tag{4.5}$$

which entails a tradeoff between unemployment close to the target rate and a low-inflation policy, weighed by a weight θ capturing the policymaker's aversion to inflation relative to unemployment. Given (4.5), it is obvious, that the policymaker is only taking account of the effects his actions are having in the current period, not of effects in coming periods.

[3]As in Masson (1995, p. 574), the one-period approach reduces the complexity of the problem and allows for a closed-form solution, but excludes policy actions with an eye on future reputation.

4.2.2 Discretionary Exchange Rate Policy

If the policymaker pursues a discretionary exchange rate policy, he will set Δe_t as to minimize (4.5), subject to (4.4).[4] It follows that:

$$\Delta e_t = \frac{\alpha}{\alpha+\theta}(E\Delta e_t + k + \delta ur_{t-1}) \tag{4.6}$$

The magnitude of devaluation is positively correlated with α and δ and negatively with θ. α determines the effectiveness of a devaluation in reducing unemployment, i.e. the higher α, the higher the marginal benefit from unemployment reduction through devaluation. Higher values for δ imply that past unemployment will be carried on to the next period by a larger extent, increasing present unemployment. As the marginal benefit from unemployment reduction is increasing in present unemployment, this provides an additional incentive for devaluation to the policymaker. On the other hand, a higher value of θ leads to a higher marginal cost from devaluation, therefore providing an incentive to devalue less.

With devaluation given by (4.6), the loss of the policymaker is:

$$L_t^D = \frac{\alpha\theta}{\alpha+\theta}(E\Delta e_t + k + \delta ur_{t-1})^2 \tag{4.7}$$

If we do not take expected devaluation as given, but instead assume rational expectations, this implies that the public knows the tradeoff faced by the policymaker. Consequently, the public knows the level of devaluation desired by the policymaker and sets its expectations accordingly, so that in equilibrium expected matches actual devaluation. (4.6) and (4.7) become:

$$E\Delta e_t = \Delta e_t = \frac{\alpha}{\theta}(k + \delta ur_{t-1}) \tag{4.8}$$

$$L_t^D = \frac{\alpha(\alpha+\theta)}{\theta}(k + \delta ur_{t-1})^2 \tag{4.9}$$

4.2.3 Fixed Exchange Rate and Time-Inconsistency

In contrast to a discretionary exchange rate policy, if the policymaker decides to keep the exchange rate fixed ($\Delta e_t = 0$), the ensuing loss is:

$$L_t^F = \alpha(E\Delta e_t + k + \delta ur_{t-1})^2 \tag{4.10}$$

If this policy is credible ($E\Delta e_t = 0$), the loss becomes:

$$L_t^F = \alpha(k + \delta ur_{t-1})^2 \tag{4.11}$$

[4] Derivation of equations (4.6) and (4.7) is given in the appendix, section C.1.1.

As the loss from a discretionary exchange rate policy with rational expectations, (4.9), is strictly greater than the loss from a credible fixed exchange rate regime, (4.11)[5], the policymaker has an incentive to fix the exchange rate, given that this policy is fully credible. The gain from having a credible fixed exchange rate versus a discretionary exchange rate with rational expectations can be derived by subtracting (4.11) from (4.9). The incentive to fix, I_t, is:

$$I_t = \frac{\alpha^2}{\theta}(k + \delta ur_{t-1})^2 > 0 \tag{4.12}$$

The gains from having a fixed exchange rate are the higher, the higher the responsiveness parameter α and the lower inflation aversion θ. An effective devaluation-unemployment tradeoff leads to high devaluation expectations, which in turn require higher actual devaluation to at least keep unemployment constant. In this case the policymaker has a lot to gain from credibly tying his hands with a fixed exchange rate. On the other hand, the higher inflation aversion, the higher the policymaker's self-discipline to not resort to devaluation for employment stimulation. In this case, less is to be gained from giving up policy flexibility.

Yet, a commitment to keep the exchange rate fixed will not be credible due to a time-inconsistency problem, as first described by Kydland and Prescott (1977). Once inflation expectations have been formed, the policymaker has an incentive to cheat on his commitment to keep the exchange rate fixed, as this will further reduce his loss. This can be shown by comparing (4.7) and (4.10), the loss functions for given devaluation expectations[6]:

$$L_t^F - L_t^D = \frac{\alpha^2}{\alpha + \theta}(E\Delta e_t + k + \delta ur_{t-1})^2 > 0 \tag{4.13}$$

Given devaluation expectations, the loss from pursuing a discretionary exchange rate policy, i.e. devaluation, is smaller than the loss from maintaining the exchange rate parity, thus, the policymaker has an incentive to cheat on his commitment to keep the exchange rate fixed. As expectations are formed rationally, the public is aware of this incentive to cheat and does not trust in the announced commitment to fix the exchange rate. Devaluation expectations are positive. In equilibrium, expected devaluation matches actual devaluation, which are both positive, despite the initial announcement to maintain a fixed exchange rate.

[5]See appendix, C.1.2.

[6]See appendix, C.1.3.

Even though a fixed exchange rate arrangement is socially optimal, it cannot be achieved without a credible mechanism that effectively commits the policymaker to a no-devaluation policy.

4.2.4 Political Cost of Devaluation and Incomplete Information

Without a credible commitment mechanism the policymaker has no incentive to maintain a fixed exchange rate, as he can always reduce the loss function by devaluing at least a little. Instead, if the policymaker were to face additional personal cost from devaluation—which will be called political cost throughout the remainder of this chapter—the incentive to devalue would be lessened. If these political cost exceed the potential gain from devaluation, expressed by (4.13), the policymaker will instead decide to keep the exchange rate fixed.

We have argued in chapter 2 that the currency board draws its stability and credibility from the legal commitment made to the currency board, among other things. While such a legal commitment presents an obstacle to dismantling the currency board, it can never completely prevent the exit from the currency board and an accompanying devaluation. Generally, all fixed exchange rate regimes are revocable. What differs are the obstacles to policymakers to engage in devaluation. Under a pure currency board, where the exchange rate is set forth by law, changes to the exchange rate can only be achieved through a sufficient majority in parliament. The proposed change has to be brought forth to parliament, will be openly discussed, and a majority has to be assured. This procedure presents higher cost to policymakers than devaluing a standard peg, where devaluation might just require a decision of the president of the central bank or the minister of economic affairs.

Take for example the present-day currency boards discussed in chapter 3. Argentina, Bulgaria, and Estonia all show strong legal commitment to the currency board. Obstacles to abandoning the currency board are high (but an exit is nevertheless possible, as the example of Argentina has shown), and devaluations of the exchange rate require an act of parliament. Political cost of devaluation related to the legal commitment are high in these three countries. In contrast, the legal commitment in Lithuania is lower. The central bank has the power to decide on a devaluation, after consultations with the government, and, despite law provides for devaluation only in situations of economic hardship, the political cost from a currency board exit are smaller. Hong Kong faces even less legal obstacles to abandoning the currency board, and has done so already once in 1974.

Yet, the political cost of devaluation are not only determined by the legal commitment, but also by the political commitment to the currency board. For example, in Argentina under the Menem government the currency board was considered the center- and masterpiece of economic policy, and the government de-facto tied its political fate to the currency board. Similarly, in Estonia there is a broad political as well as public consensus about the desirability of having a currency board. Any government or politician trying to abandon the currency board, therefore, risks to damage his political career. On the other hand, in Lithuania, where the currency board has been disputed and opposed for a long time, the government could even announce its intention to scrap the currency board without paying a political price. The political cost stemming from the political commitment may even compensate for a weak legal commitment, as is the case in Hong Kong, where legal commitment is weak, but political commitment to the currency board is strong.

The political commitment to the currency board not only relates to the political cost, but may also be an expression of the inflation aversion of the government, captured by θ. For example, Hong Kong, where the currency board was not introduced to avert an acute crisis caused by bad economic policy, might perform equally well without sticking to the currency board regime. When in 1974 Hong Kong abandoned the currency board, this did not lead to a loss of confidence in government policy. Consequently, we may assume that the Hong Kong government's inflation aversion is high, which is reflected in strong political commitment to the currency board. On the other hand, countries that decided to introduce the currency board to overcome a severe crisis caused by weak economic policy, as was the case in Argentina and Bulgaria, may display strong political (and legal) commitment to the currency board because they know this to be an important prerequisite of the stabilization success that may be brought by the currency board. In this case the policymaker embraces the inherent discipline brought by the currency board out of the self-awareness that he is not disciplined enough to achieve stabilization by himself.[7] In this case, political commitment is high because inflation aversion is low.

We assume the political cost of reneging the exchange rate commitment to be $\hat{c}^2$. The policymaker will maintain the exchange rate fixed if the political cost from devaluation outweigh the possible gain from devaluation, as given by (4.13). The square root of (4.13) is defined to be the temptation to devalue, T_t, and determines the critical value of political cost, c_t^*, at which

[7]Of course, the use of a male personal pronoun does not imply that policymakers are generally male. Instead, it should be considered to represent both genders.

the policymaker is indifferent to devaluation. It therefore follows that the policymaker will keep the exchange rate fixed if $\hat{c} \geq c_t^* = T_t$,[8] with

$$c_t^* = T_t = \frac{\alpha}{\sqrt{\alpha + \theta}}(E\Delta e_t + k + \delta ur_{t-1}) \tag{4.14}$$

The temptation to devalue is increasing in $E\Delta e_t$, as higher devaluation expectations increase the unemployment cost of maintaining the exchange rate fixed. As a result, higher devaluation expectations make an actual devaluation more likely.

To introduce uncertainty into the model, assume there is incomplete information about the true value of c. While the policymaker knows the true political cost of devaluation, which we term $\hat{c}$, the public does not. Instead, the public believes c is drawn from a probability distribution $c \sim \left[\underline{c}_t, \overline{c}\right]$ with $0 \leq \underline{c}_t < \overline{c}$ and $\underline{c}_t \leq \hat{c} \leq \overline{c}$.[9] Thus, the public can only form its devaluation expectations on the basis of this probability distribution. Note that the time subscript on the lower bound of the distribution allows for the public to learn about the lower boundary of the distribution by observing the exchange rate decisions of the policymaker.

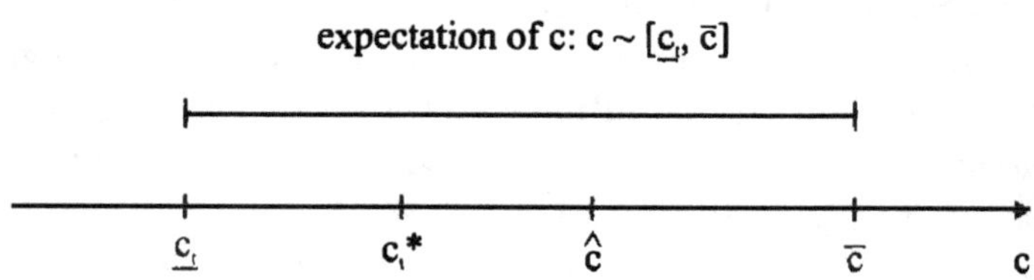

Figure 4.1: Political cost of devaluation

A possible situation in any period t is displayed in figure 4.1. $\underline{c}_t$ and $\overline{c}$ are the upper and lower bounds, respectively, of the interval, which the public believes to contain the true political cost of devaluation $\hat{c}$. The critical value c_t^* and $\hat{c}$ are both located within the interval. In the case displayed here, the policymaker does not devalue as $\hat{c}$ is greater than c_t^*.

[8] Instead we might introduce the political cost of devaluation directly to the loss function, as in Obstfeld (1994, p. 208). In this case (4.5) becomes $L_t = (ur_t)^2 + \theta(\Delta e_t)^2 + Z_t c^2$ with $Z_t = 1$ for $\Delta e_t > 0$ and $Z_t = 0$ otherwise. This approach leads to the same results.

[9] According to Obstfeld and Rogoff (1996, p. 649), it is quite plausible for the public not to know c, but to only have priors on it.

4.2.5 Possible Equilibria

We now turn to inspecting the possible equilibria in an economy whose characteristics have been laid out in the preceding sections, where the policymaker intends to maintain a fixed exchange rate by means of a currency board.[10]

With political cost of devaluation and incomplete information about the political cost, the public expects the policymaker to devalue in period t if the true political cost of devaluation is lower than a critical value c_t^*, which is determined by the temptation to devalue, (4.14). Devaluation will occur if $\hat{c} < c_t^*$ where $\underline{c_t} \leq c_t^* \leq \bar{c}$ in equilibrium. This allows for three different types of equilibria to exist: A full credibility (FC) equilibrium where $c_t^* = \underline{c_t}$, a zero credibility (ZC) equilibrium where $c_t^* = \bar{c}$, and partial credibility (PC) equilibria where $\underline{c_t} < c_t^* < \bar{c}$.

4.2.5.1 FC equilibrium

In *FC equilibrium* the fixed exchange rate commitment is fully credible. The critical value c_t^* is equal to the lower bound $\underline{c_t}$ of the distribution the public believes $\hat{c}$ to be in, and therefore, the true value $\hat{c}$ cannot be smaller than the critical value c_t^*. The probability that the temptation to devalue exceeds the political cost is zero. Consequently, no devaluation is expected and no devaluation occurs, unemployment remains unaffected. The necessary and sufficient condition for a FC equilibrium to exist is $\underline{c_t} > T_t$ when $E\Delta e_t = 0$. Assuming the fix to be credible, the temptation to devalue is smaller than any possible value of $\hat{c}$. Using (4.14), this condition becomes:

$$k + \delta u r_{t-1} \quad < \quad \frac{\underline{c_t}\sqrt{(\alpha+\theta)}}{\alpha} \tag{4.15}$$

Note that ceteris paribus (c.p.) higher unemployment, higher unemployment persistence, and higher unemployment responsiveness reduce the likeliness of an FC equilibrium, as they increase the incentive to seek unemployment reduction through devaluation, while higher inflation aversion θ and higher expectations of the public about the lower bound $\underline{c_t}$ of the probability distribution increase the likeliness of an FC equilibrium.

4.2.5.2 ZC equilibrium

A *ZC equilibrium* exists, if, should the public expect a full devaluation, as given by (4.8), the temptation to devalue exceeds any possible value of $\hat{c}$. If

[10] Obviously, the insights of the model hold true for other fixed exchange rate arrangements as well, with the difference of lower values for the political cost c.

a ZC equilibrium is realized[11], the policymaker will abandon the currency board with certainty.[12] The formal condition for the existence of a ZC equilibrium is $\bar{c} < T_t$, with devaluation expectations given by (4.8). Using (4.14), this becomes:

$$\frac{\bar{c}\theta}{\alpha\sqrt{(\alpha+\theta)}} \quad < \quad k + \delta u r_{t-1} \tag{4.16}$$

Similar to the FC case, a ZC equilibrium becomes c.p. more likely, the higher unemployment, unemployment persistence, and unemployment responsiveness, and less likely, the higher inflation aversion and the upper bound $\bar{c}$ of the probability distribution for c.

If a ZC equilibrium is realized, expected and actual devaluation are both given by (4.8), and the fully anticipated devaluation has no impact on unemployment.

We can see from (4.15) and (4.16) that it is possible for both an FC and a ZC equilibrium to exist at the same time. Whether this is the case depends not only on the parameters discussed above but even more on the beliefs of the public about the value of c, specifically on the lower and upper bounds of the probability distribution. The specific condition can be derived from (4.15) and (4.16), resulting in:

$$\frac{\bar{c}\theta}{\alpha\sqrt{(\alpha+\theta)}} \quad < \quad k + \delta u r_{t-1} < \frac{\underline{c}_t\sqrt{(\alpha+\theta)}}{\alpha}$$

which requires:

$$\bar{c} \quad < \quad \frac{\underline{c}_t(\alpha+\theta)}{\theta} \tag{4.17}$$

As has been argued before, the approach used in this model distinguishes pegged exchange rate regimes and currency boards by the political cost of devaluation. It is reasonable to believe that the higher political cost from exiting a currency board will also be reflected in the public's beliefs about the distribution of c, implying that $\underline{c}_t$ and $\bar{c}$ will also tend to be higher. As a result, it follows from (4.15) and (4.16) that c.p. it is more likely for an FC equilibrium to exist, and less likely for a ZC equilibrium to exist under a currency board in comparison to a regular peg.

[11] Note that multiple equilibria may *exist* at the same time, but only one of them can be *realized*.

[12] In the simple context of this model *abandoning* the currency board merely implies a devaluation of the exchange rate.

4.2.5.3 PC equilibria

The third type of equilibria that may possibly exist are *PC equilibria*, where $\underline{c}_t < c_t^* < \overline{c}$, and the probability of devaluation is greater than zero and less than one. As the policymaker will devalue if the true political cost $\hat{c}$ is below the critical value, and c_t^* is within the bounds of probability distribution, there is uncertainty of whether devaluation will occur or not, contrary to the FC and ZC cases. In a PC equilibrium devaluation expectations are positive and unemployment will rise without devaluation, while a devaluation will reduce unemployment. The level of expected devaluation depends, among other things, upon the critical value c_t^*, which in turn depends upon the the expectation of devaluation. So, to identify PC equilibria we first need to derive the pair of functions $c_t^*(E\Delta e_t)$ and $E\Delta e_t(c_t^*)$.

First, the function $c_t^*(E\Delta e_t)$, the critical value of political cost at which the policymaker is indifferent to devaluation, has already been derived in subsection 4.2.4. Restating (4.14):

$$c_t^* = \frac{\alpha}{\sqrt{\alpha+\theta}}(E\Delta e_t + k + \delta ur_{t-1}) \tag{4.18}$$

This function is linear in the expected devaluation rate $E\Delta e_t$. C.p., higher devaluation expectations, higher unemployment and unemployment persistence, and a higher responsiveness parameter α lead to a higher critical value c_t^*, increasing the likeliness of devaluation. Higher inflation aversion reduces the likeliness of devaluation.

Second, $E\Delta e_t(c_t^*)$ is derived by rewriting expected devaluation as $E\Delta e_t = E(\Delta e_t|\text{Devalue}) \cdot \text{prob}(\text{Devalue})$. Expected devaluation is equal to the expected magnitude of devaluation should it occur, multiplied by the probability of the policymaker actually devaluing. The probability of devaluation is given by $F_t(c_t^*) = \int_{\underline{c}_t}^{c_t^*} f(c)\,dc$, with $f(c)$ the probability function, summarizing the publics beliefs about the true value of c, and $F_t(c_t^*)$ the distribution function, determining the probability of $c \leq c_t^*$. The distribution function has the following attributes: $0 \leq F_t(c_t^*) \leq 1$ and $dF_t(c_t^*)/dc_t^* > 0$. The magnitude of devaluation $E(\Delta e_t|\text{Devalue})$ is given by (4.6). Substitution yields:[13]

$$E\Delta e_t = \frac{\alpha F_t(c_t^*)}{\alpha+\theta-\alpha F_t(c_t^*)}(k + \delta ur_{t-1}) \tag{4.19}$$

Without specifying a form for the distribution function $F_t(\cdot)$, the following properties of (4.19) can be determined:

[13] See appendix, C.1.4

P1. As $E\Delta e_t$ is increasing in $F_t(c_t^*)$ and $F_t(c_t^*)$is increasing in c_t^*, it follows that $E\Delta e_t$is increasing in c_t^* as well. The higher the critical c_t^*, the higher the likeliness of devaluation once $\hat{c} < c_t^*$, and the higher expected devaluation.

P2. As $F(\underline{c_t}) = 0$, $E\Delta e_t(\underline{c_t}) = 0$. At the lower bound of the probability distribution expected devaluation is zero.

P3. As $F(\overline{c}) = 1$, $E\Delta e_t(\overline{c}) = \frac{\alpha}{\theta}(k + \delta ur_{t-1})$. At the upper bound of the probability distribution expected devaluation equals the actual magnitude of devaluation if the policymaker decided to devalue, as given by (4.8).

A PC equilibrium exists whenever $E\Delta e_t(\cdot) = c_t^*(\cdot)$. Since $E\Delta e_t$ is likely to be non-linear, multiple PC equilibria may exist. The specific form of $F_t(\cdot)$ is unknown, which makes it impossible to determine specific PC equilibria algebraically without assuming a function for $F_t(\cdot)$. This will be done at a later stage to demonstrate how a sequence of PC equilibria over time can force the policymaker to abandon the currency board.

4.2.5.4 Graphical Representation and Multiple Equilibria

The model can be illustrated, and the existence of equilibria can be determined by use of the following diagrams:

Figure 4.2 shows possible plots for $c_t^*(E\Delta e_t)$ and $E\Delta e_t(c_t^*)$. The function for $c_t^*(E\Delta e_t)$ is linear and upward-sloping with a slope of $1/\frac{dc_t^*(\cdot)}{dE\Delta e_t} = \frac{\sqrt{\alpha+\theta}}{\alpha}$, as can be seen from (4.18). The slope and form of the function for $E\Delta e_t(c_t^*)$ are determined by the probability distribution of $c \sim [\underline{c_t}, \overline{c}]$ and satisfy property P1 given above. In this case, a uniform distribution has been assumed.

The intersecting points of each function with the abscissa (A and $\underline{c_t}$) and the $\overline{c}$-line (B and D) are as follows:

A is the intersecting point of the $c_t^*(E\Delta e_t)$-function with the abscissa. From (4.18) we get:

$$A:\ c_t^*(E\Delta e_t = 0) = \frac{\alpha}{\sqrt{\alpha+\theta}}(k + \delta ur_{t-1}) \tag{4.20}$$

B is the intersecting point of the $c_t^*(E\Delta e_t)$-function with the $\overline{c}$-line. Using (4.18) and solving $c_t^*(E\Delta e_t) = \overline{c}$ for $E\Delta e_t$, we get

$$B:\ E\Delta e_t = \frac{\sqrt{\alpha+\theta}}{\alpha}\overline{c} - (k + \delta ur_{t-1}) \tag{4.21}$$

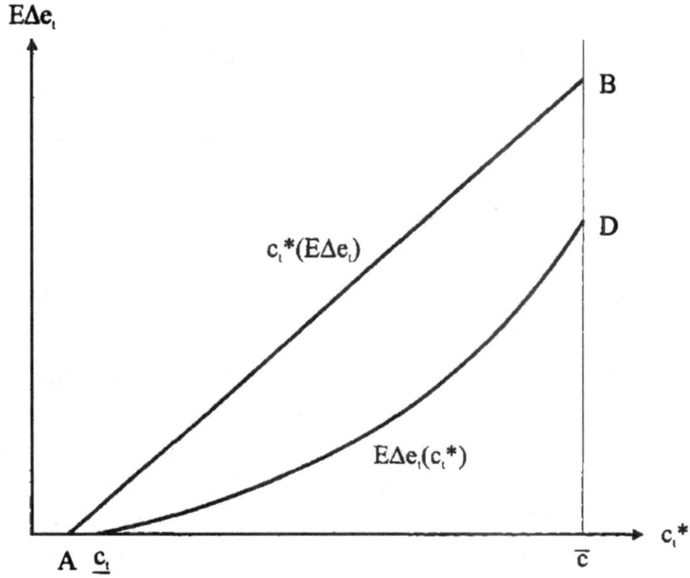

Figure 4.2: Plots for $c_t^*(E\Delta e_t)$ and $E\Delta e_t(c_t^*)$ with FC equilibrium.

$\underline{c}_t$ is the intersecting point of the $E\Delta e_t(c_t^*)$-function with the abscissa and solely determined by the lower bound $\underline{c}_t$ of the publics expectation about the true value of c. See also property P2 for (4.19).

D is the intersecting point of the $E\Delta e_t(c_t^*)$-function with the $\overline{c}$-line. As stated by property P3 for (4.19):

$$D: \; E\Delta e_t(c_t^* = \overline{c}) = \frac{\alpha}{\theta}(k + \delta ur_{t-1}) \tag{4.22}$$

In figure 4.2 only an FC equilibrium exists, as when $E\Delta e_t = 0$, $c_t^* < \underline{c}_t$, i.e. point A is situated to the left of $\underline{c}_t$. As $\frac{\alpha}{\sqrt{\alpha+\theta}}(k + \delta ur_{t-1}) < \underline{c}_t$, condition (4.15) is satisfied.

The figure demonstrates the importance of $\underline{c}_t$ for the existence of an FC equilibrium. Increasing values of $\underline{c}_t$ shift the starting point of the $E\Delta e_t(c_t^*)$-function to the right, increasing the likeliness of the existence of an FC equilibrium.

No ZC equilibrium exists, as when a full devaluation is expected, i.e. $E\Delta e_t(c_t^* = \overline{c}) = \frac{\alpha}{\theta}(k + \delta ur_{t-1})$, the corresponding value of c_t^* is lower than the upper bound $\overline{c}$, i.e. $c_t^*(E\Delta e_t = \alpha\theta^{-1}(k + \delta ur_{t-1})) < \overline{c}$, which implies that devaluation is not certain and devaluation expectations are too high. For a ZC equilibrium to exist, point D would have to be located above point B.

In that case $\frac{\alpha}{\theta}(k+\delta ur_{t-1}) > \frac{\sqrt{\alpha+\theta}}{\alpha}\bar{c} - (k+\delta ur_{t-1})$, which satisfies condition (4.16). Similar to the FC case, the public's beliefs about the distribution of c play an important role for the existence of ZC equilibria: the higher the upper bound $\bar{c}$ of the probability distribution, the higher point B, and the less likely for a ZC equilibrium to exist.

No PC equilibria exist in figure 4.2, as these require for the $c_t^*(E\Delta e_t)$- and the $E\Delta e_t(c_t^*)$-function to intersect at least once.

As a consequence of the absence of ZC and PC equilibria, the model economy represented in figure 4.2 can only realize the FC equilibrium.

Note that the existence of FC and ZC equilibria is independent of the distribution of probabilities within the interval for c, and, therefore, independent of the specific shape of the $E\Delta e_t(\cdot)$-function. All intersecting points A, B, $\underline{c}_t$, and D only depend on the parameters and variables of the model plus the upper and lower bounds of the probability function. They do not depend on the distribution of probabilities within the intervall. Therefore, given the same state of the model, the shape of the $E\Delta e_t(c_t^*)$-curve plays no role in the determination of FC and ZC equilibria. It does play a role in determining PC equilibria, though, as will become clear throughout the following paragraphs.

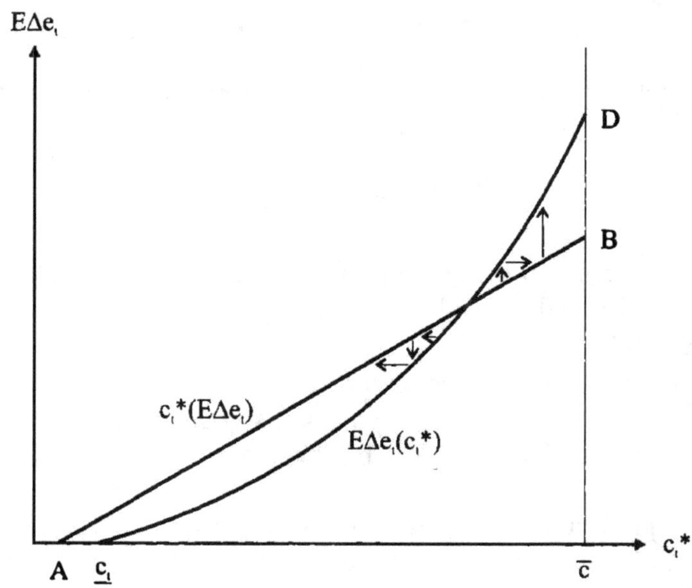

Figure 4.3: Plots for $c_t^*(E\Delta e_t)$ and $E\Delta e_t(c_t^*)$ with FC, one PC and ZC equilibria.

Now consider figure 4.3 with a different plot of $c_t^*(E\Delta e_t)$, exhibiting multiple equilibria. Again, an FC equilibrium exists with point A located to the left of $\underline{c_t}$. Also, a ZC equilibrium exists, as now point D is located above point $\overline{B}$.

As $c_t^*(E\Delta e_t)$ and $E\Delta e_t(c_t^*)$ intersect, a PC equilibrium exists in figure 4.3. It is not stable, though, as will be explained below.

In this case the same set of economic fundamentals allows for completely different economic outcomes. The state of the model economy represented by figure 4.3 allows for an FC equilibrium, in which the currency board can be maintained without generating unemployment pressure, and for an ZC equilibrium, in which the policymaker will abandon the currency board. The eventual outcome is determined by expectations, but indeterminate, i.e. neither can the policymaker enforce the realization of a certain equilibrium nor can the model predict the eventual outcome. The—in this case instantaneous—adjustment process, which determines which equilibrium is realized, is not described in the model.

Yet, we can infer some of the dynamics of the instantaneous adjustment process: Assume that at the beginning of the adjustment process in figure 4.3 initial devaluation expectations lie somewhere to the right of the PC equilibrium on the $E\Delta e_t(\cdot)$-function. As becomes clear from the $c_t^*(\cdot)$-function, this value of devaluation expectations means that the critical value c_t^*, the minimal value of political cost from devaluation for the policymaker not to devalue, has to be higher than initially assumed (indicated in the figure by an arrow to the right). This, in turn, implies a higher probability of devaluation, and results in higher devaluation expectations (indicated by an upward arrow). Eventually, the adjustment process leads to the (instantaneous) realization of the ZC equilibrium. Conversely, an adjustment process starting with lower devaluation expectations than in the PC equilibrium will result in realization of the FC equilibrium, as indicated by the left and downwards arrows.

From this reasoning it follows that the PC equilibrium in figure 4.3 is unstable, and will only be reached if initial devaluation expectations exactly match those in PC equilibrium. Any deviation will lead to realization of the FC or the ZC equilibrium.

Finally, figure 4.4 displays plots for $c_t^*(E\Delta e_t)$ and $E\Delta e_t(c_t^*)$ allowing for multiple PC equilibria. As opposed to the previous figures, we now assume that c is drawn from a density function with a single peak, which provides for the possibility of the two functions intersecting more than once. Following the reasoning throughout the previous paragraphs, the first PC equilibrium is unstable and the second stable.

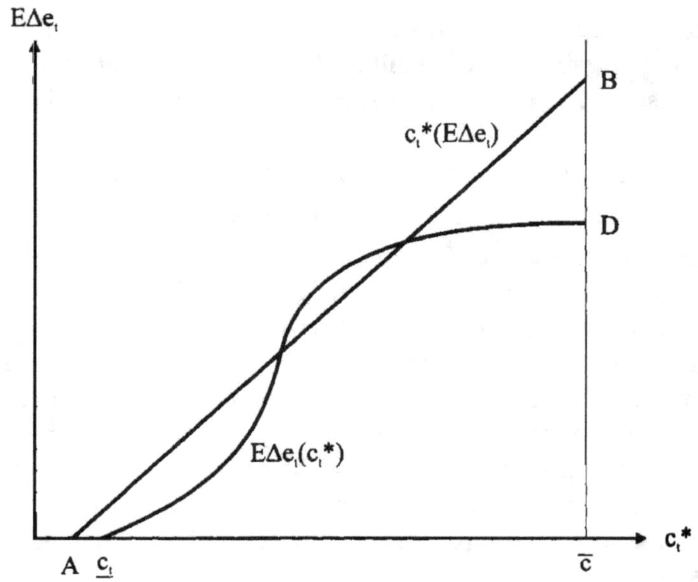

Figure 4.4: Plots for $c_t^*(E\Delta e_t)$ and $E\Delta e_t(c_t^*)$ with FC, two PC and ZC equilibria.

The figure demonstrates that the existence of PC equilibria depends on two important factors: On the relative position of the two curves in the diagram, and on the shape of the $E\Delta e_t(\cdot)$-function. The relative position of the two curves is determined by the model parameters. Combinations of parameters that render an FC equilibrium highly likely and a ZC equilibrium highly unlikely (implying the $c_t^*(\cdot)$-function to run above the $E\Delta e_t(\cdot)$-function), as well as parameters that render an FC equilibrium highly unlikely and a ZC equilibrium highly likely (implying the $c_t^*(\cdot)$-function to run below the $E\Delta e_t(\cdot)$-function), both decrease the likeliness of PC equilibria existing. The shape of the $E\Delta e_t(\cdot)$-function is determined by the probability distribution $c \sim [\underline{c}_t, \overline{c}]$, which will be discussed in more detail in the following subsection. Also note that the existence of an FC, as is the case in figure 4.4, requires the functions to intersect at least twice for a stable PC equilibrium to exist. Without an FC equilibrium only one intersection will provide for a stable PC equilibrium.

4.2.5.5 Model Parameters and Types of Equilibria

The previous subsection has clearly shown that the existence of the different types of equilibria depends on the relative position of the $E\Delta e_t(\cdot)$- and $c_t^*(\cdot)$-functions. These in turn depend on the parameters and variables of the model. For better understanding of the model and its graphical representation, this section shortly answers the question of how the existence of different types of equilibria is affected by the model's parameters and variables. These answers are derived straightforward from equations (4.18) and (4.19) and from the location of points A to D, as discussed in relation to figure 4.2.

As the model is concerned with the stability of currency boards, we will refer to the existence of only an FC equilibrium as a 'good situation', since the realization of an FC equilibrium allows for the unconditional maintenance of the currency board, and to the existence of only a ZC equilibrium as a 'bad situation'. Therefore, e.g. a worse situation denotes an increased likeliness of existence of a ZC equilibrium and a decreased likeliness of existence of an FC equilibrium.

- A higher degree of *unemployment responsiveness* α results in a worse situations for the policymaker. A more effective tradeoff between unemployment and inflation increases the temptation to devalue, and results in a higher penalty from not fulfilling devaluation expectations. Consequently, this raises devaluation expectations, again increasing the temptation to devalue.

- Higher *inflation aversion* θ leads to an improved situation. Higher marginal cost from devaluation reduce the temptation to devalue and also lower devaluation expectations.

- An increase in *past persistent unemployment* δur_{t-1} worsens chances to maintain the currency board. As high unemployment tempts the policymaker to devalue, devaluation expectations rise.

- The *probability distribution* $c \sim [\underline{c_t}, \bar{c}]$ influences the existence of equilibria in two ways: First, higher values of $\underline{c_t}$ and $\bar{c}$ improve the policymaker's situation, as they indicate that the public expects the political cost to be high, which increases the credibility of the currency board in the eyes of the public. As a consequence, devaluation expectations are lower. Second, the distribution of probabilities within the interval determines the existence of PC equilibria. Consider figure 4.2: The convex $E\Delta e_t(\cdot)$-function given there is based on a uniform distribution of probabilities within the interval $[\underline{c_t}, \bar{c}]$; every possible value of c is assigned the same probability by the public. If instead we assume that the public assigns high probabilities to higher values of c, i.e. a left-skewed probability distribution, the $E\Delta e_t(\cdot)$-function becomes even more convex. Likewise, a right-skewed probability distribution of c will render the $E\Delta e_t(\cdot)$-function less convex and, eventually, concave. Given a sufficiently concave function, two PC equilibria would exist in figure 4.2, the first unstable, the second stable. As this introduces additional equilibria less favorable than the FC equilibrium, we can conclude that the more right-skewed the probability distribution, i.e. the lower the public expects $\hat{c}$ to be, given the bounds of the interval, the worse the situation for the policymaker.

As parameters and variables of the model determine the existence and, to that extent, the realization of equilibria, the economic outcome from realization of a specific equilibrium in turn influences the existence of equilibria in subsequent periods. These dynamic effects will be explored in the following section.

4.2.6 Inter-temporal Linkages and Dynamic Effects

There are two inter-temporal linkages present in the model: First, unemployment ur_t is persistent, affecting both $c^*_{t+1}(E\Delta e_{t+1})$ and $E\Delta e_{t+1}(c^*_{t+1})$. Second, the exchange rate outcome in one period may be informative about the true value of c, leading to different devaluation expectations by the public in the next period.

Ad 1. Suppose unemployment is equal to its steady-state value. For this to be the case, $E\Delta e_t$ must equal Δe_t. (4.4) then becomes $ur_t = \sqrt{\alpha}(k + \delta ur_{t-1})$. Setting $ur_t = ur_{t-1} = \overline{ur}$ we get:

$$\overline{ur} = \frac{\sqrt{\alpha}k}{1-\sqrt{\alpha}\delta} \tag{4.23}$$

Now suppose the policymaker announces to keep the exchange rate fixed at the beginning of period t. At the end of period t he will stick to this announcement either in the FC case, or in the PC case, if $\hat{c} > c^*_t$. In the FC case devaluation expectations are zero, and unemployment will stay at its steady-state level. In the PC case devaluation expectations are positive, and unemployment will rise in the present period. With unemployment persistence, unemployment will also rise in subsequent periods by an amount determined by the autoregressive coefficient $\sqrt{\alpha}\,\delta$, which can be derived from (4.4). As can be seen from (4.18) and (4.19), this will affect both $c^*_{t+1}(E\Delta e_{t+1})$ and $E\Delta e_{t+1}(c^*_{t+1})$. Relating to figure 4.2, the result is a parallel-shift of the c^*-function to the right, as point A shifts to the right and point B shifts downward, and a counterclockwise rotation of the $E\Delta e$-function around point $\underline{c}_t$, as point D shifts upwards.

Ad 2. Suppose that in period t the equilibrium is PC, but the policymaker does not devalue, i.e. $\hat{c} \geq c_t^*$. The public observes the policy-action of not-devaluing and learns that $\hat{c} \geq c_t^*$. Consequently, when forming devaluation expectations for period $t+1$, the public knows that $\hat{c}$ must lie within the range $[c_t^*, \bar{c}]$.[14] Other things being equal, this will lead to lower devaluation expectations in $t+1$. Relating to figure 4.2, the result is a shift of point $\underline{c}$ to the right.

Note that this kind of learning does not take place in FC or ZC equilibria. In those cases the decision of whether or not to devalue is independent of $\hat{c}$. Therefore, no inferences about the true political cost can be made.

The inter-temporal effects resulting from the realization of an FC equilibrium are small. Providing unemployment in $t-1$ was at its steady-state level, there are no effects on unemployment. Also, no learning occurs and, therefore, the state of economy will remain unchanged. An FC equilibrium produces inter-temporal effects only, if unemployment in $t-1$ was above its steady-state level. In this case it leads to a reduction of unemployment. This effect will be explored at later stages of this chapter.

Realization of a PC equilibrium leads to two competing effects. On the one hand, unfulfilled devaluation expectations increase unemployment and make maintaining the currency board more costly. On the other hand, the public learns about the true political cost of abandoning the currency board, which increases the credibility of the exchange rate commitment. The combined effect from the realization of a PC equilibrium is illustrated in figure 4.5.

In period t (indicated by dashed curves), multiple equilibria exist. Suppose the outcome is the stable PC equilibrium represented by point P. If the resulting c_t^* is lower than the true devaluation cost $\hat{c}$, the policymaker will not devalue. Since devaluation expectations are positive, unemployment rises. The public observes the policymaker maintaining the exchange rate parity and learns that the true political cost must be higher than the threshold level c_t^* at point P.

In period $t+1$ (indicated by solid curves) the functions for $c_{t+1}^*(E\Delta e_{t+1})$ and $E\Delta e_{t+1}(c_{t+1}^*)$ change due to the outcome of the previous period. As described before, the $c_{t+1}^*(E\Delta e_{t+1})$-function shifts to the right, due to $ur_t > ur_{t-1}$. The new run of the $E\Delta e_{t+1}(c_{t+1}^*)$-function depends on three factors: First, higher unemployment in the previous period raises $E\Delta e_{t+1}(\bar{c})$ and point D becomes D'. Second, due to the learning process, the public now

[14] Bayesian learning occurs. See Irwin (2001, p. 14).

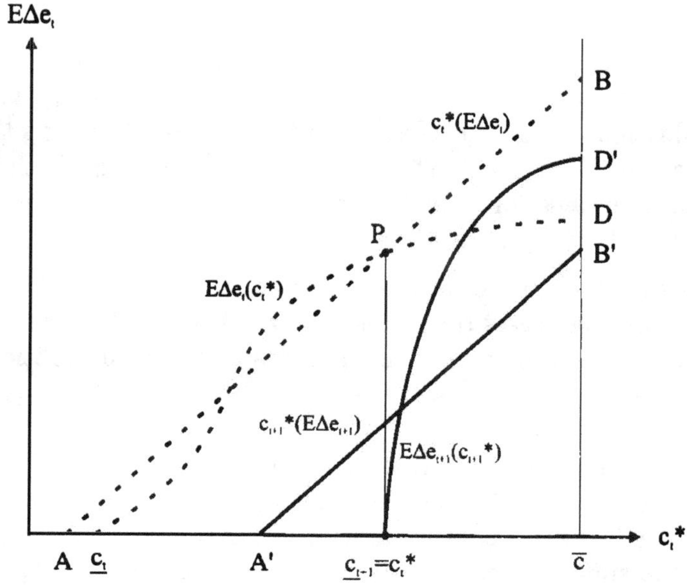

Figure 4.5: Inter-temporal shift from PC equilibrium to other.

knows that $\hat{c} \geq c_t^*$. Therefore, the lower bound of the public's density function of c now becomes $\underline{c_{t+1}} = c_t^*$. Finally, the shape of the curve between points $\underline{c_{t+1}}$ and D' depends on the probability distribution for c between the new lower bound $\underline{c_{t+1}}$ and the upper bound $\bar{c}$, which is represented by the shape of the function in t along the segment PD.

With the outcome as drawn in figure 4.5, multiple equilibria still exist in period $t+1$: An FC equilibrium ($A' < \underline{c_{t+1}}$), a ZC equilibrium ($B' < D'$), an unstable PC equilibrium (the intersection of the two functions), but no stable PC equilibrium. However, this need not be the case. Had the unemployment effect been less strong (meaning less-pronounced shifts of the points A, B and D), there might have been a second (stable) PC equilibrium but no ZC equilibrium. Had the unemployment effect been even less strong and the learning effect stronger, there might have been only an FC equilibrium.

Obviously, the inter-temporal linkages of the model allow for a variety of outcomes in the next period. Therefore, the following section will explore the consequences of realization of one equilibrium in period t on the state of the model economy in period $t+1$ in more detail.

4.2.7 Stability of the Currency Board

This section explores the the dynamics of the model in more depth. First, the learning effect from realization of a PC equilibrium, which increases the credibility of the currency board, is examined in subsection 4.2.7.1. In subsection 4.2.7.2 we take a closer look at the unemployment effect, which is the counterpart of the learning effect, and tends to weaken the exchange rate arrangement. Subsection 4.2.7.3 then demonstrates how a sequence of PC equilibria over time can eventually force the policymaker to abandon the currency board, no matter how high the political cost from devaluation. Finally, subsection 4.2.7.4 examines how a sufficiently high adverse shock may lead to the breakdown of the currency board arrangement, but may also, if the arrangement withstands the resulting unemployment pressure, strengthen the exchange rate commitment for future periods.

4.2.7.1 Gains from Increased Credibility

The learning effect from a PC equilibrium without devaluation, outlined in section 4.2.6, can increase the stability of the currency board. As the public realizes that they have underestimated the level of political cost from devaluation, and that the policymaker is more determined to maintain the currency board than initially expected, devaluation expectations in the next period are reduced. If the gain from increased credibility is not outweighed by the rise in unemployment, which we prove to be the case, the policymaker will find himself in a more comfortable situation in the following period.

This point is illustrated in figure 4.6. Assume the policymaker has just introduced the currency board and the public is uncertain about the policymaker's determination to maintain the currency board. As a result, the lower bound of the probability distribution, $\underline{c_t}$, is relatively low, and only a PC equilibrium can be realized in period t (solid curves). Observing the policymaker maintaining the currency board, the public realizes that the political cost from devaluation have to be higher than initially assumed and they adjust their devaluation expectations for the following period accordingly. The outcome is an FC equilibrium in period $t+1$, as shown by the dashed curves in the figure.

In this case the stability of the currency board is being tested. Passing the test, it gains the credibility necessary for the public to fully believe in the sustainability of the currency board, the first-best situation with unemployment eventually at its steady-state level and zero devaluation.

Whether a PC equilibrium in period t really leads to a stabilization of the currency board, in the sense of increasing the likeliness of an FC equilibrium

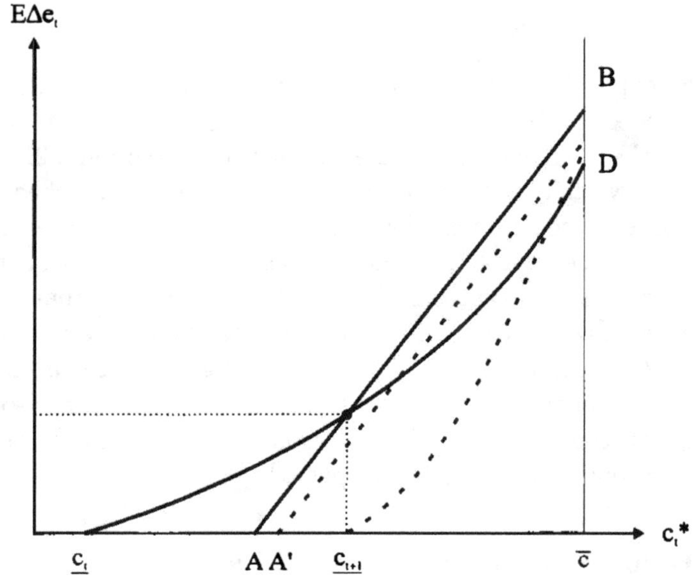

Figure 4.6: Credibility gain improving stability of the currency board.

existing in the following period, depends on the combined effects increased unemployment and the credibility gain have on the situation in period $t+1$. From the condition for the existence of an FC equilibrium, (4.15), we know that increasing unemployment reduces, and gained credibility increases the likeliness of an FC equilibrium. The question is, which effect dominates, i.e. does the right-shift of $\underline{c}_t$, due to gained credibility, outweigh the right-shift of point A, due to increased unemployment?

Assume unemployment in period $t-1$ was at its steady-state level, $ur_{t-1} = \overline{ur}$, given by (4.23). In period t a PC equilibrium is realized with $E\Delta e_t > 0$. If the policymaker does not devalue, unemployment in period t is given by:[15]

$$\begin{aligned} ur_t &= \sqrt{\alpha}(E\Delta e_t + k + \delta\overline{ur}) \\ &= \overline{ur} + \sqrt{\alpha}E\Delta e_t \end{aligned} \tag{4.24}$$

We know from subsection 4.2.5.4 that in period t point A in figure 4.6 is located at $A = \frac{\alpha}{\sqrt{\alpha+\theta}}(k + \delta\overline{ur})$. In period $t+1$ point A' is located to the right of point A, due to the unemployment effect. With unemployment in period t given by (4.24), we get:

$$A' = \frac{\alpha}{\sqrt{\alpha+\theta}}[k + \delta(\overline{ur} + \sqrt{\alpha}E\Delta e_t)]$$

[15]See appendix, C.1.5.

$$= \quad A + \frac{\delta\alpha^{\frac{3}{2}}}{\sqrt{\alpha+\theta}} E\Delta e_t \tag{4.25}$$

We can also calculate the position of point $\underline{c_{t+1}} = c_t^*$, which is located at the intersection of the $c_t^*(\cdot)$- and the $E\Delta e_t(\cdot)$-functions. From (4.18) we get:

$$\begin{aligned} \underline{c_{t+1}} &= c_t^* = \frac{\alpha}{\sqrt{\alpha+\theta}}(E\Delta e_t + k + \delta ur_{t-1}) \\ &= A + \frac{\alpha}{\sqrt{\alpha+\theta}} E\Delta e_t \end{aligned} \tag{4.26}$$

No FC equilibrium exists in period $t+1$ if $\underline{c_{t+1}}$ is located further to the left than A', i.e. if $\underline{c_{t+1}} < A'$:

$$\begin{aligned} A + \frac{\alpha}{\sqrt{\alpha+\theta}} E\Delta e_t &< A + \frac{\delta\alpha^{\frac{3}{2}}}{\sqrt{\alpha+\theta}} E\Delta e_t \\ 1 &< \delta\sqrt{\alpha} \end{aligned} \tag{4.27}$$

Condition (4.27) states that an FC equilibrium in period $t+1$ will exist after realization of a PC equilibrium in period t, if the autoregressive coefficient of unemployment, $\delta\sqrt{\alpha}$, is less than unity. This condition must always hold, as an autoregressive coefficient greater or equal one would lead to an infinite increase of unemployment over time. It, therefore, follows that the realization of a PC equilibrium without devaluation always result in the existence of an FC equilibrium in the next period.

This result has consequences for the existence of PC equilibria in the next period, as well. In figure 4.6 no stable PC equilibrium exists in period $t+1$. A stable PC would only exist if the two functions intersect in a point where the slope of the $c_t^*(\cdot)$-function is steeper than the slope of the $E\Delta e_t(\cdot)$-function. For this to be the case in the figure, point A' would have to be located to the right of point $\underline{c_{t+1}}$. But we have just proven the opposite to be true after the realization of a PC equilibrium. With point A' to the left of point $\underline{c_{t+1}}$ a stable PC equilibrium can only exist if the functions intersect at least twice. A necessary, but not sufficient, condition for this is the $E\Delta e_t(\cdot)$-function being concave. It, therefore, follows that, after the realization of a PC equilibrium in period t, no stable PC equilibrium exist in period $t+1$, if the $E\Delta e_{t+1}(\cdot)$-function is convex or linear, or, equivalent to that, if the $E\Delta e_t(\cdot)$-function is convex or linear within the interval $[c_t^*, \bar{c}]$. This, in turn, requires, as has been explained in 4.2.5.5, the probability distribution for c to be sufficiently right-skewed, i.e. within the given interval the public expect the political cost to be rather low.

We conclude that the credibility gained from realizing a PC equilibrium without devaluation always stabilizes the currency board in the sense that in the next period a FC equilibrium exists—which, if realized, is the optimal outcome for the model-economy—and that, under certain conditions, no stable PC equilibrium exists, reducing the possibility of multiple equilibria.

It has to be noted, though, that the PC equilibrium in figure 4.6 might also lead to the existence of a ZC equilibrium in period $t+1$. The learning effect affects only the condition for an FC equilibrium, but not the condition for a ZC equilibrium, (4.16). Thus, the unemployment effect from the realization of the PC equilibrium weakens the condition for the existence of a ZC equilibrium. This connection will be explored in the following subsection.

4.2.7.2 Destabilization through Unemployment

This subsection demonstrates how the realization of a PC equilibrium in period t can lead to the existence of a ZC equilibrium in period $t+1$.

The condition for the existence of a ZC equilibrium, (4.16), depends on ur_{t-1}, $\bar{c}$ and other parameters of the model, but not on $\underline{c_t}$. Assuming unemployment in $t-1$ was at its steady state level, i.e. $ur_{t-1} = \overline{ur}$, the realization of a PC equilibrium without a devaluation leads to the following two effects, as discussed in subsection 4.2.6: Firstly, as $E\Delta e_t > \Delta e_t$, unemployment rises so that $ur_t > \overline{ur}$. Secondly, the public learns that $\underline{c_{t+1}} = c_t^* > \underline{c_t}$. Only the first effect affects the condition for existence of a ZC equilibrium in period $t+1$. Higher unemployment increases the likeliness of a ZC equilibrium existing, while the learning effect has no impact on the existence of ZC equilibria. Consequently, the realization of a PC equilibrium without a devaluation leads to a weaker condition for the existence of a ZC equilibrium in the next period.

This conclusion can be verified by again looking at figure 4.5. Increased unemployment in $t+1$ led to shifts of points A, B, and D to A', B', and D', respectively. The learning effect led to a shift of point $\underline{c_t}$ to $\underline{c_{t+1}}$. Remember that the existence of a ZC equilibrium depends solely on the relative location of points B and D. The location of these is only affected by increased unemployment, but not by the learning process.

We know from (4.24) that, after a PC equilibrium without devaluation, unemployment is given by:

$$ur_t \;=\; \overline{ur} + \sqrt{\alpha} E\Delta e_t$$

Clearly, $ur_t > \overline{ur}$ when $E\Delta e_t > 0$. Substituting expected devaluation in PC equilibrium from (4.19) yields:[16]

$$k + \delta ur_t = (k + \delta \overline{ur}) \left[1 + \frac{\delta \alpha^{3/2} F_t(c_t^*)}{\theta + \alpha(1 - F_t(c_t^*))} \right] \tag{4.28}$$

The left-hand term of (4.28) is part of the condition for a ZC equilibrium, (4.16). In period t, with unemployment in period $t-1$ at its steady-state level, this term was $k + \delta ur_{t-1} = k + \delta \overline{ur}$. In period $t+1$, after the realization of a PC equilibrium in period t, the term is given by (4.28). Evidently, the term in period $t+1$ is greater by the factor in square brackets, which means that the condition for the existence of a ZC equilibrium in period $t+1$ is weaker by the same factor.

The term in square brackets is increasing in α and δ. Higher unemployment responsiveness and persistence can present a threat to the sustainability of the currency board. On the other hand, the term is decreasing in θ, as higher inflation aversion of the policymaker reduces devaluation expectations.

4.2.7.3 Destabilization through a Sequence of PC Equilibria

While sections 4.2.7.1 and 4.2.7.2 were mostly concerned with the existence of FC and ZC equilibria, this section demonstrates how, under certain conditions, a sequence of realized PC equilibria can eventually lead to the abandonment of the currency board. If the realization of a stable PC equilibrium in one period results in the existence of a stable PC equilibrium in the following period, and if the new PC equilibrium is also realized, it follows that $c_t^* < c_{t+1}^*$: Due to the learning effect the public learns that $\underline{c_{t+1}} = c_t^*$. The realization of a PC equilibrium in period $t+1$ implies that $c_{t+1}^* > \underline{c_{t+1}}$ and therefore $c_t^* < c_{t+1}^*$.

If it is possible to realize an indefinite sequence of PC equilibria this implies that c_t^* can rise indefinitely over time. Since the policymaker will devalue if $c_t^* > \hat{c}$, he will eventually be forced to renege on the exchange rate commitment, regardless of how high the political cost of devaluation.

To allow for an analytical solution of the model, Irwin (2001, p. 17) assumes that the public's beliefs about the true value of c can be represented by a Pareto distribution so that $F_{t+1}(c) = 1 - (\underline{c_{t+1}}/c)^2$ for $c \geq \underline{c_{t+1}}$.[17]

[16] See appendix, C.1.6.

[17] While Irwin (2001, pp. 17–18) stresses that the "distribution has been chosen so that an analytic solution of the model can be derived, and not because it is more plausible than any other prior probability distribution", we know from subsection 4.2.7.1 that for a PC equilibrium to exist in period $t+1$, the probability distribution has to provide for

The learning effect implies that $\underline{c_{t+1}} = c_t^*$ and therefore $F_{t+1}(c_{t+1}^*) = 1 - \left(c_t^*/c_{t+1}^*\right)^2$. Note that the distribution has no upper bound.

Substitution into (4.19) yields:

$$E\Delta e_{t+1}(c_{t+1}^*) = \frac{\alpha(c_{t+1}^*)^2 - \alpha(c_t^*)^2}{\theta(c_{t+1}^*)^2 + \alpha(c_t^*)^2}(k + \delta ur_t) \tag{4.29}$$

Substituting (4.29) into the equation for c_{t+1}^*, (4.18), and solving for c_{t+1}^*, yields (the negative root is disregarded as it represents an unstable PC equilibrium, instead only the positive root is considered):[18]

$$c_{t+1}^* = \frac{\alpha}{2\theta}\Bigg[\sqrt{\alpha+\theta}(k + \delta ur_t) + \sqrt{(\alpha+\theta)(k+\delta ur_t)^2 - \frac{4\theta}{\alpha}(c_t^*)^2}\Bigg] \tag{4.30}$$

Unemployment ur_t is itself a function of c_t^*. In a PC equilibrium without devaluation, the unemployment rate is (Irwin 2001, pp. 19–20):

$$ur_t = \frac{\sqrt{\alpha+\theta}c_t^*}{\sqrt{\alpha}} \tag{4.31}$$

Substituting (4.31) into (4.30) yields:

$$c_{t+1}^* = \frac{\alpha}{2\theta}\sqrt{\alpha+\theta}\left(k + \sqrt{\frac{\alpha+\theta}{\alpha}}\delta c_t^*\right) + \frac{\alpha}{2\theta}\sqrt{(\alpha+\theta)\left(k + \sqrt{\frac{\alpha+\theta}{\alpha}}\delta c_t^*\right)^2 - \frac{4\theta}{\alpha}(c_t^*)^2} \tag{4.32}$$

For a PC equilibrium to actually exist in period $t+1$, the following necessary and sufficient conditions have to hold: $c_t^* < c_{t+1}^*$, as has been explained above, and a real numbers solution to (4.32) has to exist, i.e. the term under the square root sign needs to be positive.

If we assume $\alpha > \theta$, a necessary and sufficient condition for the existence of a stable PC equilibrium in $t+1$ is (Irwin 2001, p. 20):

$$c_t^*[2\sqrt{\theta} - \delta(\alpha+\theta)] \leq \sqrt{\alpha}\sqrt{(\alpha+\theta)}k \tag{4.33}$$

a concave $E\Delta e(\cdot)$-function, at least along some segments. The Pareto distribution results in a function for $E\Delta e(\cdot)$ that is concave along the whole interval $[\underline{c}, \overline{c}]$.

[18]See appendix, C.1.7.

Suppose this condition is satisfied. In this case a PC equilibrium in t without devaluation will lead to the existence of a stable PC equilibrium in $t+1$ such that $c^*_{t+1} > c^*_t$. This will obviously hold true for all other periods, as well. Furthermore, if the term in square brackets in (4.33) is negative, this condition will hold, regardless of how high c^*_t. This will be the case if:

$$\delta \ > \ \frac{2\sqrt{\theta}}{\alpha+\theta} \tag{4.34}$$

As a result, if unemployment persistence δ is high enough to satisfy (4.34), and if the assumptions made are satisfied, there is at least the possibility of a succession of PC equilibria eventually forcing the policymaker to devalue, regardless how high the value of $\hat{c}$. In this case unemployment rises to such an extent over time that the policymaker will eventually be forced to abandon the currency board, regardless of the offsetting credibility gains associated with the public learning about the true value of c.

4.2.7.4 Employment-Decreasing Shocks

This section explores the question of how employment-decreasing shocks to a currency board can lead to the destabilization and abandonment of the exchange rate arrangement.[19] We do this by assuming a model-economy, in which only an FC equilibrium exists, and then introducing a shock to the unemployment function, examining how the economy is affected by this shock. We chose an FC-equilibrium-only situation since this case represents the most stable situation for the currency board. Shocks during a less stable situation will have even worse effects on the model-economy.

Assume the model is in a state that allows for the existence of an FC equilibrium only, which is consequently realized. This implies that the condition for existence of an FC equilibrium, (4.15), is fulfilled, and the condition for existence of a ZC equilibrium, (4.16), is not fulfilled. To eliminate the possible existence of a PC equilibrium we might also assume the following condition to hold:

$$\begin{aligned} c^*_t(E\Delta e_t = \alpha/\theta(k+\delta ur_{t-1})) \ &< \ \underline{c_t} \\ k+\delta ur_{t-1} \ &< \ \frac{\underline{c_t}\theta}{\alpha\sqrt{(\alpha+\theta)}} \end{aligned} \tag{4.35}$$

Condition (4.35) states that at the maximum level of devaluation expectations the resulting value of c^*_t is smaller than the starting point $\underline{c_t}$ of the

[19] The only real economy reference in our model is unemployment. Therefore, such unemployment-decreasing shocks may be seen as a proxy for adverse real shocks, as they have been discussed throughout subsection 2.2.3 on optimum currency areas.

$E\Delta e_t(\cdot)$-function. If this is the case, it is impossible for both functions to intersect, and no PC equilibria can exist. Yet, this is a very strong condition, and, assuming the probability function of the public is not extremely right-skewed, still no PC equilibria may exist without the condition holding.

In a manner similar to Obstfeld (1997, p. 63), we now introduce an unexpected, exogenous, employment-decreasing shock η_t into the unemployment equation, which we assume to affect the economy only once, at the beginning of period $t = 1$. Equation (4.4) becomes:

$$\begin{aligned} ur_t &= \sqrt{\alpha}\left[(E\Delta e_t - \Delta e_t) + k + \delta ur_{t-1} + \eta_t\right], \\ \eta_1 &> 0, \quad \eta_{t>1} = 0 \end{aligned} \tag{4.36}$$

Consequently, locations of points A, B, D in figures 4.2–4.5 change accordingly, to represent the shock: $A : \frac{\alpha}{\sqrt{\alpha+\theta}}(k + \delta ur_{t-1} + \eta_t)$, $B : \frac{\sqrt{\alpha+\theta}}{\alpha}\overline{c} - (k + \delta ur_{t-1} + \eta_t)$ and $D : \frac{\alpha}{\theta}(k + \delta ur_{t-1} + \eta_t)$. As can be seen, the shock will act as a shift parameter for the curves. With $\eta_t > 0$, point A shifts to the right by $\frac{\alpha}{\sqrt{\alpha+\theta}}\eta_t$, point B shifts down by η_t and point D shifts up by $\frac{\alpha}{\theta}\eta_t$. Obviously, point $\underline{c_t}$ is unaffected.

Two critical values of the shock can be calculated: First, the magnitude of the shock leading to the existence of an ZC equilibrium, and second, the magnitude of the shock leading to the disappearance of the FC equilibrium.

Ad 1. A shock of a magnitude sufficient to provide for the existence of a ZC equilibrium can have two consequences: If other equilibria still exist, it means the economy has become vulnerable to speculative attacks, and high devaluation expectations can become self-fulfilling by leading to the realization of a ZC equilibrium. If no other equilibria exist, the shock will certainly lead to a break-down of the currency board.

The critical size of the shock can be calculated by examining the shifts of points B and D caused by $\eta_t > 0$. If the combined shifts are greater than the initial distance between both points, a ZC equilibrium will ensue. Algebraical:

$$\eta_t > \frac{\overline{c}\theta}{\alpha\sqrt{\alpha+\theta}} - (k + \delta ur_{t-1}) \tag{4.37}$$

Condition (4.37), which resembles the ZC condition, (4.16), states that a shock will lead to the existence of a ZC equilibrium if the unemployment impetus from the shock, η_t ($\sqrt{\alpha}\,\eta_t$ is additional unemployment generated by the shock), outweighs the difference between the critical unemployment impetus (first term on the right side) and the actual unemployment impetus (second term on the right side), given full devaluation expectations.

Ad 2. A shock that leads to the disappearance of the FC equilibrium enforces the realization of a new, less favorable equilibrium. Depending on the available equilibria (stable PC only, ZC only, stable PC and ZC) this either increases the unemployment cost of maintaining the currency board (if a PC equilibrium is realized) or even leads to the abandonment of the exchange rate parity (ZC equilibrium).

The critical magnitude of the shock can be determined by observing the shift of point A caused by $\eta_t > 0$. If the shift is greater than the initial distance between points A and $\underline{c}_t$, the FC equilibrium will cease to exist. Algebraical:

$$\eta_t \quad > \quad \frac{\underline{c}_t\sqrt{\alpha+\theta}}{\alpha} - (k + \delta ur_{t-1}) \tag{4.38}$$

Similar to condition (4.37), condition (4.38) resembles the condition for the existence of an FC equilibrium, (4.15). A shock will lead to the disappearance of the FC equilibrium if the unemployment impetus from the shock, η_t, exceeds the difference of the maximum unemployment impetus compatible with an FC equilibrium (the first term on the right side) and the actual unemployment impetus (the second term on the right side), given no devaluation expectations.

Conditions (4.37) and (4.38) underline the importance the model parameters have on the stability of our model-economy: Higher unemployment responsiveness, α, increases the susceptibility of the economy to shocks, as the increased efficiency of the devaluation-unemployment tradeoff tempts the policymaker to reduce his loss by engaging in devaluation. Likewise, high past persistent unemployment, δur_{t-1}, increases the unemployment cost from maintaining the exchange rate, and makes a devaluation more likely. On the other hand, higher inflation aversion, θ, and high lower and upper bounds of the probability function, $\underline{c}_t$ and $\overline{c}$, increase the credibility of the exchange rate commitment and reduce the vulnerability to shocks.

Depending on economic fundamentals and the public's beliefs, the shock can push the economy out of the FC equilibrium, and thereby increase the cost of maintaining the currency board in the present and subsequent periods (condition (4.38) holds), or even lead to the instant abandonment of the currency board (condition (4.37) holds). Which of both conditions will be met first, depends on the parameters: Condition (4.38) may hold while (4.37) does not, and vice versa.

While this section concerns itself with an economy initially being in an FC-only situation, the above results also hold true for other constellations.

The stability of the economy when facing a shock does not only depend on the model parameters examined so far, though. The distribution of probabilities within the interval $[\underline{c}_t, \overline{c}]$ plays an important role as well.

Figures 4.7 and 4.8 represent model economies with the same economic fundamentals, but different distributions of probabilities within the interval $[\underline{c}_t, \overline{c}]$: In figure 4.7 the underlying probability distribution is sufficiently right-skewed for the $E\Delta e_t(\cdot)$-function to be concave, and in figure 4.8 the probability distribution is slightly left-skewed. Each graph in both figures illustrates a different magnitude of the shock: The upper left graph represents the economy without a shock, $\eta_t = 0$, the upper right graph illustrates a shock of sufficient magnitude to allow for the existence of a ZC equilibrium, and the lower right graph illustrates a larger shock that causes the FC equilibrium to disappear.

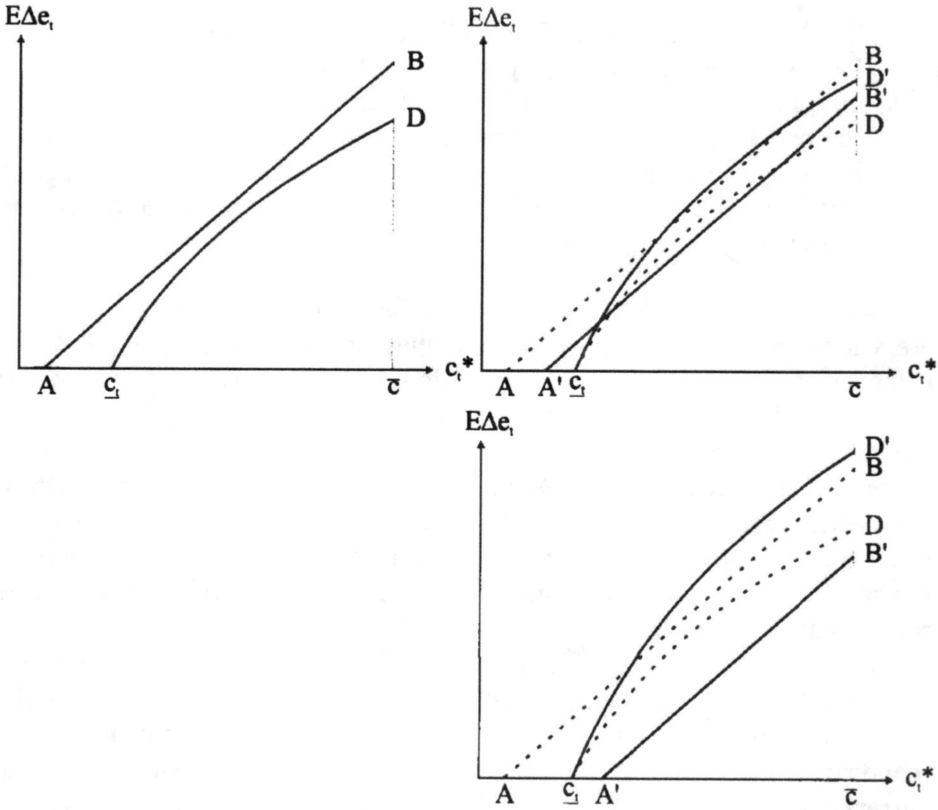

Figure 4.7: Employment shock with right-skewed probability function.

As explained previously, and obvious from figures 4.7 and 4.8, the distribution of probabilities within a given interval does not affect the (non-)

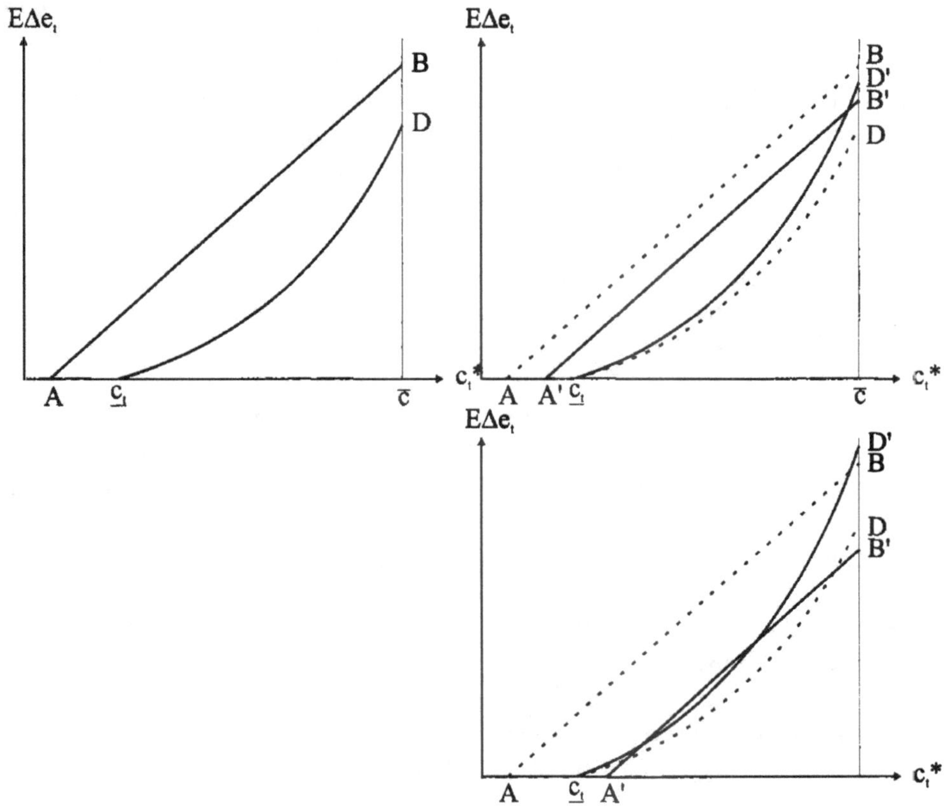

Figure 4.8: Employment shock with left-skewed probability function.

existence of FC and ZC equilibria, but the existence of PC equilibria. Consider figure 4.7: A small shock, insufficient for the existence of a ZC equilibrium, could already create a stable PC equilibrium and leave the economy vulnerable to a speculative attack that would not lead to the collapse of the currency board, but increase the unemployment cost of maintaining it. This is not the case in figure 4.8. There, no PC equilibria will exist until a ZC equilibrium exists.

Likewise, consider the upper right graphs in both figures: In both cases an FC, a ZC and an unstable PC equilibrium exist, the level of the PC equilibrium being the difference between both figures. This difference has consequences in respect to the instant adjustment taking place in every period, as discussed in section 4.2.5.4. If initial devaluation expectations at the beginning of the adjustment process are higher than in the PC equilibrium, the adjustment process will end up in realization of the ZC equilibrium, otherwise the FC equilibrium will be realized. As a result, relatively low initial devaluation expectations will lead to realization of an ZC equilibrium in case of the right-skewed probability distribution, as compared to the case of a left-skewed probability distribution, where only relatively high devaluation expectations lead to the collapse of the currency board.

Finally, consider the lower right graph of both figures: Here the magnitude of the employment shock is sufficiently high for the FC equilibrium to cease to exist. While in 4.7 this leads to unconditional exit from the currency board, as only a ZC equilibrium exists, figure 4.8 also provides for a PC equilibrium with relatively low devaluation expectations, and the eventual outcome depends on the instant adjustment process.

Given the interval $[\underline{c}_t, \overline{c}]$, it follows that the higher the probabilities the public assigns to lower values within the interval, the lower the employment-reducing shock η_t leading to the existence of a stable PC equilibrium, and the higher the corresponding devaluation expectations if the PC equilibrium is realized.

Curiously, if the shock does not lead to the abandonment of the currency board, it can even serve to strengthen the model-economy

Assume again that unemployment before the shock was at its steady-state level. If the shock does not lead to the abandonment of the currency board, two possibilities arise: First, an FC equilibrium is realized, second, a PC equilibrium without devaluation is realized. The effect of these two equilibria on the location of points A, B and D is summarized in table 4.1.

	FC equilibrium in period t	**PC equilibrium in period t**
Unemployment in t	$ur_t = \overline{ur} + \sqrt{\alpha}\,\eta_t$	$ur_t = \overline{ur} + \sqrt{\alpha}\,\eta_t + \sqrt{\alpha}\,E\Delta e_t$
Location of A, B and D in period $t-1$	$A^0 = \frac{\alpha}{\sqrt{\alpha+\theta}}(k + \delta\overline{ur})$ $B^0 = \frac{\sqrt{\alpha+\theta}}{\alpha}\overline{c} - (k + \delta\overline{ur})$ $D^0 = \frac{\alpha}{\theta}(k + \delta\overline{ur})$	
Location of A, B and D in period t with $\eta_t > 0$	$A = A^0 + \frac{\alpha}{\sqrt{\alpha+\theta}}\,\eta_t$ $B = B^0 - \eta_t$ $D = D^0 + \frac{\alpha}{\theta}\,\eta_t$	
Location of A, B and D in period $t+1$	$A' = A^0 + \delta\sqrt{\alpha}\,\frac{\alpha}{\sqrt{\alpha+\theta}}\,\eta_t$ $B' = B^0 - \delta\sqrt{\alpha}\,\eta_t$ $D' = D^0 + \delta\sqrt{\alpha}\,\frac{\alpha}{\theta}\,\eta_t$	$A' = A^0 + \delta\sqrt{\alpha}\,\frac{\alpha}{\sqrt{\alpha+\theta}}(\eta_t + E\Delta e_t)$ $B' = B^0 - \delta\sqrt{\alpha}(\eta_t + E\Delta e_t)$ $D' = D^0 + \delta\sqrt{\alpha}\,\frac{\alpha}{\theta}(\eta_t + E\Delta e_t)$

Table 4.1: Location of points A, B and D after a shock.

In the FC case the result is non-ambiguous: In period $t+1$ all points shift back in the direction of their initial steady-state positions since the autoregressive coefficient of unemployment, $\delta\sqrt{\alpha}$, has to be less than unity, as we have argued in subsection 4.2.7.1. This strengthens the condition for the existence of an FC equilibrium and weakens the condition for the existence of a ZC equilibrium. If the economy remains in FC equilibrium, the shock has had barely no impact on the economy, except for a short increase in unemployment, which will return to its steady-state level over time.

In the PC case we again have two effects to consider: The credibility gain from not devaluing, as explained in subsection 4.2.7.1, and the unemployment effect. The credibility gain improves the situation of the model-economy. The impact of the unemployment effect depends on whether the combined impact of the employment shock and positive devaluation expectations on unemployment in period $t+1$ is smaller than the impact of just the employment shock on unemployment in period t. The unemployment-situation in period $t+1$ will have improved, compared to period t, if $\delta\sqrt{\alpha}(\eta_t + E\Delta e_t) < \eta_t$, or:

$$E\Delta e_t < \frac{1-\delta\sqrt{\alpha}}{\delta\sqrt{\alpha}}\eta_t \tag{4.39}$$

If the autoregressive coefficient of unemployment is sufficiently small, unemployment in period $t+1$ is lower than in period t, and consequently the condition for the existence of a ZC equilibrium is also weaker than in period t. But even with a rise in unemployment, the increase is lower compared to a PC equilibrium that did not result from a shock.

If the economy manages to return to an FC equilibrium in period $t+1$ after realizing a PC equilibrium from a shock, the situation will have improved compared to before the shock. While the increase in unemployment is only temporary as unemployment eventually returns to its steady-state level, the credibility gain is permanent. Therefore, the economy will be less vulnerable to speculative attacks or further shocks.

4.2.7.5 Conclusion

This subsection has highlighted some of the important advantages, but also drawbacks of the currency board system. The credibility effect, explored in 4.2.7.1, explains why a currency board can be a very effective and successful instrument for stabilization: If a currency board is introduced to end an acute economic crisis, such as the hyperinflation and currency crises in Argentina and Bulgaria, this stabilization attempt might initially not be very credible in the eyes of economic agents, as the policymaker has previously also failed to stabilize the economy. Consequently, devaluation expectations will initially be rather high. But, if the policymaker has set high enough political cost for the currency board exit—highlighting once again why a strong legal and political commitment to the currency board is essential, especially if the currency board is implemented during an economic crisis—the high devaluation expectations may still not prompt the policymaker to devalue (realization of a PC equilibrium without devaluation). This firm commitment to a no-devaluation policy, despite potentially high real cost from unfulfilled devaluation expectations, reveals to the public the policymaker's sincerity to maintain the currency peg. Consequently, the public lower devaluation expectations for the following period by an extent, that at least makes it *possible* for the currency board commitment to be fully credible in the following period (existence of an FC equilibrium). This effect is evident for both Argentina (see section 3.3) and Bulgaria (see section 3.5), where the introduction of the currency board led to a rapid decline in inflation and interest rates, and a strong resumption of growth.

On the other hand, 4.2.7.2 and 4.2.7.3 have also highlighted the potentially destabilizing role of unemployment. As long as the currency board is not fully credible, maintaining it leads to increasing unemployment pressure, or, if we take unemployment in the model to be a proxy for the real economy, to increasing real cost. In the model, one very important factor defining the destabilizing impact of unemployment is the degree of unemployment persistence, δ. If we assume unemployment persistence to be influenced by labor market flexibility, we may conclude that unemployment tends to undermine the stability of the currency board and the economy in general the more, the less flexible labor markets are. The more flexible labor markets are, the less likely is a build-up of unemployment over time, which might eventually tempt the policymaker to resort to devaluation. This conclusion also conforms to our repeated assertions throughout section 2.2, where we have stressed the importance of labor market flexibility.

We may now also shed some light on a question we have raised in section 3.6: What is the possible connection between rigid currency board design, implying high political cost, $\hat{c}$, and high levels of unemployment, as we have observed them in some of the currency boards examined in chapter 3. We have asserted that a government introducing a currency board to end an acute crisis would have to show strong legal and political commitment to the currency board, so the currency board could gain sufficient credibility to effectively stabilize the economy. In our model, potential reasons for a currency crisis are low inflation aversion of the government, θ, and high unemployment responsiveness to inflation, α. We have seen in subsections 4.2.2 and 4.2.3 that the consequence of these two factors under discretionary exchange rate policy would be high inflation, yet unchanged unemployment. Under such circumstances, the gains from having a credible fixed exchange rate are very high. Yet, we also know that with high unemployment responsiveness and low inflation aversion the temptation to devalue is very high, and, therefore, the political cost from devaluation have to be high to ascertain the sustainability of the currency board. Consequently, our model explains why countries such as Argentina or Bulgaria had no other choice but to opt for a relatively rigid currency board arrangement.

On the other hand, having a currency board in an economy where unemployment is highly responsive to inflation is not only bringing large gains, but also more risks. High unemployment responsiveness implies that, whenever the commitment to the currency board is doubtful and devaluation expectations are positive, or when a negative shock hits the economy, as has been elaborated in 4.2.7.4, unemployment increases rather strongly. To mitigate this exposure to unemployment to some extent, once again labor market flexibility is needed, to reduce the amount of unemployment that is carried on to future periods.

This, while certainly being simplified account, shows that there must not necessarily be a causal connection between rigid currency board design and high levels of unemployment. Instead, both may be, at least in cases such as Argentina and Bulgaria, the manifestation of an environment where unemployment is sensible to unexpected inflation, whether positive or negative.

4.2.8 Loss from Exit

This subsection aims at examining the cost from exiting the currency board. As we have seen from the preceding discussion, there are two cases, when the currency board will be abandoned: First, if a ZC equilibrium is realized, regardless of the true political cost of devaluation. Second, if a PC equilibrium is realized, and the critical value c_t^* is greater than the true political cost. What can the model tell us about the economic circumstances associated with these two cases?

The question is easy to answer in the case of the ZC equilibrium, as it has been discussed before. From equation (4.8) we know that if the policymaker devalues, consequence of a realized ZC equilibrium, devaluation and expected devaluation are given by:

$$E\Delta e_t = \Delta e_t = \frac{\alpha}{\theta}(k + \delta ur_{t-1})$$

As the devaluation offsets devaluation expectations exactly, unemployment is only determined by previous unemployment and unemployment persistence, namely:

$$ur_t = \sqrt{\alpha}(k + \delta ur_{t-1}) \qquad (4.40)$$

The resulting loss is given by (4.9):

$$L_t^{D,ZC} = \frac{\alpha(\alpha+\theta)}{\theta}(k+\delta ur_{t-1})^2$$

Note that the loss from realizing a ZC equilibrium is the maximum loss the policymaker can incur. Devaluation is the same as under discrete exchange rate management and fully matched by devaluation expectations, which is why devaluation does not even reduce unemployment. Besides α and θ, therefore, a crucial determinant of the policymaker's loss is persistent unemployment. The higher unemployment persistence δ and the higher the unemployment pressure generated over past periods—which in turn is also positively correlated with δ—the higher the policymaker's loss before, and in the period of exit from the currency board. And even after an exit from the currency board, given an exchange rate policy where devaluation and devaluation expectations match, unemployment will decline slower, the higher unemployment persistence.

If the exit from the currency board occurs when in PC equilibrium, devaluation expectations are lower than in the ZC case as the public is not certain of the policymaker devaluing. In PC equilibrium devaluation expectations are given by (4.19):

$$E\Delta e_t = \frac{\alpha F_t(c_t^*)}{\alpha+\theta-\alpha F_t(c_t^*)}(k+\delta ur_{t-1})$$

Notice that with F_t approaching 1, expected devaluation in the PC case increases until eventually matching expected devaluation in the ZC case. To determine the magnitude of devaluation in the PC case, substitute (4.19) into (4.6). This yields:

$$\Delta e_t = \frac{\alpha}{\alpha+\theta-\alpha F_t(c_t^*)}(k+\delta ur_{t-1}) \tag{4.41}$$

Clearly, actual devaluation outweighs devaluation expectations for all values $F_t < 1$, while also being lower than in ZC equilibrium. The resulting surprise devaluation will reduce unemployment and lead to lower unemployment compared to the ZC case:

$$ur_t = \frac{\sqrt{\alpha}\theta}{\alpha+\theta-\alpha F_t(c_t^*)}(k+\delta ur_{t-1}) \tag{4.42}$$

Obviously, with devaluation and unemployment both being lower than in the ZC case, the policymaker's loss will also have to be lower:

$$L_t^{D,PC} = \frac{\alpha\theta(\alpha+\theta)}{(\alpha+\theta-\alpha F_t(c_t^*))^2}(k+\delta ur_{t-1})^2 \tag{4.43}$$

The implications of currency board exit will be discussed again and in more detail in subsection 4.3.7, where some policy implications will be presented, as well.

4.3 The Model with Debt

This section extends the model to introduce effects from foreign-currency denominated debt. The presence of currency substitution and foreign currency debt, specifically debt denominated in the anchor currency, is a property found in many currency board economies, as we could show to some extent throughout chapter 3. Foreign currency debt has also played an important role in the recent breakdown of the Argentinean currency board in early 2002, as the devaluation led to the de-facto insolvency of many firms and banks, prompting the government to freeze bank deposits to prevent the breakdown of the banking system. Both, insolvencies and the bank freeze still have a devastating impact on the Argentinean economy.

A growing body of literature, stimulated by the experience of the Asian Crisis in 1997, concerns itself with the effects of foreign currency debt on the balance sheets of firms and the economy as a whole. There is sufficient reason to believe that foreign currency debt per se has recessionary consequences in the circumstance of a devaluation of the domestic currency, counteracting the stimulative effect so far assumed in the model. Consequently, this section aims to explore the effect foreign currency debt has on the desirability and stability of a currency board and on the conditions and the resulting loss from currency board exit.

The section is organized as follows: Subsection 4.3.1 presents two distinct channels through which foreign currency debt can have an effect on the model economy. A brief survey of the literature concerned with the effects the financial sector and the financial structure of firms can have on the real economy is given. The impact of these effects on unemployment is evaluated in subsection 4.3.2, and a new unemployment equation is formulated. Subsection 4.3.3 then examines the resulting general changes for exchange rate policy, exchange rate setting, and the desirability of a currency board. Subsections 4.3.4, 4.3.5, and 4.3.6 are devoted to examining in detail how the presence of foreign currency debt affects the stability of the currency board, its dynamics and resilience to shocks. Eventually, subsection 4.3.7 inspects the levels of loss to the policymaker, unemployment, and devaluation upon currency board exit and concludes.

4.3.1 Possible Effects of Foreign-Currency Debt on the Model Economy

In this subsection we will examine how the presence of foreign currency-denominated debt in our model economy may alter the results obtained from the basic model. There are two possible channels, which may possibly alter model outcomes: First, the presence of foreign currency debt can alter the preferences of the policymaker regarding the tradeoff between unemployment and inflation. Second, if firms take on foreign currency debt, a devaluation, through the resulting balance sheet effects, can have recessionary effects, weakening or even suspending the inflation unemployment tradeoff.

How the presence of foreign-currency denominated debt alters the behavior of the policymaker can be demonstrated by introducing some simple modifications to the basic model, which serve to demonstrate the qualitative consequences for the model. Assume the policymaker is not only concerned about unemployment and changes to the exchange rate, but also about changes in the level of government debt.[20] This is expressed by the following loss function:

$$L_t = (ur_t)^2 + \theta(\Delta e_t)^2 + \gamma(\Delta B_t)^2, \qquad \gamma > 0 \tag{4.44}$$

with γ a weight factor and ΔB_t the change in the level of government debt measured in domestic currency units. As the change in government debt is squared, this loss function applies only for $\Delta B_t \geq 0$, which we show to imply $\Delta e_t \geq 0$.

We further assume that the government holds only one loan of infinite maturity with the constant foreign currency interest rate i_a. The present value of government debt in local currency units, assuming the exchange rate decided on in period t will be kept indefinitely, is given by:

$$B_t = \sum_{n=t}^{\infty}\left(\frac{i_a \exp(e_t)}{(1+i_a)^n}D\right) = \exp(e_t)D \tag{4.45}$$

where D the nominal value of the loan in foreign currency units. Expressing (4.45) in logs and defining $\Delta B_t = B_t - B_{t-1}$ yields:

$$\Delta B_t = e_t - e_{t-1} = \Delta e_t \tag{4.46}$$

[20] This approach goes along the lines of Obstfeld (1994, pp. 200-206). In that model the policymaker has to finance exogenously given government consumption and debt service on *domestic*-currency denominated debt from tax income and income on foreign-currency denominated assets. The policy variables are the tax rate and the exchange rate. Under certain circumstances this setting leads to multiple equilibria and vulnerability to self-fulfilling currency crises. While Obstfelds model assumes domestic currency debt and foreign currency assets, which can lead to destabilization, the approach presented here assumes foreign currency debt, which leads to stabilization.

Substituting (4.46) back into the loss function, (4.44), yields:

$$L_t = (ur_t)^2 + \theta' (\Delta e_t)^2, \qquad \theta' = \theta + \gamma > \theta \tag{4.47}$$

As we can see from (4.47), the presence of foreign-currency denominated debt effectively increases the policymaker's aversion against devaluation. This is a straightforward result if the policymaker is concerned about the level of government debt: A devaluation reduces the value of the domestic currency relative to the foreign currency. As a consequence, the domestic currency value of debt, which in this case is correlated with the real terms value of debt, increases. While this effect should be noted, we will not explore it further in this chapter.

A growing body of literature, dating back as far as to Fisher (1933), is concerned with the second channel: the real effects of financial and credit markets. In the canonical real business cycle model and the textbook Keynesian IS-LM model financial and credit markets only determine the real interest rate, but do not otherwise affect the real economy, that is, they adopt the underlying assumptions of the Modigliani and Miller (1958)-theorem, which states that financial structure is both indeterminate and irrelevant to real economic outcomes. In contrast, the alternative view sees deteriorating credit-market conditions—sharp increases in insolvencies and bankruptcies, rising real debt burdens, collapsing asset prices, and bank failures—not as passive reflections of a declining real economy, but as major depressing factors themselves. Recent experiences in Scandinavia, Latin America, Japan, and other East Asian countries have been cited as instances where distressed banking systems and adverse credit-market conditions contributed to serious macroeconomic contractions, and have spurred further academic work in this field (Bernanke, Gertler, and Gilchrist 1998, p. 1).

In a recent paper, Krugman (1999) summarizes the stylized facts of the Asian crisis, and, for lack of existing models to address these facts, calls for a "third-generation" (Krugman 1999, p. 32) currency crisis model, which should incorporate these factors. One of the three stylized facts highlighted are balance sheet problems: the explosion in the the domestic currency value of dollar debt had disastrous effects on firms, and worsened the prospects for recovery after the crisis. In the simple model devised by Krugman as a first step towards such a third-generation model, a reduction of capital inflows leads to a deterioration of the real exchange rate, which in turn reduces the net worth of firms by increasing the domestic currency value of foreign debt, and reduces their ability to borrow and to invest. Under certain conditions, such a setting can lead to multiple equilibria and self-fulfilling currency crises. In that case, either the real exchange rate deteriorates, or, if stabilization of the exchange rate is attempted, output is reduced.

While in the Krugman-model the outcome of the crisis in the presence of foreign currency debt is either a deterioration of the exchange rate *or* a contraction in output, the model serves to underline the potential adverse effects from foreign debt. Furthermore, as pointed out by Jeanne (1999), the model would, in accordance with data from the Asian crisis, predict both a deterioration of the exchange rate *and* a contraction in output, if the financial disruption reduced not only the investment flow, but also the productivity of capital and labor.

The main aspect of Krugmans model in respect to this section's model with debt, the importance of firms' balance sheets for the real economy, has been examined by an extensive body of recent literature, such as Bernanke, Gertler, and Gilchrist (1996, 1998), Kiyotaki and Moore (1997), Céspedes, Chang, and Velasco (2000), and Caballero and Krishnamurthy (2000, 2001, 2002).[21]

Kiyotaki and Moore (1997), for example, develop a stylized model, in which land (as a proxy for a durable and productive asset) serves as both a factor of production and as a source of collateral for loans to producers. Some firms are credit constrained, and are highly levered in that they have borrowed heavily against the value of their landholdings. A (temporary) shock (for example a devaluation reducing the net value of firms with foreign debt) lowers the value of land and hence of producers' collateral. This, in turn, tightens borrowing constraints, forces credit constrained companies to reduce spending and production, which eventually reduces land value further. The process is summarized in figure 4.9. In equilibrium the marginal productivity of the constrained firms is higher than that of the unconstrained firms, as the constrained firms cannot borrow as much as they want, and aggregate output is reduced.

The works of Caballero and Krishnamurthy follow along the lines of Kiyotaki and Moore (1997). Instead of assuming financial constraints to be on the microeconomic individual firm level, Caballero and Krishnamurthy (2001) assume an aggregate borrowing constraint on the country level, reflecting conditions faced by emerging economies. While this does not change the basic results of the model, the authors show that if domestic financial markets are underdeveloped, firms will choose excessive foreign currency liabilities and will not adequately precaution against adverse shocks, increasing the economies vulnerability to adverse balance sheet effects.

Another recent paper by Choi and Cook (2002) examines the impact external and internal shocks have on the economy under either a flexible

[21] For a more detailed survey of literature up to 1998 see Bernanke, Gertler, and Gilchrist (1998, pp. 40–45).

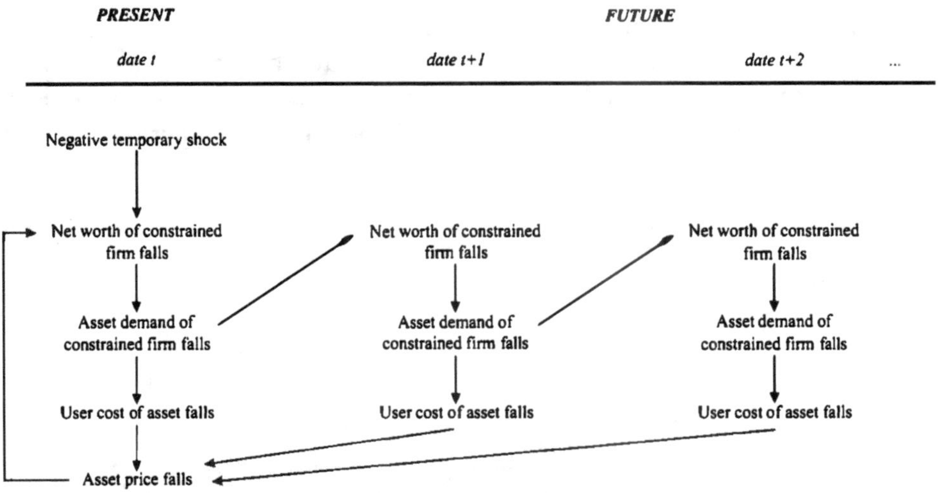

Kiyotaki and Moore (1997, p. 213).

Figure 4.9: Amplification of shock through balance sheet effects.

exchange rate with inflation targeting or a fixed exchange rate. While the papers presented above concerned themselves with the financial structure of non-financial firms, Choi and Cook examine the bank balance sheet channel instead. They conclude that, with banks facing a mismatch in the currency denomination of their assets and liabilities, a fixed exchange rate offers more stability compared to a flexible exchange rate regime. Furthermore, their model shows that under a flexible exchange rate shocks tend to have a worse impact on GDP than under a fixed exchange rate.

Assuming, as seems reasonable from the body of literature reviewed here, that in the presence of foreign-currency denominated debt a devaluation may lead to a contraction of aggregate output through balance sheet effects, a devaluation also reduces labor demand. Depending on labor supply, this possibly leads to an increase in unemployment, to some extent offsetting the employment increasing effect from a devaluation as stated by unemployment equation (4.4). To demonstrate how this effect can possibly alter the currency board model and the behavior of the policymaker, the following sections will incorporate the balance sheets effect into the model and examine the resulting changes in model behavior.

4.3.2 Unemployment

If, in the presence of foreign-currency denominated debt, a devaluation leads to a contraction of aggregate output, as has been argued in the preceding section, the resulting reduction in labor demand will possibly also affect unemployment. In section 4.2.1 we have assumed that labor market equilibrium requires a constant expected real wage of 1, or, in log terms, $w_t - Ee_t = 0$. This condition is satisfied by the labor supply and demand functions LS and LD, respectively, displayed in figure 4.10.

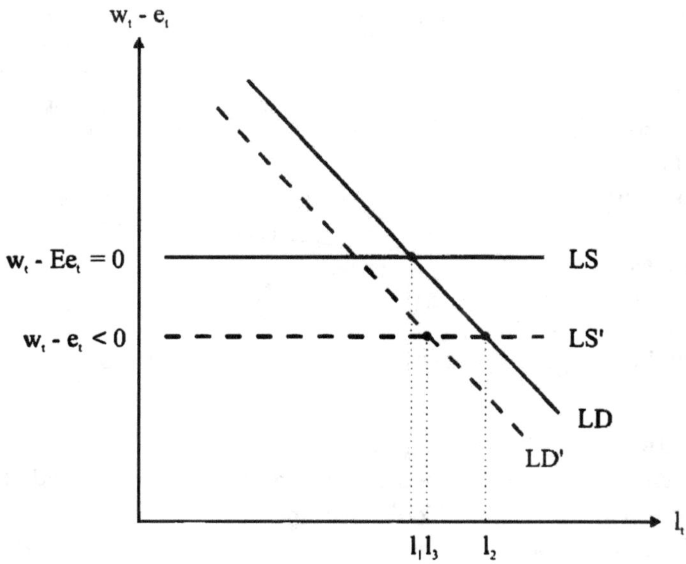

Figure 4.10: Increase in unemployment through reduction in labor demand caused by devaluation.

At the end of period $t-1$ workers and firms agree to a nominal wage w_t, at which workers will supply all labor demanded by firms in period t. Following from the horizontal labor supply curve, the agreed nominal wage will always equal the expected exchange rate in period t. The eventual amount of labor employed in period t then depends on the policymaker's decision of whether to devalue or not. We consider three different cases:

1. The exchange rate matches the expected exchange rate, i.e. $e_t = Ee_t$ or $\Delta e_t = E\Delta e_t$. This situation corresponds to the realization of either an FC or a ZC equilibrium. As the expected real wage corresponds to the realized real wage, employment will be at the level l_1, desired when negotiating w_t in period $t-1$.

2. The exchange rate exceeds the expected exchange rate, i.e. $e_t > Ee_t$ or $\Delta e_t = E\Delta e_t$. By devaluing in excess of the publics expectations the policymaker drives down the real wage and thereby increases em-

ployment. In figure 4.10 this corresponds to a shift of the labor supply function from LS to LS', which leads to employment of $l_2 > l_1$.

3. The exchange rate exceeds the expected exchange rate *and* in the presence of foreign-currency denominated debt the devaluation leads to a reduction in labor demand. Here, the increase in employment through a reduction of the real wage is partly offset by the reduction in labor demand: The labor supply function shifts down from LS to LS' and the labor demand function shifts to the left from LD to LD'. As a consequence, employment is l_3 with $l_2 > l_3 \geq l_1$.[22]

Cases 1 and 2 are captured by the initial unemployment equation (4.4). The effect we are interested in in this section is described by case 3. To account for the effects of foreign-currency denominated debt, the unemployment equation is modified as follows:

$$ur_t = \sqrt{\alpha}\left[(E\Delta e_t - (1-\beta)\Delta e_t) + k + \delta ur_{t-1}\right], \quad 0 < \beta < 1 \quad (4.48)$$

with the coefficient β expressing to what extend the reduction in labor demand from devaluation offsets the employment-increasing effect from lowering the real wage through devaluation. The higher the debt burden of the economy, the higher β.

The loss function remains unchanged as the preferences of the policymaker are unchanged by the presence of debt. Yet, with the modified unemployment equation we need to specify clearer bounds for the model parameters to avoid mathematical exceptions. Therefore:

$$L_t = (ur_t)^2 + \theta(\Delta e_t)^2, \qquad \theta > \alpha\beta(1-\beta) \quad (4.49)$$

4.3.3 Discretionary and Fixed Exchange Rate Policy

If the policymaker pursues a discretionary exchange rate policy, he will set Δe_t as to minimize his loss function (4.5), subject to the modified unemployment function (4.48). The optimal change in the exchange rate is:

$$\Delta e_t = \frac{\alpha(1-\beta)}{\alpha(1-\beta)^2 + \theta}(E\Delta e_t + k + \delta ur_{t-1}) \quad (4.50)$$

[22]We only consider cases in which the reduction in labor demand partly or at most completely offsets the increase in employment through the reduction of the real wage. While there is no reason to believe that a devaluation in combination with balance sheet effects may not in practice lead to an overall reduction in employment, allowing for this effect would unnecessarily complicate the model. The inclusion of such an effect into the present model introduces an implausible incentive for revaluation of the currency that would have to be accounted for.

The resulting loss then is:

$$L_t^D = \frac{\alpha\theta}{\alpha(1-\beta)+\theta}(E\Delta e_t + k + \delta ur_{t-1})^2 \tag{4.51}$$

Assuming rational expectations, i.e. $E\Delta e_t = \Delta e_t$, equations (4.50) and (4.51) become:

$$\Delta E e_t = \Delta e_t = \frac{\alpha(1-\beta)}{\theta - \alpha\beta(1-\beta)}(k + \delta ur_{t-1}) \tag{4.52}$$

$$L_t^D = \frac{\alpha\theta\left(\alpha(1-\beta)^2+\theta\right)}{\left(\theta-\alpha\beta(1-\beta)\right)^2}(k+\delta ur_{t-1})^2 \tag{4.53}$$

Alternatively, if the policymaker pursues a fixed exchange rate policy, i.e. $\Delta e_t = 0$, the loss of the policymaker, given devaluation expectations is:

$$L_t^F = \alpha(E\Delta e_t + k + \delta ur_{t-1})^2 \tag{4.54}$$

and, assuming the commitment to fix the exchange rate is credible, i.e. $E\Delta e_t = 0$:

$$L_t^F = \alpha(k+\delta ur_{t-1})^2 \tag{4.55}$$

Obviously, the loss from pursuing a fixed exchange rate policy is not affected by the presence of foreign currency debt, since, without devaluation, no recessionary effects from debt can arise. Equations (4.54) and (4.55) are the same as (4.10) and (4.11), respectively.

How does the presence of foreign currency debt affect exchange rate policy and the choice of an exchange rate regime? Under discretionary exchange rate policy we have to distinguish two cases when examining the loss-minimizing magnitude of devaluation, given by (4.50) and (4.52): In the case of $\alpha \leq \theta$ devaluation in the presence of debt will always be lower than without debt (i.e. $\beta = 0$). The presence of debt reduces the inflation-unemployment trade-off, thus reducing the marginal employment benefit from devaluation while the marginal cost from devaluation remain unchanged. As a consequence, the policymaker devalues less.

In the case of $\alpha > \theta$, devaluation in the presence of debt will be higher for low values of β and lower for high values of β, compared to the situation without debt. Here, the relative efficiency of the unemployment-inflation tradeoff is high and the policymaker compensates for the weakening of the tradeoff through the debt-effect by devaluing even more. Therefore, contrary to what might have been expected, the presence of foreign currency debt may in certain situations increase the devaluation desired by the policymaker, and, given rational expectations, also lead to higher devaluation expectations.

Obviously, in both cases optimal devaluation will converge towards zero as β approaches unity since the increasing debt-effect will eventually wipe out any unemployment benefits from devaluation.

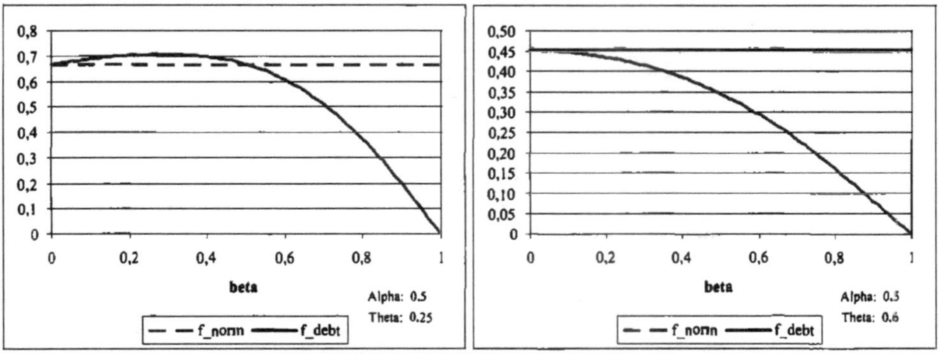

$$f\_debt : \frac{\alpha(1-\beta)}{\alpha(1-\beta)^2+\theta} \qquad f\_norm : \frac{\alpha}{\alpha+\theta}$$

Figure 4.11: Magnitude of devaluation (equation (4.50)) with and without debt.

These results are confirmed by figure 4.11, which displays the devaluation factors[23] with debt, *f_debt*, and without debt, *f_norm*, of devaluation equation (4.50) for the cases $\alpha > \theta$ (left-hand graph) and $\alpha \leq \theta$ (right-hand graph).[24]

Under discretionary exchange rate policy the loss of the policymaker given devaluation expectations, (4.51), is higher than the loss without debt. This can be seen by comparing the factors before of the bracket terms: $\frac{\alpha\theta}{\alpha+\theta} < \frac{\alpha\theta}{\alpha(1-\beta)^2+\theta}$ holds true for all possible values of β. This result is intuitive,

[23]Please not that for all following figures aiming to assess the impact of the presence of foreign-currency denominated debt on model behavior by numerical evaluation, only *factors* are compared. Otherwise, numerical values for expected devaluation, unemployment, and so on would have to be specified as well. In this case, equation (4.6) (optimal devaluation without debt) and (4.50) (optimal devaluation with debt) differ only by the first factor term on the right hand side. They share the second term on the right hand side, $(E\Delta e_t + k + \delta ur_{t-1})$. Since this also holds true for all following comparisons in this section, differences between equations without and with debt can be determined by just evaluating the factor terms. The values of these factors, usually labelled *f_norm* for the factor without debt, and *f_debt* for the factor with debt, are indicated on the ordinate of the figures.

[24]As we attempt to compare equations, values of α and θ are indicated in the figure. Plots for equation (4.52) lead to the same qualitative results, therefore no extra figure is given.

considering that the policymaker's scope for policy action is diminished by the debt-effect, and reducing unemployment by a certain amount becomes more costly.

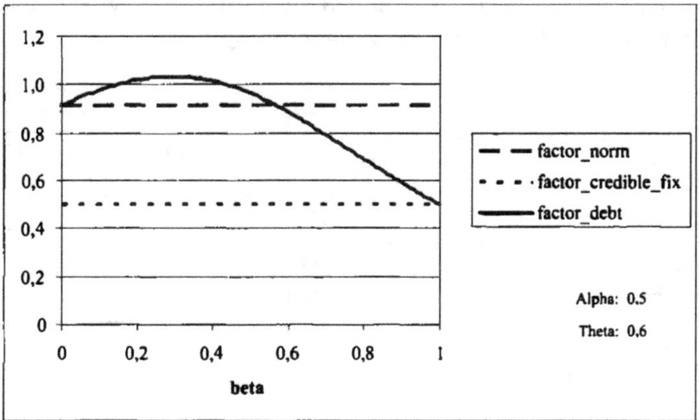

$$factor\_norm : \frac{\alpha(\alpha+\theta)}{\theta} \qquad factor\_debt : \frac{\alpha\theta\left(\alpha(1-\beta)^2+\theta\right)}{(\theta-\alpha\beta(1-\beta))^2}$$

$$factor\_credible\_fix : \alpha$$

Figure 4.12: Loss comparison for flexible and fixed exchange rate.

Interestingly, though, this result does not apply when assuming rational expectations, (4.52), as shown by figure 4.12. The figure displays the loss from discretionary exchange rate policy with rational expectations without debt ($factor\_norm$), the loss from discretionary exchange rate policy with rational expectations with debt ($factor\_debt$), and the loss from fixed exchange rate policy with credible commitment, which is obviously not affected by the presence of foreign currency debt ($factor\_credible\_fix$). For relatively low levels of foreign currency indebtedness the loss from pursuing a discretionary exchange rate policy exceeds the loss in a situation without debt. This is again due to the increased cost of reducing unemployment in the presence of debt. But for higher levels of indebtedness the loss is actually lower than in a situation without debt, converging towards the loss level of a credible fixed exchange rate as β increases. While this result might be perplexing at first sight, it can be easily explained: At high levels of foreign currency indebtedness the policymaker's ability to resort to devaluation for employment stimulation is severely limited. A high level of debt imposes a quasi-rule on exchange rate policy. With rational expectations the public knows that the policymaker is left with little scope for devaluation, which leads to lower devaluation expectations and consequently a lower loss to the policymaker.

Ultimately, as β approaches unity, expected and actual devaluation approach zero and the exchange rate regime becomes a de-facto fixed exchange rate system, resulting in the same loss for the policymaker as a credible fixed exchange rate system.

Yet, these results might have to be put into perspective. Unlike in the model without debt, long-run unemployment with debt is not independent of the exchange rate system. Without debt, steady-state unemployment is given by (4.23), regardless of whether a credible fixed exchange rate or a discretionary exchange rate with rational expectations is in place.[25] But with debt, discretionary exchange rate policy will lead to higher long-run unemployment than a credible fixed exchange rate.

Suppose a credible fixed exchange rate regime is in place. In steady-state, $E\Delta e_t = \Delta e_t$ has to hold. Additionally, $\Delta e_t = 0$. Substituting into the modified unemployment equation, (4.48), yields:

$$ur_t = \sqrt{\alpha}\,[k + \delta ur_{t-1}]$$

Substituting $\overline{ur} = ur_t = ur_{t-1}$ and solving for $\overline{ur}$ yields steady-state unemployment under a fixed exchange rate:

$$\overline{ur}^F = \frac{\sqrt{\alpha}k}{1 - \sqrt{\alpha}\delta} \tag{4.56}$$

Obviously, steady-state unemployment is the same as without debt, which is due to the fact that without devaluation there can be no unemployment-increasing debt-effect. Substituting (4.56) into loss function (4.55) yields the steady-state loss from a fixed exchange rate:

$$\overline{L}^F = \frac{\alpha k^2}{(1 - \sqrt{\alpha}\delta)^2} \tag{4.57}$$

Now, suppose a discretionary exchange rate regime with rational expectations is in place. Once again, in steady-state equilibrium $E\Delta e_t = \Delta e_t$ has to hold. Substituting this into the unemployment function yields:

$$ur_t = \sqrt{\alpha}\,[\beta\Delta e_t + k + \delta ur_{t-1}]$$

Clearly, unemployment under a discretionary exchange rate regime has to be higher, since, even though expected devaluation matches actual devaluation,

[25] This is due to the fact that in steady-state equilibrium $E\Delta e_t = \Delta e_t$. When substituting into the unemployment equation without debt, (4.4), both terms are eliminated from the equation, always yielding the same steady-state unemployment, regardless of the exchange rate regime.

unemployment is increased by the debt-effect, $\beta\Delta e_t$. Setting $\overline{ur} = ur_t = ur_{t-1}$ and substituting Δe_t by (4.52) yields steady-state unemployment under a flexible exchange rate:

$$\overline{ur}^D = \frac{\left(\frac{\alpha^{\frac{3}{2}}\beta(1-\beta)}{\theta-\alpha\beta(1-\beta)} + \sqrt{\alpha}\right)k}{1-\delta\left(\frac{\alpha^{\frac{3}{2}}\beta(1-\beta)}{\theta-\alpha\beta(1-\beta)} + \sqrt{\alpha}\right)} \tag{4.58}$$

Equation (4.58) confirms the notion that steady-state unemployment under a discretionary exchange rate regime is higher than both in the case without debt, (4.23), and in the case of a fixed exchange rate (4.56): For all $\beta > 0$, the fraction term in the brackets is greater than zero and consequently steady state unemployment is always greater than in the case of $\beta = 0$.[26] Substituting steady state unemployment into the discretionary exchange rate policy loss function, (4.53), yields the steady state loss:

$$\overline{L}^D = \frac{\alpha\theta(\alpha(1-\beta)^2+\theta)k^2}{\theta^2(1-\sqrt{\alpha}\delta)^2 - \beta(1-\beta)(2\theta(\alpha-\alpha^{\frac{3}{2}}\delta) - \alpha^2\beta(1-\beta))} \tag{4.59}$$

Numeric evaluation, shown in figure 4.13, reveals that, despite higher unemployment in steady state, the basic properties of (4.59) are the same as those of (4.53), discussed above. The loss from a discretionary exchange rate policy with debt is higher for relatively low values of β and lower for relatively high values of β, compared to the situation without debt, eventually approaching the level of loss from a fixed exchange rate. At a certain level of indebtedness the disciplining effect from debt, which lowers devaluation expectations, overcompensates for the restrained ability to reduce unemployment, leading to a lower loss than in a situation without debt.

If we consider the case of $\delta = 0$ (left-hand graph in figure 4.13) the levels of the loss factors are identical whether in steady state or not (compare with figure 4.12). An obvious result, since without unemployment persistence the level of unemployment, and, therefore, also the policymaker's loss, depend only on the current period policy actions and not on past economic outcomes. For increasing values of δ the loss levels increase. This is obviously due to positive unemployment persistence, which increases unemployment and therefore loss levels. Additionally, the maximum of the *factor_debt*-curve increases, and the range of values of β leading to a lower loss with discretionary exchange rate policy with debt, compared to the situation without debt, narrows. These effects stem from the combined effect of both a higher δ *and* higher steady state unemployment, as their product enters the loss function

[26] Remember that we have specified $\theta > \alpha\beta(1-\beta)$ in (4.49).

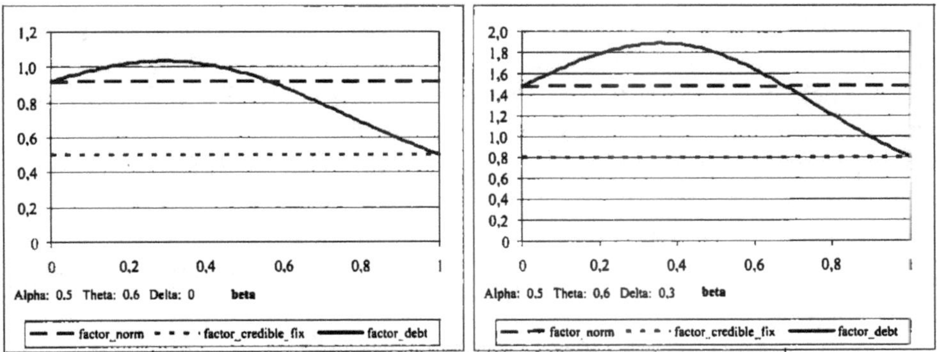

$$factor\_norm : \frac{\alpha(\alpha+\theta)}{\theta(1-\sqrt{\alpha}\delta)^2} \qquad factor\_credible\_fix : \frac{\alpha}{(1-\sqrt{\alpha}\delta)^2}$$

$$factor\_debt : \frac{\alpha\theta(\alpha(1-\beta)^2+\theta)}{\theta^2(1-\sqrt{\alpha}\delta)^2-\beta(1-\beta)(2\theta(\alpha-\alpha^{\frac{3}{2}}\delta)-\alpha^2\beta(1-\beta))}$$

Figure 4.13: Steady state loss comparison for flexible and fixed exchange rate.

(see (4.53)). The higher δ, the more pronounced the impact of steady state unemployment on the loss. Additionally, the higher δ, the higher $\overline{ur}^D$ itself. A higher δ therefore expands the range of values of β in which the presence of debt leads to a higher policy loss, and narrows the range of values that lead to a lower loss.

We conclude that in the long run the relative benefits or detriments of introducing foreign currency debt into an economy with a flexible exchange rate depend not only on the level of indebtedness, expressed by β, as concluded from the discussion of equations (4.50) to (4.55), but also on the level of unemployment persistence, δ. Since steady state unemployment in an economy with debt depends on the chosen exchange rate regime, and the gap between $\overline{ur}^F$ and $\overline{ur}^D$ is widened by increasing values of δ, the performance of a discretionary exchange rate regime, in terms of loss to the policymaker, relative to the performance of a fixed exchange rate system, is worsened by increasing values of δ. Therefore, the policy loss expressed by the period to period flexible exchange rate loss function, (4.53), understates the long-run loss from a flexible exchange rate, the more, the higher δ.

Yet, these results do not undermine the validity of the period to period loss function (4.53). In each period of the model the policymaker chooses an exchange rate regime, i.e. he either devalues or not. This decision is solely based on the current-period outcomes achievable, which in turn are limited by the model parameters *and* previous-period unemployment. Therefore, given previous-period unemployment, the loss of the policymaker is either (4.53) or (4.55), depending on whether he chooses a flexible or fixed exchange rate and assuming rational expectations or a credible fix, respectively.

The debt-modified period to period loss functions, (4.53) and (4.55), also affect the choice of an exchange rate regime, specifically the desirability of having a fixed exchange rate. The incentive to fix, i.e. the difference of (4.55) and (4.53), is now given by:

$$I_t = \frac{\alpha^2\left(\theta(1-\beta^2)+\alpha\beta^2(1-\beta)^2\right)}{(\theta-\alpha\beta(1-\beta))^2}(k+\delta ur_{t-1})^2 \tag{4.60}$$

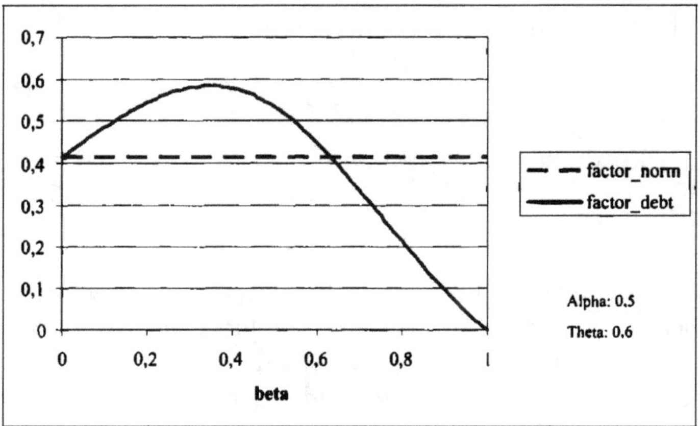

$factor\_norm : \frac{\alpha^2}{\theta}$

$factor\_debt : \frac{\alpha^2\left(\theta(1-\beta^2)+\alpha\beta^2(1-\beta)^2\right)}{(\theta-\alpha\beta(1-\beta))^2}$

Figure 4.14: Incentive to fix with and without debt.

As figure 4.14 shows, low levels of indebtedness increase the desirability of having a fixed exchange rate, while for higher levels of β the incentive to fix approaches zero. With high indebtedness, the debt acts as a disciplining device for exchange rate policy and the gains from instituting an exchange rate commitment as an additional disciplining device decrease.

The problem of time-inconsistency is still existent in the presence of foreign currency debt, yet to a lesser extent. Once devaluation expectations have been formed, the loss from devaluation, (4.51), is smaller than the loss from maintaining the exchange rate fixed, (4.54). The policymaker has an incentive to renege on a given exchange rate commitment. The incentive can be calculated by subtracting (4.54) from (4.51):

$$L_t^F - L_t^D = \frac{\alpha^2(1-\beta)^2}{\alpha(1-\beta)^2+\theta}(E\Delta e_t + k + \delta ur_{t-1})^2 \tag{4.61}$$

Alternatively, taking the square root of (4.61), we get the temptation to devalue:

$$T_t = \frac{\alpha(1-\beta)}{\sqrt{\alpha(1-\beta)^2+\theta}}(E\Delta e_t + k + \delta ur_{t-1}) \tag{4.62}$$

For all values $\beta > 0$ the incentive to cheat on the exchange rate commitment is reduced, compared to the situation without debt. This will c.p. lead to reduced devaluation expectations and increased stability of the subsequently discussed currency board model as the policymaker has less to gain from devaluation.

We may, therefore, conclude from this subsection that, assuming the presence of foreign-currency denominated debt has indeed the presumed effect on unemployment in case of a devaluation, allowing or even encouraging economic agents to use the anchor currency as parallel money for transactions, contracts, and as store of value, as has been the case in Argentina, where the US dollar was made parallel legal tender upon currency board introduction, may be beneficial for the stability of a currency board. The presence of any level of foreign currency debt reduces the temptation to devalue, so the policymaker has less incentive to resort to devaluation for employment stimulation. Furthermore, we have seen that especially relatively high levels of debt lead to increased monetary policy discipline, regardless of the exchange rate regime, as the tradeoff between unemployment and inflation diminishes. All these factors should lead to lower devaluation expectations and, therefore, higher currency board stability. Both will be examined throughout the following subsections.

4.3.4 Model Equilibria

The preceding subsection has shown the presence of foreign currency debt to reduce the policymaker's temptation to devalue. Since the existence of all three types of equilibria, full credibility (FC) equilibrium, zero credibility (ZC) equilibrium, and partial credibility (PC) equilibrium depends on the temptation to devalue, the conditions for existence of these equilibria are affected by the presence of debt as well.

In 4.2.5.1 we have shown the condition for the existence of an FC equilibrium to be $\underline{c_t} > T_t$ with $E\Delta e_t = 0$. The temptation to devalue T_t is reduced by the presence of foreign currency debt. But there is no reason to assume that the publics beliefs about the true value of c, $c \sim [\underline{c_t}, \overline{c}]$, are affected by indebtedness. Consequently, the presence of debt should strengthen the condition for existence of an FC equilibrium. Using (4.62) and rearranging terms we get:

$$k + \delta ur_{t-1} \quad < \quad \frac{\underline{c_t}\sqrt{(\alpha(1+\beta)^2+\theta)}}{\alpha(1-\beta)} \tag{4.63}$$

which confirms this notion. Note that an increasing β will strengthen the condition more than proportionally as the denominator on the right-hand side of (4.63) decreases.

The condition for an ZC equilibrium, as stated in 4.2.5.2, is $\bar{c} < T_t$, with devaluation expectations given by (4.52), i.e. the public expects a full devaluation. Again, indebtedness does not affect the upper bound of the publics beliefs about the true value of c, $\bar{c}$, but reduces the temptation to devalue T_t. Therefore, we might expect the condition for the existence of an ZC equilibrium to be weakened. Yet, while devaluation expectations for the FC equilibrium are the same with or without debt, $E\Delta e_t = 0$, devaluation expectations for the ZC equilibrium are given by (4.52), which is affected by debt. In subsection 4.3.3 we have shown that for $\alpha > \theta$ and low values of β the presence of foreign currency debt can lead to higher devaluation expectations. Higher devaluation expectations will c.p. increase the temptation to devalue, thus strengthening the condition for an ZC equilibrium. Therefore, the overall effect depends on the model parameters and the relative strength of the opposite effects.

Substituting (4.62) and (4.52) into the ZC equilibrium condition, we get:

$$\frac{\bar{c}(\theta - \alpha\beta(1-\beta))}{\alpha(1-\beta)\sqrt{(\alpha(1-\beta)^2+\theta)}} \quad < \quad k + \delta ur_{t-1} \tag{4.64}$$

Numerical evaluation shows that for values of α sufficiently higher than θ, the resulting increase in devaluation expectations for lower values of β overcompensates for the otherwise reduction in the temptation to devalue, so that the net effect is a strengthening of the condition for the existence of a ZC equilibrium for low values of β. This case is illustrated by the J-curve in figure 4.15. In all other cases the condition for a ZC equilibrium to exist is weakened in the presence of debt, i.e. a ZC equilibrium is less likely to exist.

The existence of PC equilibria again depends on the pair of functions $c_t^*(E\Delta e_t)$ and $E\Delta e_t(c_t^*)$. $c_t^*(\cdot)$ is determined by the temptation to devalue, (4.62):

$$c_t^* \quad = \quad \frac{\alpha(1-\beta)}{\sqrt{\alpha(1-\beta)^2+\theta}}(E\Delta e_t + k + \delta ur_{t-1}) \tag{4.65}$$

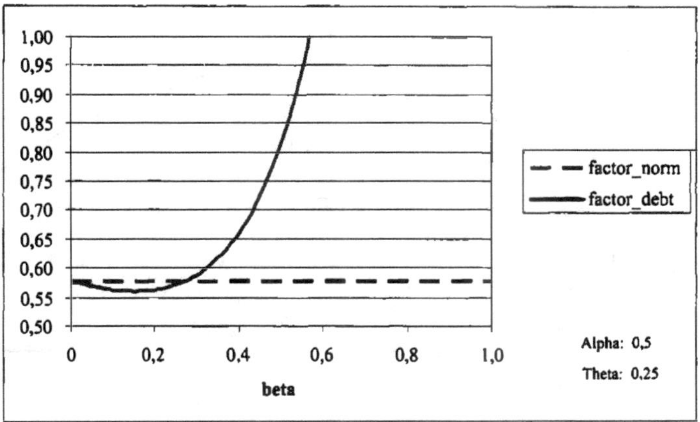

$$factor\_norm : \frac{\theta}{\alpha\sqrt{\alpha+\theta}}$$

$$factor\_debt : \frac{\theta-\alpha\beta(1-\beta)}{\alpha(1-\beta)\sqrt{\alpha(1-\beta)^2+\theta}}$$

Figure 4.15: Condition for ZC equilibrium with and without debt.

and, as has been discussed previously, is lower than in the case without debt, given devaluation expectations. Since the policymaker will devalue if $c_t^* > \hat{c}$, devaluation is less likely to occur.

As described in 4.2.5.3, the function for devaluation expectations given c_t^* can be obtained by rewriting expected devaluation as the product of expected devaluation under discretionary exchange rate policy and the probability of devaluation: $E\Delta e_t = E(\Delta e_t|\text{Devalue}) \cdot \text{prob}(\text{Devalue})$. Substituting $F_t(c_t^*)$ for the probability of devaluation and (4.52) for the magnitude of devaluation yields:

$$E\Delta e_t = \frac{\alpha(1-\beta)F_t(c_t^*)}{\alpha(1-\beta)(1-\beta-F)+\theta}(k+\delta ur_{t-1}) \qquad (4.66)$$

The probability of devaluation, i.e. the probability of $c_t^* > \hat{c}$ given c_t^*, is independent of the presence of debt. The magnitude of devaluation, (4.52), on the other hand, is generally reduced by $\beta > 0$, except for the case of $\alpha > \theta$ combined with a relatively low β, where it may exceed devaluation without debt. With (4.66) the product of the probability and the magnitude of devaluation, it follows that expected devaluation under the currency board will also be generally lower with foreign currency debt—stabilizing the currency board—except for the case of $\alpha > \theta$ and a low β. This result is confirmed by numerical evaluation as shown in figure 4.16.

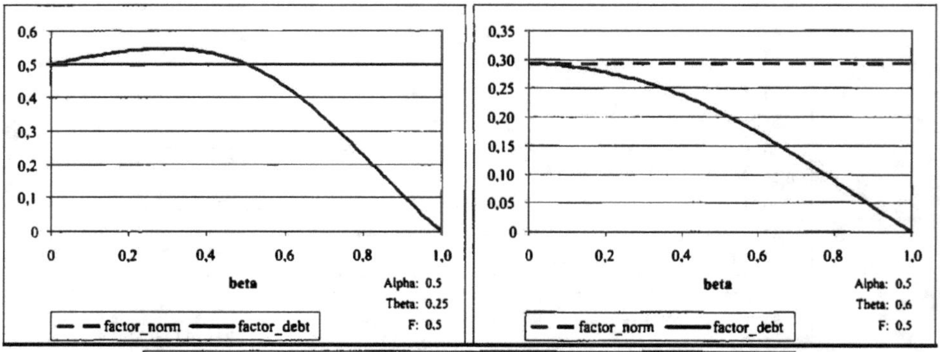

$factor\_norm: \frac{\alpha F_t(c_t^*)}{\alpha+\theta-\alpha F_t(c_t^*)}$ $\quad factor\_debt: \frac{\alpha(1-\beta)F_t(c_t^*)}{\alpha(1-\beta)(1-\beta-F)+\theta}$

Figure 4.16: Devaluation expectations in PC equilibrium with and without debt.

4.3.5 Graphical Representation and Interpretation of the Modified Model

The previous subsection has demonstrated that all types of equilibria, the FC equilibrium, the ZC equilibrium, and PC equilibria are affected by the presence of foreign-currency denominated debt. To allow for a better understanding of these changes, this subsection inspects changes in the graphical representation of the model with debt vis a vis the model without debt, as displayed in figure 4.17. We start by examining the intersecting points A, B, $\underline{c}_t$, and D:

A: The intersecting point of the $c_t^*(\cdot)$-function with the abscissa is:

$$A: \; c_t^*(E\Delta e_t = 0) = \frac{\alpha(1-\beta)}{\sqrt{\alpha(1-\beta)^2+\theta}}(k+\delta ur_{t-1}) \tag{4.67}$$

Due to the properties of $c_t^*(\cdot)$-function discussed previously, A shifts to the left with increasing values of β. Consequently, in the model with debt A is located further to the left compared to the model without debt.

B: The end point of the $c_t^*(\cdot)$-function. Solving $c_t^*(E\Delta e_t) = \bar{c}$ for $E\Delta e_t$, we get from (4.65):

$$B: \; E\Delta e_t = \frac{\sqrt{\alpha(1-\beta)^{2}}}{\alpha(1-\beta)}c - (k+\delta ur_{t-1}) \tag{4.68}$$

Increasing values of β lead to higher values of $E\Delta e_t$, resulting in an upward-shift of point B, which is consequently located above B in the model without debt.

$\underline{c}_t$: The lower bound of the publics expectation about the true value of c. Since the beliefs of the public about the political cost of devaluation remain untouched by the presence of debt, point $\underline{c}_t$ is unchanged.

D: The end point of the $E\Delta e_t(\cdot)$-function. Here, the probability of devaluation is unity and, therefore, $E\Delta e_t$ in point D equals expected devaluation under discretionary exchange rate policy, (4.52).

$$D: \ E\Delta e_t(c_t^* = \bar{c}) = \frac{\alpha(1-\beta)}{\theta - \alpha\beta(1-\beta)}(k + \delta ur_{t-1}) \tag{4.69}$$

Therefore, as has become clear from the discussion of (4.52), two cases have to be distinguished: If $\alpha \leq \theta$, point D shifts down in the presence of debt. If $\alpha > \theta$, point D shifts up for low values of β, and down otherwise. It follows that the location of point D in the model with debt compared to the model without debt depends on the other model parameters.

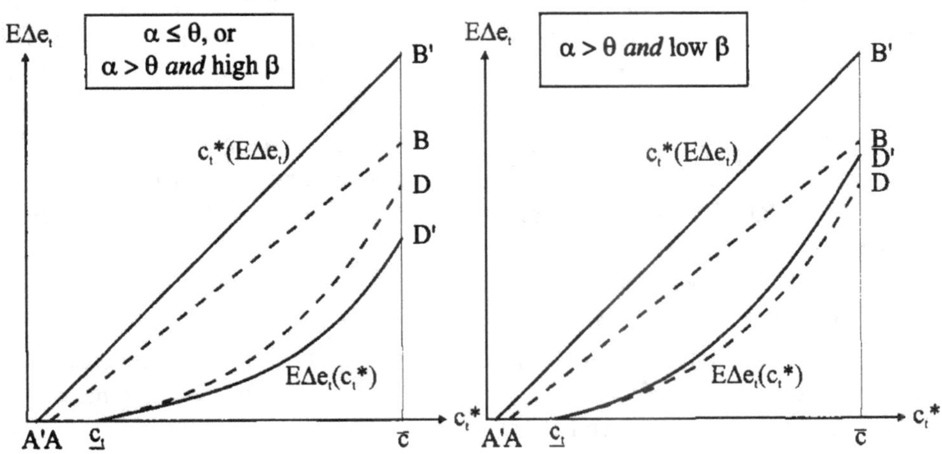

Figure 4.17: Graphical representation of the model with debt (solid curves) compared to model without debt (dashed curves).

In addition to the shift of the points, the $c_t^*(\cdot)$-function, whose slope is now $\frac{\sqrt{\alpha(1-\beta)^2+\theta}}{\alpha(1-\beta)}$, becomes steeper with increasing values of β, while the change in the slope of the $E\Delta e_t(\cdot)$-function is ambiguous. For $\alpha > \theta$ and low values of β the slope increases while it decreases otherwise.

These effects are summarized in figure (4.17) where points A, B, and D and dashed curves represent the model without debt, while points A', B', and D' and solid curves represent the model with debt. Obviously, in the case of $\alpha \leq \theta$ or $\alpha > \theta$ in combination with relatively high values of β, (left-hand side graph), the stability of the currency board is actually increased by the presence of foreign-currency denominated debt. The likeliness of an FC equilibrium increases, while the likeliness of an ZC equilibrium decreases. Additionally, PC equilibria tend to improve. This is shown in figure 4.18, where the economy without debt exhibits two stable (SPC_1 and SPC_2) and one unstable ($USPC_1$) PC equilibrium while in the presence of debt only one stable (SPC_1') and one unstable ($USPC_1'$) equilibrium exist. In an economy with debt the first stable PC equilibrium is now to be found in SPC_1', to the lower left of its initial point SPC_1. The state of the economy associated with this stable PC equilibrium is more favorable in the presence of debt than without: The critical value c_t^* is lower, therefore the policymaker is less likely to abandon the currency board if this equilibrium is realized, and devaluation expectations are reduced, lowering the unemployment cost if the currency board is maintained. In general, all stable equilibria exhibit a tendency to improve if we introduce debt into the model. This is due to the shifts of points A, B, and D *and* the changes in slope of the functions $c_t^*(\cdot)$ (steeper) and $E\Delta e_t(\cdot)$ (flatter): A stable PC equilibrium may lead to the existence of a previously not-existing FC equilibrium (as is the case with SPC_2); a stable PC equilibria may improve in terms of lower values of c_t^* and $E\Delta e_t$ (SPC_1 to SPC_1'); a ZC equilibrium may disappear and be replaced by a stable PC equilibrium (not shown in figure 4.18). Additionally, unstable PC equilibria tend to shift to the upper right, as shown by the shift from $USPC_1$ to $USPC_1'$. This is an improvement, considering the instantaneous adjustment process leading to the realization of a particular equilibrium. An unstable PC equilibrium at a higher level allows for relatively high devaluation expectations at the beginning of the adjustment process to lead to the realization of an equilibrium with relatively low devaluation expectations, whereas the previously lower level unstable PC equilibrium would have led the adjustment process to end up in an equilibrium with relatively high devaluation expectations.[27]

In the case of $\alpha > \theta$ and a relatively low value of β, shown by the right-hand graph in figure 4.17, the overall effects are not as clear-cut as in the previous case. While the changes in $c_t^*(\cdot)$ stabilize the model economy, the changes in $E\Delta e_t(\cdot)$ destabilize it. As $\underline{c_t}$ is not affected by the debt-effect,

[27] This effect has already been discussed in 4.2.7.4. See also 4.2.5.4 and discussion of figure 4.3.

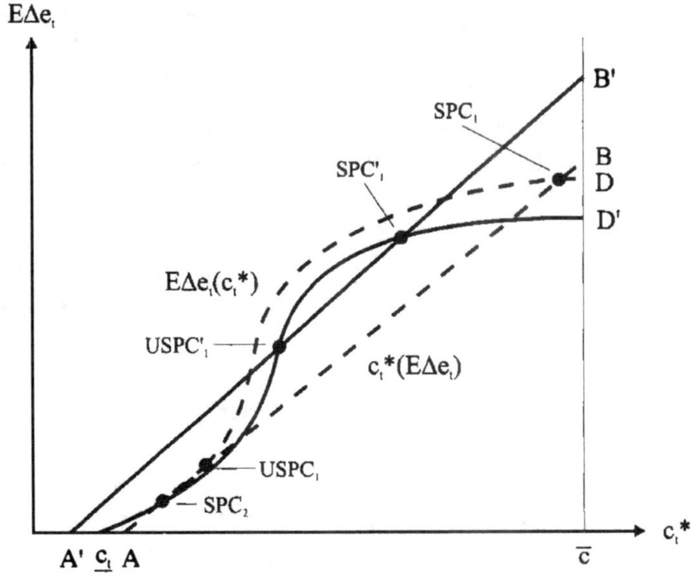

Figure 4.18: Effect of debt on the presence of PC equilibria.

the likeliness of an FC equilibrium existing still increases. On the other hand, the simultaneous upward-shifts of B and D preclude a general assertion on whether the likeliness of the existence of a ZC equilibrium increases or decreases. This depends on the relative strength of the shifts, which, in turn, depends on the specific values of the model parameters, as summarized in the condition for a ZC equilibrium, (4.64). Also, the increasing slopes of *both* $c_t^*(\cdot)$ and $E\Delta e_t(\cdot)$ rule out any non-ambiguous conclusions about the impact on PC equilibria. The steeper $c_t^*(\cdot)$-function tends to shift them to the lower left while the steeper $E\Delta e_t(\cdot)$-function shifts them to the upper right.

Overall, we may nevertheless conclude that under most parametrical combinations the introduction of foreign currency debt into the economy will stabilize the model, making it more likely that an FC equilibrium exists and is realized while at the same time reducing the likeliness of existence and realization of a ZC equilibrium. The only exception to this conclusion is the case of $\alpha \gg \theta$, combined with low values of β. In this case the likeliness of both, an FC, and a ZC equilibrium existing is increased.

4.3.6 Model Dynamics and Resilience to Shocks

The basic dynamics of the model do not change through the presence of debt. The credibility effect, as discussed in 4.2.7.1, still strengthens the currency board, and the unemployment effect, as discussed in 4.2.7.2, weakens the currency board. Furthermore, as this brief section will show, the resilience of the model economy to shocks is altered in the same fashion, as the presence of debt has affected the general stability of the currency board: The likeliness of a shock leading to the disappearance of an FC equilibrium is lowered and the likeliness of a shock creating an ZC equilibrium is either increased or lowered, depending on the model parameters.

Assume again an economy where only an FC equilibrium exists. The unemployment equation including the unemployment-decreasing shock now is:

$$\begin{aligned} ur_t &= \sqrt{\alpha}\left[(E\Delta e_t - (1-\beta)\Delta e_t) + k + \delta ur_{t-1} + \eta_t\right], \qquad (4.70) \\ \eta_1 &> 0, \quad \eta_{t>1} = 0 \end{aligned}$$

From this unemployment equation the resulting location of points A, B, and D in the graphical representation (see figure 4.17) now is:

$A: \frac{\alpha(1-\beta)}{\sqrt{\alpha(1-\beta)^2+\theta}}(k + \delta ur_{t-1} + \eta_t)$

$B: \frac{\sqrt{\alpha(1-\beta)^2+\theta}}{\alpha(1-\beta)}\overline{c} - (k + \delta ur_{t-1} + \eta_t)$

$D: \frac{\alpha(1-\beta)}{\theta-\alpha\beta(1-\beta)}(k + \delta ur_{t-1} + \eta_t)$

With $\eta_t > 0$, point A shifts to the right, but by less than in the case of $\beta = 0$, point B shifts down by η_t, the same amount with or without debt, and point D shifts up by either more ($\alpha > \theta$ and low β) or less (otherwise) than without debt.

These results already indicate what will be proven below: With A shifting right by less than without debt, a shock is less likely to lead to the disappearance of the FC equilibrium. With B shifting down by the same amount, and D shifting up by either more or less than without debt, an increase or decrease of the likeliness of a ZC equilibrium appearing depends on the model parameters.

Let us first examine the magnitude of the shock leading to the disappearance of the FC equilibrium. For the FC equilibrium to disappear, the shift of point A resulting from the shock has to be greater than the initial distance between points A and $\underline{c}_t$, i.e. if:

$$\underline{c}_t - \frac{\alpha(1-\beta)}{\sqrt{\alpha(1-\beta)^2+\theta}}(k + \delta ur_{t-1}) < \frac{\alpha(1-\beta)}{\sqrt{\alpha(1-\beta)^2+\theta}}\eta_t$$

Rearranging terms gives the condition for the shock leading to the disappearance of the FC equilibrium:

$$\eta_t > \frac{\underline{c}_t\sqrt{\alpha(1-\beta)^2+\theta}}{\alpha(1-\beta)} - (k+\delta ur_{t-1}) \tag{4.71}$$

Since the right-hand side fraction is greater for $\beta > 0$ than for $\beta = 0$, the condition is weakened, and consequently the currency board with debt is strengthened in the sense that a shock is less likely to lead to the disappearance of the FC equilibrium. This is the same result we got when inspecting the condition for existence of an FC equilibrium, (4.63)—not surprisingly, as the FC equilibrium condition is part of (4.71).

Similarly, a shock will lead to the appearance of an ZC equilibrium if the combined shifts of points B and D through the shock are greater than the initial distance between both points, i.e. if:

$$\frac{\sqrt{\alpha(1-\beta)^2+\theta}}{\alpha(1-\beta)}\overline{c} - \frac{\alpha(1-\beta)}{\theta-\alpha\beta(1-\beta)}(k+\delta ur_{t-1}) < \eta_t + \frac{\alpha(1-\beta)}{\theta-\alpha\beta(1-\beta)}\eta_t$$

Rearranging terms yields the condition for a shock leading to the existence of a ZC equilibrium:

$$\eta_t > \frac{\overline{c}(\theta-\alpha\beta(1-\beta))}{\alpha(1-\beta)\sqrt{\alpha(1-\beta)^2+\theta}} - (k+\delta ur_{t-1}) \tag{4.72}$$

As with (4.71), equation (4.72) closely resembles the condition for existence of a ZC equilibrium with debt, (4.64). Therefore, the condition is strengthened in the case of $\alpha \gg \theta$ and low values of β, i.e. a shock is more likely to lead to the existence of a ZC equilibrium in the presence of debt, and weakened in all other cases.

It follows that the basic dynamic behavior of the model and resilience to shocks, as they have been explored in subsections 4.2.6 and 4.2.7 have not qualitatively changed through the presence of debt, and the results from subsections 4.3.4 and 4.3.5 can be applied: With debt the model becomes more robust with respect to FC equilibria while the robustness with respect to ZC equilibria depends on the model parameters.

4.3.7 Loss from Exit and Conclusion

How does the loss with debt compare to the loss without debt? To answer this question we cannot just examine the existing loss functions. The presence of debt reduces the effectiveness of the unemployment-devaluation tradeoff, increasing the stability of the currency board. The unemployment pressure that eventually forces the policymaker to abandon the currency board has to be higher with debt than without debt. Therefore, it does not suffice to just compare the factor terms of the loss functions with and without debt, but the unemployment pressure term $(k + \delta ur_{t-1})$ has to be considered as well.

We start by asking, at which value of $(k + \delta ur_{t-1})$ the policymaker is indifferent to devaluation or maintaining the exchange rate parity. This is the case if the political cost from devaluation, $\hat{c}$, match the temptation to devalue, (4.62), i.e. if:

$$\begin{aligned} c_t^* = \hat{c} &= T_t \\ \hat{c} &= \frac{\alpha(1-\beta)}{\sqrt{\alpha(1-\beta)^2+\theta}}(E\Delta e_t + k + \delta ur_{t-1}) \end{aligned}$$

Substituting (4.66) for expected devaluation, and rearranging terms yields:

$$(k + \delta ur_{t-1}) = \frac{\alpha(1-\beta)(1-\beta-F)+\theta}{\alpha(1-\beta)\sqrt{\alpha(1-\beta)^2+\theta}}\hat{c} \tag{4.73}$$

(4.73) is the level of unemployment pressure, at which the policymaker is just indifferent to devaluing or not. As figure 4.19 clearly shows, unemployment pressure $(k + \delta ur_{t-1})$ has to be higher for all $\beta > 0$ for the policymaker to be indifferent to devaluation. The presence of debt stabilizes the currency board and reduces the effectiveness of devaluation lowering unemployment. Consequently, the policymaker refrains from devaluation at levels of unemployment pressure that would have triggered devaluation in an economy without debt.

From (4.73) we proceed to determine expected devaluation. As expressed in (4.66), expected devaluation is:

$$E\Delta e_t = \frac{\alpha(1-\beta)F_t(\hat{c})}{\alpha(1-\beta)(1-\beta-F)+\theta}(k + \delta ur_{t-1})$$

Substituting (4.73) into this equation yields:

$$E\Delta e_t = \frac{F_t(\hat{c})}{\sqrt{\alpha(1-\beta)^2+\theta}}\hat{c} \tag{4.74}$$

Furthermore, devaluation can be determined from (4.50):

$$\Delta e_t = \frac{\alpha(1-\beta)}{\alpha(1-\beta)^2+\theta}(E\Delta e_t + k + \delta ur_{t-1})$$

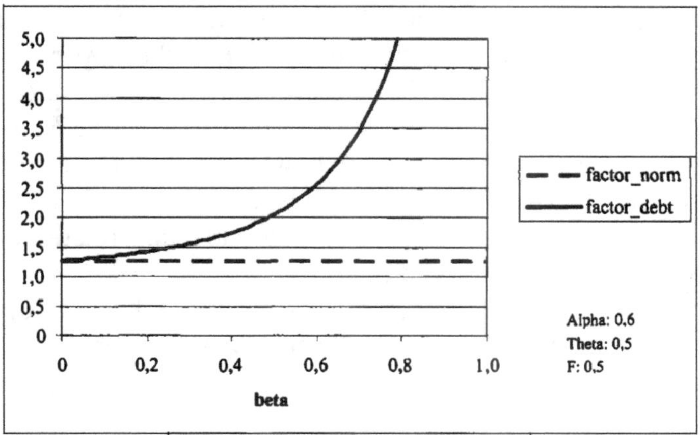

$$factor\_norm : \frac{\alpha(1-F)+\theta}{\alpha\sqrt{\alpha+\theta}}$$

$$factor\_debt : \frac{\alpha(1-\beta)(1-\beta-F)+\theta}{\alpha(1-\beta)\sqrt{\alpha(1-\beta)^2+\theta}}$$

Figure 4.19: Unemployment pressure, at which policymaker is indifferent to devaluation.

Substituting (4.73) and (4.74) into this equation yields:

$$\Delta e_t = \frac{1}{\sqrt{\alpha(1-\beta)^2+\theta}}\hat{c} \qquad (4.75)$$

We find that both expected devaluation, (4.74), and actual devaluation, (4.75), are higher with debt than without, i.e. with $\beta > 0$. While perhaps a surprising result—we have concluded debt to stabilize the currency board and therefore *lower* devaluation expectations might be expected—this result is due to our findings expressed in (4.73). The unemployment pressure under which the policymaker is eventually indifferent to devaluation is considerably higher in an economy with debt. Consequently, once the policymaker does devalue, the need for offsetting devaluation is higher than without debt and, despite the reduced effectiveness of the devaluation-unemployment tradeoff, even minor reductions of unemployment can lead to major reductions of the policymaker's loss. As a result, both expected devaluation and actual devaluation are higher.[28]

[28]This becomes even clearer when considering the basic loss function of the policymaker, (4.5). Both unemployment and devaluation are squared. When the policymaker devalues, unemployment is higher compared to an economy without debt, due to the higher unemployment pressure. Formal proof of this is given in equation (4.76). Higher unemployment leads to a more than proportional increase of the policymaker's loss, the more, the

Also, note that expected devaluation is less than actual devaluation, unless the true political cost from devaluation equal the upper bound of the publics beliefs about the true political cost, i.e. $\hat{c} = \overline{c}$, in which case devaluation can only occur by realization of a ZC equilibrium, where $F_t(\overline{c}) = F_t(\hat{c}) = 1$. This result is consistent with the basic functioning of the model, in which the public cannot be certain of devaluation unless a ZC equilibrium is realized. If devaluation follows from a PC equilibrium, expected devaluation will always be less than actual devaluation.

Given expected devaluation, actual devaluation, and unemployment pressure, we can now determine unemployment, which is given by (4.48):

$$ur_t = \sqrt{\alpha}\left[(E\Delta e_t - (1-\beta)\Delta e_t) + k + \delta ur_{t-1}\right]$$

Substituting (4.73), (4.74), and (4.75) into this equation, we get:

$$ur_t = \frac{\theta}{\sqrt{\alpha}(1-\beta)\sqrt{\alpha(1-\beta)^2+\theta}}\hat{c} \tag{4.76}$$

In the presence of debt the policymaker is willing to bear a higher unemployment burden before he eventually devalues, and even in the period of devaluation unemployment is still higher in an economy with debt, as shown by (4.76). As both unemployment and devaluation are higher than without debt, clearly, the policymaker's loss when exiting the currency board has to be higher as well. We can easily verify this by using the original loss function, (4.49):

$$L_t = (ur_t)^2 + \theta\,(\Delta e_t)^2$$

and substituting (4.75) and (4.76) for devaluation and unemployment, respectively, which yields:

$$L_t = \frac{\theta}{\alpha(1-\beta)^2}\hat{c} \tag{4.77}$$

This is the obvious downside of having an economy with foreign currency debt: The price of gained stability is reduced flexibility to exit the currency board and thereby ease the unemployment pressure on the economy. While foreign-currency denominated debt introduces higher stability to the currency board, and may therefore be beneficial in reaching the minimal-loss

higher indebtedness β. On the other hand, the reduction in the devaluation-unemployment tradeoff is only proportional to β. Consequently, the policymaker can reduce his loss from higher unemployment by devaluing more than he would without debt, regardless of how ineffective the devaluation-unemployment tradeoff has become.

FC equilibrium, the economic cost in the case of an exit from the currency board are unproportionally higher. In case of an economic crisis the policymaker is more reluctant to give up the currency board, and is willing to incur higher real cost, in this case unemployment, before eventually deciding to devalue. Yet, once the policymaker decides to devalue the disruption from devaluation or, synonymous, inflation is considerably higher than without debt.

These conclusions also apply to the level of the political cost of devaluation. Higher political cost, e.g. setting down the rules of the currency board in the constitution or tying the policymaker's political fate to the success of the currency board, can significantly increase the stability of the currency board, if these actions are reflected in the publics beliefs about the political cost, i.e. increased values of $\underline{c_t}$ and $\bar{c}$. But again, increasing the political cost implies raising the stakes: There is more to win but also more to lose. The more the policymaker has to lose from exiting the currency board, the more reluctant he is to do so. Therefore, once he is forced to exit, the higher are unemployment, devaluation, and, consequently, the loss, as equations (4.75) to (4.77) clearly show.

The results confirm, to some extent, the Argentinean experience. Under the Argentinean currency board both political cost as well as the presence of foreign-currency denominated debt have been high, as described throughout section 3.3. These two factors contributed to the rapid and successful stabilization of the Argentinean economy during the first years after currency board introduction. Later, though, the economy began to struggle, as it was hit by a series of adverse economic shocks, and unemployment started to rise to very high levels. The sustainability of the currency board became increasingly doubtful as unemployment pressure continued to rise, possibly reflecting the realization of subsequent PC equilibria. Under a more flexible arrangement with lower obstacles to currency board exit, the government might have opted for abandoning the currency board at a much earlier stage, avoiding increasing real costs of maintaining the currency board. Yet, the government, especially under president Menem, was highly committed to the currency board, and the design provided for high legal obstacles to abandoning it. Also, as the degree of de-facto dollarization was relatively high, the effectiveness of stimulating the economy through a devaluation of the peso was doubtful.

As economic conditions continued to deteriorate at increasing speed, the government still fought against exiting the currency board, mainly motivated by the fact that the largest share of government debt was denominated in dollars, and a devaluation would have increased the already unsustainable government debt service burden.[29] Only when Argentina was unable to service its debt anymore and entered into default, did the government eventually decide to scrap the currency board. Note that the following severe recession, partly caused by insolvencies of enterprises and an almost-breakdown of the banking sector due to the increased real value of dollar liabilities, may even hint to the possibility of β having been greater than one in Argentina, a case we have excluded in the model in order to allow for an analytical solution. If this had been the case, implying that devaluations actually have a negative impact on employment, it may have further explain the government's aversion to exit the currency board.

Note that the parameters α and θ have exactly the opposite effect on loss function (4.77) than usual, as for example on (4.51) or (4.54). A higher responsiveness parameter reduces the loss while higher inflation aversion increases it. Again, this can be explained by the tradeoff between stability and flexibility: A higher responsiveness parameter indicates a more effective devaluation-unemployment tradeoff. With devaluation more effective in reducing unemployment, the temptation to devalue is higher and the policymaker will already devalue under less unemployment pressure, also requiring a lesser devaluation. On the other hand, with higher inflation aversion the policymaker is more reluctant to devalue and will only devalue under higher unemployment pressure, implying high economic cost on currency board exit.

[29]The modelling of this behavior has been provided in subsection 4.3.1, where we have shown that the government's concern over the levels of foreign currency debt it owes leads to a de-facto increase of inflation aversion, reducing the government's disposition to resort to devaluation.

5

Concluding Remarks

5.1 Currency Board Selection

Choosing a currency board for monetary and exchange rate arrangement provides the greatest benefits in an economy with a very effective devaluation-unemployment tradeoff (i.e. a high value of α in the model), where the policymaker has low inflation aversion (a low value of θ). Devaluation expectations aside, an effective devaluation-unemployment tradeoff might be considered positive to have. It would enable the policymaker to keep unemployment close to the target level through surprise devaluation while avoiding high inflation. Yet, devaluation expectations matter. If the public is aware of the unemployment-reducing effectiveness of devaluations, which assuming rational expectations implies, it foresees that the policymaker has a lot to gain from creating surprise devaluation and is willing to accept relatively high levels of inflation. This willingness to accept high levels of inflation is even higher with low inflation aversion. Consequently, the public's devaluation expectations will be high. In equilibrium, where expected matches actual devaluation, the policymaker has to generate high inflation just to match devaluation expectations. As a result, unemployment is unaffected but inflation is high, and so is the loss to the policymaker. The higher the policymaker's potential to pursue an activist economic policy, i.e. the more effective surprise devaluations are and the lower the policymaker's inflation aversion, the higher the inflation bias of pursuing a discretionary exchange rate policy will be.

In such a situation, the policymaker has a lot to gain from tying his own hands. If he manages to establish a credible fixed exchange rate regime, thus giving up the flexibility of policy intervention, he will drive down his loss considerably. Assuming that the fixed exchange rate regime is fully credible, unemployment will be same as it would have been under a flexible exchange rate, since inflation expectations are reduced by the same degree as actual inflation. However, inflation is wiped out, and the economy is better off.

This incentive to fix increases even further in the presence of relatively low levels of foreign-currency denominated debt. With such debt, devaluations do not only have an unemployment reducing effect, but an additional recessionary component, brought about by the balance sheet channel of financial and non-financial firms. This reduces the policymaker's ability to at least match devaluation expectations under a flexible exchange rate regime, and, therefore, result in either higher unemployment or higher inflation, increasing the loss to the policymaker. Consequently, there is even more to gain from establishing a credible fixed exchange rate regime.

For relatively high levels of debt the picture is different. Here, the debt effect becomes more and more of a disciplining device. As the recessionary component of devaluations becomes more severe, the policymaker loses most of his ability to pursue an activist economic policy. This is reflected in lower devaluation expectations. From a certain level of indebtedness on this indirect gain from lowered devaluation expectations outweighs the direct cost from the diminished ability to reduce unemployment, leading to a lower loss to the policymaker. Eventually, as indebtedness approaches the level where it wipes out any potential unemployment reduction benefits, the policymaker has no other option than to pursue a de-facto fixed exchange rate policy. At this point, there is nothing to be gained from establishing a de-jure fixed exchange rate. The presence of debt suffices to effectively tie the hands of the policymaker and there is no additional gain to be had from also tying them voluntarily.

Four of the five present-day currency boards discussed in chapter 3 have introduced their currency boards in response to high levels of inflation. While it is difficult to asses the effectiveness of the inflation-unemployment tradeoff in each particular case, discretionary policies had failed to maintain price stability. Growing inflation expectations were offsetting any potentially beneficial effects inflation might have had, and a return to a low-inflation policy under the monetary regime in place would have entailed high real economic costs, particularly in unemployment, given the high levels of inflation expectations. This was particularly true in the case of Argentina, which had had a culture and long history of high inflation. Additionally, the country's inflation history had also led to currency substitution and informal dollarization, reducing the stimulating impact of increased inflation, or, requiring even higher increases in inflation to achieve the same stimulus on the real economy. In such an environment a return to low levels of inflation, given the government's long-standing and firm reputation for pursuing inflationary policies, requires a radical departure from present policies, such as the introduction of a currency board, to quickly and credibly bring down inflation expectations.

While such a radical departure from existing monetary institutions, combined with the adoption of a new arrangement that credibly ties the hands of policymakers, may serve to quickly bring down inflation, and thereby solve the most pressing problem of new currency board countries, the currency board will also have to be sustained over the medium term. To ensure the sustainability, a number of important preconditions have to be kept in mind at the time of currency board selection, or have to be implemented quickly after that, as has been stressed in subsection 2.2: A suitable anchor currency has to be chosen in order to prevent misalignment of business cycles in the currency board country and in the anchor country; factor and goods markets need to be flexible, so necessary adjustments can be made by changes in prices instead of adjustments of real aggregates, such as consumption and income; the financial sector has to be robust and prudently supervised so that banks can cope with periods of stress in the absence of a lender of last resort; austere fiscal policies have to keep budget deficits in check to ensure that government debt burdens remain relatively low.

The importance to consider these factors when introducing a currency board has recently been highlighted dramatically by the experience of Argentina. Argentina had a lot to gain from introducing a currency board, but it also had to erect high barriers to exit from the currency board, to break inflation expectations. However, inflexible markets, a series of external shocks, leading to increasing adjustment pressures, as well as rising government debt levels led to mounting pressure on the currency, and rising interest rates, which in turn further increased the adjustment pressure on the economy and government finances. The inability of markets and government finances to adjust to these pressures eventually led to the exit from the currency board. Yet, as the political cost from exit had been set very high, this only happened at a stage when government finances had collapsed and pulled the economy into a severe recession.

5.2 Currency Board Stability

Once a currency board has been established, the policymaker will only stick to it as long as it is his loss minimizing option. The circumstances where the policymaker has the most to gain from selecting a currency board are the same where the incentive to exit from the currency board is the highest: An effective devaluation-unemployment tradeoff may tempt the policymaker into cheating on the exchange rate commitment and to reduce unemployment at low inflation cost. The lower the policymaker's inflation aversion, the lower his self-discipline to refrain from devaluation.

The options to increase the stability of the currency board, i.e. reducing the likeliness of an exit, are twofold: Tying the hands of the policymaker more effectively and/or ameliorating the economic conditions under which the currency board operates.

The most obvious measure to increase the stability of the currency board by tying the hands of the policymaker is to set the political cost from exiting as high as possible.[1] One potential way to increase the political cost is to set high legal obstacles to currency board exit, by setting forth in law the rules of the currency board, specifically the anchor currency and exchange rate, the backing requirement, and the convertibility undertaking. Especially in the context of the model, it is important to make it difficult to change the level of the exchange rate, for example by requiring an act of parliament to do so, as currency board designs in Argentina, Bulgaria, and Estonia require.[2] Yet, not only are political cost determined by the legal commitment, but also by the policymaker's political commitment to the currency board. If the policymaker faces a loss of face when abandoning the currency board, he will be very reluctant to do so.

Besides raising the political cost of an exit from the currency board, it is also very important to make these cost as transparent as possible. The publics beliefs about the true political cost have an essential role in determining devaluation expectations, which in turn seriously affect the stability of the currency board. High transparency should therefore increase the publics beliefs about the true political cost and stabilize the currency board. As the model has shown, beliefs can be more important than the real cost. The level of the political cost will raise the threshold of pain up to which the policymaker will stick to the currency board. The public's beliefs, however, determine the existence of equilibria, specifically multiple equilibria, under which the breakdown of the currency board can be enforced by a self-fulfilling speculative attack.

Consequently, stabilization may even result from cheating the public into having high expectations about the political cost. The policymaker could try to systematically deceive the public about the level of political cost from devaluation and thus reap stabilization gains without tying his hands too

[1]See also Flood and Marion (1997). The authors examine possible consequences and drawbacks of raising c in the Obstfeld (1994) model. They propose that in some cases raising c may lead to destabilization, instead of stabilization.

[2]Enoch and Gulde (1997, pp. 7–9) devote one section of their paper to the legal issues of establishing a currency board.

much. Yet, as the model assumes rational expectation formation, it is doubtful whether this attempt of deception would eventually work. Furthermore, failed deception might even lead to destabilization as the policymaker becomes untrustworthy in the public's perception.

As has been discussed in 4.2.7.5, political cost from currency board exit have to be particularly high if the currency board is intended to achieve stabilization after an economic crisis. Firstly, such a crisis may well result from low inflation aversion of the policymaker and an effective unemployment-inflation tradeoff. In this case, the temptation to devalue will be high, implying that the policymaker is relatively willing to abandon the currency board to achieve unemployment reduction. In this case, for the currency board to be sustainable, political cost have to be high, offsetting the high temptation to devalue. Secondly, initial devaluation expectations right after introduction of the currency board may be rather high due to the bad inflation record history of the policymaker. Again, for these bad expectations not to lead to immediate abandonment of the currency board, political cost have to be relatively high, so the policymaker will not resort to devaluation at the first signs of real economic stress stemming from still positive devaluation expectations.

Once the policymaker has proven his determination to maintain the currency board, rapid stabilization is possible through the credibility effect, which always provides for the existence of an FC equilibrium after realization of a PC equilibrium, as we have shown in 4.2.7.1. This potential for rapid monetary stabilization is particularly evident from the hyperinflation currency board countries. In both Argentina and Bulgaria did the introduction of the currency board lead to a swift reduction in inflation, while not dragging down the real economy at the same time. This indicates that inflation expectations were drastically and effectively reduced by the installation of the new monetary regimes.

Another measure to increase the stability of a currency board is to actively encourage informal dollarization of the economy. By legalizing and encouraging bank deposits and loans denominated in the currency board's anchor currency, as well as denominating public debt in this currency, the policymaker signals confidence in the domestic currency and the currency board, and reduces the stimulative impulse from a devaluation, thus limiting his policy options. This measure corresponds to the policy pursued under the Argentinean currency board, where the economy was highly dollarized and the US dollar was made legal tender parallel to the peso. This may well have contributed to the extremely high aversion of abandoning the currency board in Argentina, where the decision to exit from the currency board was only taken at a point where government finances and the economy had already started collapsing.

However, we have shown that under certain conditions dollarization, while increasing the likeliness of the currency board being a fully credible exchange rate commitment, may also further the possibility of a breakdown of the currency board. This is the case when unemployment responsiveness to inflation relative to inflation aversion is high, and the level of indebtedness is relatively low. In this situation, should the policymaker decide to abandon the currency board, the debt effect leads the policymaker to devalue by even more than in the case without debt, to compensate for the reduced effectiveness of devaluation in reducing unemployment. Consequently, devaluation expectations tend to be higher, destabilizing the currency board and allowing for successful speculative attacks against the currency board.

The fourth potential measure to increase the stability of the currency board is to lower unemployment persistence. Unemployment persistence prevents unemployment from quickly falling back to its steady state level, and may bring about a build-up of unemployment, as high unemployment increases devaluation expectations, which, absent of an offsetting devaluation, raise unemployment again, and so forth.

The role of unemployment persistence is particularly important in those economies trying to end a currency crisis by means of a currency board. If, as was perhaps the case in Bulgaria and Argentina, such a crisis is due to high unemployment responsiveness, introduction of a currency board leaves the economy vulnerable to high unemployment pressure. Any realization of a PC equilibrium, implying positive and unfulfilled devaluation expectations, or exposure to adverse real shocks will tend to have a marked impact on unemployment. If, on top of this, unemployment persistence is high, unemployment pressure may quickly accumulate, leading to high real cost, and threatening the sustainability of the currency board.

Consequently, countries introducing a currency board should seek to lower unemployment persistence. If we take unemployment persistence to be related to labor market flexibility, potential measures of achieving this include deregulation of the labor market, enhancing the effectiveness of the job finding process, and increasing the willingness and ability to rejoin the labor force.[3]

All the measures described in this section tend to increase the stability of the currency board. The measures aiming to enhance the economic environment in which the currency board operates—influencing the publics beliefs and reducing unemployment persistence—are non-ambiguously beneficial, or

[3]For papers on unemployment persistence, labor market deregulation, and policy implications, e.g. see Arulampalam, Booth, and Taylor (1998), Blanchard (1991), Blanchard and Giavazzi (2001), Pissarides (1992).

at least neutral, and should therefore be pursued unconditionally when deciding to set up a currency board. This also includes the preconditions discussed in section 2.2—market flexibility, adequate choice of an anchor currency, prudent financial sector supervision and regulation, and austere fiscal policy—as well as measures furthering the fulfillment of these conditions, which are not or only indirectly incorporated into the currency board model developed in chapter 4. On the other hand, the benefit of measures aiming to reduce the policymaker's room to manoeuvre is ambiguous. The increased stability from increasing the political cost of devaluation or informal dollarization comes at a cost, as will be explained in the following subsection, and therefore requires a conscious evaluation of the trade-off involved.

5.3 The Risks

Rigidly tying the hands of the policymaker to enhance the sustainability of any fixed exchange rate regime (i.e. setting a very high level of $\hat{c}$ in context of the model) is not a win-only strategy. If it were, all existing fixed exchange rate systems short of formal dollarization should be currency boards, which they obviously are not.[4] Rather, it can be seen as rasing the stakes in a gamble. The more constrained the policymaker's options of economic policy are, the higher are the odds of establishing a fully credible fixed exchange rate. But, in the case of failure, the loss will also be higher.

Increased political cost of devaluation will lead the policymaker to tolerate higher unemployment pressure, before eventually deciding to devalue. Once devaluation is then undertaken, it will be by a larger extend than otherwise with lower political cost, and the disruption to the economy as well as the loss will be higher.

Dollarization of the economy aggravates the consequences of an exit even more. The higher the level of foreign-currency denominated debt, the less effective the devaluation-unemployment tradeoff. Therefore, unemployment

[4]Fischer (2001) examines the validity of the bipolar view of exchange rate regimes. According to this often advocated view, intermediate exchange rate regimes between hard pegs and floats are not sustainable. Fischer concludes that the last decade has indeed witnessed a hollowing out of the middle of the distribution of exchange rate regimes. Yet, Levy-Yeyati and Sturzenegger (2002a) show that when using a de-facto instead of a de-jure classification of exchange rate regimes, as compiled in their de-facto classification database (Levy-Yeyati and Sturzenegger 2002b), many de-jure floats turn out to be de-facto dirty floats ("fear of floating", a term initially coined by Calvo and Reinhart (2000)) and that de-facto pegs outnumber de-jure pegs. They call this phenomenon of shying away from explicitly committing to a peg "fear of pegging" (Levy-Yeyati and Sturzenegger 2002a, p. 1).

pressure will have to be high until the policymaker decides to devalue. Yet, once he decides to devalue, the reduced effectiveness of devaluation in reducing unemployment means that the magnitude of devaluation has to be very high, resulting in a disruptive exit from the currency board.

These conclusions in particular apply to instances where currency boards are introduced for economic stabilization. During a currency crisis there is a lot to gain from introducing a currency board. As has been shown throughout chapter 3, the aspect of stabilization has been the leading rationale for the introduction of almost all present-day currency boards, whether it was the relatively mild crisis of confidence surrounding Hong Kong's return to the currency board in 1983, or the acute currency and hyperinflation crises leading to the introduction of currency boards in Argentina 1991 and Bulgaria 1997. Yet, currency board introduction during a crisis requires a very high commitment to the currency board to restore confidence, leaving countries with few exit options. On top of that, introduction of a currency board during a crisis may also indicate that unemployment responsiveness is high, implying that unemployment cost from lack of confidence in the exchange rate arrangement or from shock adjustment tend to be high, particularly if unemployment responsiveness is high. If we dramatize this conclusion we might say that, to achieve economic stabilization of a monetary crisis, currency board countries heavily expose themselves to real disturbances and rigidly tie their hands from ameliorating such disturbances.

Once again, the outstanding example for the aforementioned potential risks of having a currency board is Argentina. The country profited greatly from the stabilization success of the currency board, which was achieved through high cost from exit and strong political commitment towards the monetary arrangement, and furthered by a high degree of dollarization. Yet, once the exit from the currency board took place, it was extremely disruptive—real GDP is estimated to have fallen by more than 20% until November 2002—entailing a large devaluation of the currency, which lost over 70% of its value in the first nine months of 2002. Dollarization, especially liability dollarization, which had tended to stabilize the currency board, posed a devastating burden in the presence of the large devaluation, particularly on households and firms with dollar liabilities but peso incomes.

During the last decade of the twentieth century, currency boards have often been advocated and implemented as a monetary regime promoting monetary stabilization. But while stabilization achievements were highlighted by currency board proponents and easily visible, especially in post-crisis economies, the potential risks of having a currency board were often not fully considered, or even neglected, partly due to the pressing need for stabilization in a crisis and the relative easiness of achieving it by means of a currency board.

5.4 Outlook

This thesis has confirmed the often-expressed and often-witnessed notion that indeed a currency board is a very suitable arrangement for prompt monetary stabilization. It achieves this by lending credibility to monetary policy and effectively driving devaluation/inflation expectations down. Yet, as this thesis has clearly shown, such stabilization is not to be had for free. The high obstacles to exit, such as a high political penalty on the policymaker, as well as perhaps high levels of dollarization, which lend credibility and stability to the currency board, also entail sizeable downside risks for the economy, should the currency board come under pressure or even be abandoned. The benefits and risks of the currency board system are symmetric; the more credible the design, the higher the potential loss.

While very strict and rigid currency board design still makes sense in high inflation environments, where the policymaker has a bad track record of low monetary stability and monetary policy intervention, as well as a high incentive to so, potential risks of strict currency board design have at least to be taken into account. Also, countries intending to introduce a currency board, as well as those already having one, should try to implement non-ambiguous supporting reforms and measures that do not carry downside risks to the greatest extent possible—such as a transparent and understandable currency board arrangement, flexible markets, an adequate anchor currency, a strong financial sector, and prudent fiscal policies—thereby reducing the necessity of compensating for the lack of a supportive economic environment to the currency board by even stricter currency board design.

The experience of Argentina will prompt countries considering to introduce a currency board to think twice, before tying their hands, and renouncing monetary policy intervention powers that might be necessary to prevent potential excesses of overly rigid monetary policy. Furthermore, the end of socialism in eastern Europe, which eventually led to the establishment of most of the currency boards discussed in chapter 3, was a unique historical event, so no repeated wave of currency board establishment is to be expected. Additionally, all of the remaining countries that introduced currency boards in the 1990s, except for Bosnia, look set to abandon their currency boards in the foreseeable future. Estonia and Lithuania may do so as early as 2006, the earliest possible date at which they might join the euro zone. Bulgaria will have to wait at least until 2009, as it will not join the EU before 2007, but the country has already expressed its intention to also abandon the currency board in exchange for introduction of the euro. In the medium-term, the revival of the currency board system, as presented in chapter 3, may well prove to be short-lived.

Appendix A

Currency Boards 1849–2002 Overview

Table A.1: Currency boards from 1849 to 2002. An overview

Country[1]	Est'd	Exit	Colonial Power	Independence	Anchor Currency[2]
Abu Dhabi	1966	1973	UK	1971	UK-£
Aden and Aden protectorate (part of Yemen)	1951	1972	UK	1967	UK-£
Argentina	1902	1914			gold
Argentina	1927	1929			gold
Argentina	1991	2002			US-$
Bahamas [UK]	1916	1974	UK	1973	UK-£, US-$
Bahrain [UK]	1965	1973	UK	1971	UK-£
Barbados [UK]	1937	1973	UK	1966	UK-£
Bermuda [UK]	1915		UK		UK-£, US-$

[1] Today's name given in parentheses, if applicable.

[2] Multiple currencies indicate change of anchor currency during currency board operation.

Table A.1: (continued)

Country	Est'd	Exit	Colonial Power	Indepen-dence	Anchor Currency
Bosnia	1997				DM, euro
British Guiana (Guyana)	1937	1965	UK	1966	UK-£
British Honduras (Belize)	1894	1981	UK	1981	US-$, UK-£, US-$
British Solomon Islands (Solomon Islands)	1930	1940	UK	1978	AUS-£
British Somaliland (part of Somalia)	1942	1961	UK	1960	UK-£
Brunei	1952	1973	UK	1983	UK-£
Bulgaria	1997				DM, euro
Burma	1947	1952	UK	1948	UK-£
Cameroons (part of Cameroon and Nigeria)	1916	1959	UK	1959	UK-£
Cayman Islands	1933	1961	UK		UK-£
Cayman Islands	1972		UK		US-$
Ceylon (Sri Lanka)	1884	1950	UK	1948	Idian rupee
Cyprus	1928	1964	UK	1960	UK-£
Danzig (Gdansk, Poland)	1923	1924			UK-£
Djibouti	1949		France	1977	US-$
Dubai	1966	1973	UK	1971	gold
Eritrea	1942	1945	Italy, Ethiopia	1993	UK-£
Estonia	1992				DM, euro

Table A.1: (continued)

Country	Est'd	Exit	Colonial Power	Independence	Anchor Currency
Ethiopia	1942	1945			UK-£
Falkland Islands	1899		UK		UK-£
Faroe Islands (part of Denmark)	1940				UK-£, DK-krona
Fiji	1913	1975	UK	1970	UK-£
Gambia	1913	1971	UK	1965	UK-£
Gibraltar	1927		UK		UK-£
Gold Coast (Ghana)	1913	1958	UK	1957	UK-£
Hong Kong	1935	1941	UK	1998	UK-£
Hong Kong	1945	1974	UK	1998	UK-£, US-$
Hong Kong	1983		UK	1998	US-$
Iraq	1931	1949	UK	1932	UK-£
Ireland	1928	1943	UK	1921	UK-£
Italian Somaliland (part of Somalia)	1941	1959	Italy	1960	UK-£
Jamaica	1933	1961	UK	1962	UK-£
Kenya	1897	1966	UK	1963	UK-£
Kuwait	1961	1969	UK	1961	UK-£
Leeward Islands (Anguilla, Antigua and Barbuda, St Kitts and Nevis, Montserrat)	1935	1983	UK		UK-£, US-$
Liberia	1913	1944			UK-£
Libya	1950	1956	UK, France	1951	UK-£

Table A.1: (continued)

Country	Est'd	Exit	Colonial Power	Indepen-dence	Anchor Currency
Lithuania	1994				US-$, euro
Malaya (part of Malaysia)	1899	1942	UK	1963	UK-£
Malaya (part of Malaysia)	1946	1967	UK	1963	UK-£
Maldive Islands (Maldives)	1849	1967	UK	1965	idian rupee, UK-£
Malta	1949	1965	UK	1964	UK-£
Mauritius	1849	1967	UK	1964	idian rupee, UK-£
New Zealand	1850	1856	UK	1907	UK-£
Nigeria	1913	1959	UK	1960	UK-£
North Borneo (part of Malaysia)	1881	1942	UK	1963	spanish-$, UK-£
North Borneo (part of Malaysia)	1946	1967	UK	1963	UK-£
North Russia (part of Russia)	1918	1920			UK-£
Northern Rhodesia (Zambia)	1940	1956	UK	1964	UK-£
Nyasaland (Malawi)	1940	1956	UK	1966	UK-£
Oman	1970	1974			UK-£
Palestine (Israel)	1927	1951	UK	1948	UK-£
Panama	1904	1931			US-$
Philippines	1903	1918	USA	1946	US-$
Philippines	1923	1942	USA	1946	US-$

Table A.1: (continued)

Country	Est'd	Exit	Colonial Power	Independence	Anchor Currency
Philippines	1945	1948	USA	1946	US-$
Qatar	1966	1973	UK	1971	gold
Sarawak (part of Malaysia)	1927	1942	UK	1963	UK-£
Sarawak (part of Malaysia)	1946	1967	UK	1963	UK-£
Seychelles	1849	1966	UK	1976	indian rupee, UK-£
Sierra Leone	1913	1964	UK	1961	UK-£
Singapore	1899	1942	UK	1967	UK-£
Singapore	1946	1973	UK	1967	UK-£
Southern Rhodesia (Zimbabwe)	1940	1956	UK	1965	UK-£
St Helena	1970	1975	UK		UK-£
Sudan	1957	1960	UK	1956	UK-£
Swaziland	1974	1986	UK	1968	SA-rand
Tanganyika (Tanzania)	1920	1966	UK	1961	UK-£
Togoland (part of Ghana)	1914	1958	UK	1957	UK-£
Tonga	1936	1974	UK	1970	AUS-£, AUS-$
Transjordan (Jordan)	1927	1964	UK	1946	UK-£
Trinidad and Tobago	1935	1964	UK	1962	UK-£
Uganda	1919	1966	UK	1962	UK-£

Table A.1: (continued)

Country	Est'd	Exit	Colonial Power	Independence	Anchor Currency
Western Samoa	1920	1973	New Zealand	1962	NZ-£, NZ-$
Windward Islands (Grenada, St Vincent and the Grenadines, St Lucia, Dominica)	1935	1983	UK	1974-1979	UK-£, US-$
Yemen Arab Republic (part of Yemen)	1964	1971			UK-£
Zanzibar (Tanzania)	1936	1966	UK	1961	UK-£

Sources: Schuler (1992, appendix), Gosh, Gulde, and Wolf (1998, p. 8).

Appendix B

Design Features of Present Currency Boards

Table B.1: Design features of five modern currency boards: Argentina, Bulgaria, Estonia, Hong Kong, and Lithuania. An overview

	Argentina	**Bulgaria**	**Estonia**	**Hong Kong**	**Lithuania**
Law governing the currency board setup	Convertibility Law (CL) of 1991	Law on the Bulgarian National Bank (LoBNB)	Law of the Republic of Estonia on the Security for the Estonian Kroon (LoSEK) The law for the establishment of the Bank of Estonia makes no reference to the law providing for the currency board system	No legislation dedicated to the currency board setup	Law on the Credibility of the Litas (LoCL)

Table B.1: (continued)

	Argentina	Bulgaria	Estonia	Hong Kong	Lithuania
Institutional setting	Currency board was maintained and operated by independent Banco Central de la República Argentina (BCRA).	Currency Board maintained and operated by independent Bulgarian National Bank (BNB). Separate Issue Department for currency board operation, while Banking Department pursues limited central bank functions with excess reserve.	Currency Board maintained and operated by independent Bank of Estonia (BOE). Separate Issue Department for currency board operation, while Banking Department pursues limited central bank functions with excess reserve.	De-facto currency board maintained and operated by Hong Kong Monetary Authority (HKMA), whose duties include but also exceed typical central bank functions by far.	Currency Board is maintained and operated by independent Bank of Lithuania (BOL).
Anchor currency, official exchange rate	US$1 = 1 peso	1 Deutsche mark = 1,000 lev (July 1, 1997–December 31, 1998) 1 euro = 1,955.83 lev (January 1, 1999–July 4, 1999) 1 euro = 1.95583 lev (July 5, 1999–present)	1 Deutsche mark = 8 kroon (June 20, 1992–December 31, 1998) 1 euro = 15.6466 kroon (January 1, 1999–present)	US$1 = HK$7.8	US$1 = 4 litas (April 1, 1994–February 1, 2002) 1 euro = 3.4528 litas (February 2, 2002–present)
Legal fixation of level of exchange rate and power to change.	Level of exchange rate set forth by CL. Can only be changed by act of parliament.	Level of exchange rate set forth by LoBNB. Can only be changed by act of parliament.	Not fixed by law. BOE has right to revalue exchange rate. Devaluation only through parliament.	Not fixed by law. Level of exchange rate set by HKMA and Financial Secretary.	Not fixed by law. Re- or devaluation through BOL after consulting government.
Backing rule	At least 100% of the monetary base. (CL)	Foreign exchange reserves have to cover all liabilities of BNB. (LoBNB)	Foreign exchange reserves have to cover monetary base. (LoSEK)	Basic law (BL) and Exchange Fund Ordinance (EFO) require 100% backing of notes issued.	Foreign exchange reserves have to cover monetary base. (LoCL)

Table B.1: (continued)

	Argentina	Bulgaria	Estonia	Hong Kong	Lithuania
(a) coverage of monetary base	Operationally, monetary base is defined as cash in circulation, and deposits of financial entities with central bank.	Monetary liabilities consist of all bank notes and coins in circulation, account balances held with BNB (including gov't deposit). (LoBNB)	Monetary base includes cash in circulation, currency in current and fixed date accounts held with BOE. (LoSEK)	Operationally, both stock and flow of monetary base are fully backed by foreign reserves.	Monetary base includes notes and coins in circulation, account balances held with BOL, and litas-denominated securities and other promissory notes of BOL. (LoCL)
(a) eligible assets for backing	Reserves are to be invested in deposits, other interest-bearing transactions, or national or foreign public bonds payable in gold, precious metals, US$ or other foreign exchange. Maximum of 30% domestic dollar denominated bonds. (CL and BCRA charter)	Eligible assets include foreign-currency denominated bank notes and coins, foreign currency funds held with foreign financial institutions, SDRs, debt instruments issued by foreign institutions, forward or repurchase agreements with foreign institutions, and gold. (LoBNB)	Gold and foreign-currency denominated assets. (LoSEK)	The entire backing portfolio of the monetary base is made up of US$ assets. None of these are claims on the domestic government.	Reserves include foreign-currency denominated bank notes and coins, foreign currency deposits held in foreign institutions, and foreign-currency denominated securities. (LoCL and Law on the Bank of Lithuania (LoBOL))
Convertibility undertaking	Legally one-way, although two-way in practice. Central bank is required to sell foreign exchange for pesos at the official exchange rate. Central bank is permitted to buy foreign exchange at market rate. (CL)	BNB is required to sell and buy lev at the spot rate, which must not deviate from the official rate by more than 0.5%, without limit. (LoBNB)	Euro have to be bought and sold from/to licensed banks without a spread. (LoSEK)	Certificates of Indebtedness have to be bought and sold at the determined exchange rate. (EFO) Operationally, licensed banks can convert their HK$ balance in clearing accounts at HKMA into US$ at official exchange rate.	BOL is required to sell foreign exchange at official exchange rate. In other direction, bank guarantees free exchange of anchor currency in litas without specifying applicable exchange rate. (LoCL)

Table B.1: (continued)

	Argentina	Bulgaria	Estonia	Hong Kong	Lithuania
Lender of last resort (LoLR) capabilities	Generally, BCRA was prohibited from acting as LoLR. Exceptions: Allowed to grant rediscounts and advance to financial institutions in temporary illiquidity, as long as backing requirement is not violated. (BCRA charter)	No LoLR action, except where emergence of liquidity risk that may affect stability of banking system. Only short-term and collateralized assistance to solvent banks. Only up to extent of excess reserves. (LoBNB)	Only in cases of systemic and emergency situations. Limited to excess reserves. (LoSEK)	Yes, no restrictions. EFO stipulates that Exchange Fund assets to be used for maintaining stability and integrity of monetary and financial systems. Operationally, on a case-to-case basis.	Up to extent of excess reserves. (LoBOL)
Scope for discretionary monetary policy besides LoLR	Reserve requirements, liquidity requirements, rediscount operations (limited) (BCRA charter).	Reserve requirements (LoBNB)	Reserve requirements, liquidity requirements, certificates of deposit, open market operations (planned, after EU accession).	Discount window, open-market operations, Treasury-bills.	Reserve requirements, rediscount operation, collateralized loans to banks, Treasury-bills, open market operations (LoBOL).
Lending to the government	No. But BCRA was allowed to buy government securities on secondary market. (BCRA charter)	No. BNB must also not buy domestic securities. (LoBNB)	No. BOE must also not buy government securities. (LoSEK)	No special statutory provision. But operationally, has not happened.	No direct lending. But government securities may be purchased in secondary market. (LoBOL)
Commitment to the currency board	Strong political commitment.	Moderate (political unaminity with desultory voices for abandonment). Yet to be tested.	Strong public and political commitment (full political unanimity).	Strong political commitment.	Initially very weak. Introduction was disputed and opposed by BOL. Repeated announcements and plans by government and BOL to abolish currency board. Recently, commitment has increased.

Table B.1: (continued)

	Argentina	**Bulgaria**	**Estonia**	**Hong Kong**	**Lithuania**
Dollarization of the economy	Very high. Dollar was parallel legal tender.	Relatively high.	Rather low.	High?	Medium (higher than Estonia, lower than Bulgaria).

Sources: Chapter 3, Tsang (1999, pp. 57–63), Tsang (2000, pp. 15–18), Nenovsky, Hristov, and Mihaylov (2002, pp. 12–13).

Appendix C

Derivation of Equations

C.1 The Standard Model

C.1.1 Derivation of Devaluation and Loss Equations (4.6) and (4.7)

Substituting unemployment equation (4.4) into the loss function (4.5) yields:

$$L_t = \left(\sqrt{\alpha}\left[(E\Delta e_t - \Delta e_t) + k + \delta ur_{t-1}\right]\right)^2 + \theta(\Delta e_t)^2 \quad (C.1)$$

To minimize the loss function, differentiate respect to Δe_t and set equal to zero:

$$\frac{dL_t}{d\Delta e_t} = 2\alpha(\Delta e_t - E\Delta e_t - k - \delta ur_{t-1}) + 2\theta\Delta e_t = 0 \quad (C.2)$$

Solving for Δe_t yields equation (4.6):

$$\Delta e_t = \frac{\alpha}{\alpha+\theta}(E\Delta e_t + k + \delta ur_{t-1})$$

Substituting (4.6) back into (C.1) gives:

$$\begin{aligned} L_t &= \alpha\left(1 - \frac{\alpha}{\alpha+\theta}\right)^2 (E\Delta e_t + k + \delta ur_{t-1})^2 \\ &\quad + \theta\left(\frac{\alpha}{\alpha+\theta}\right)^2 (E\Delta e_t + k + \delta ur_{t-1})^2 \end{aligned} \quad (C.3)$$

Equation (C.3) can be simplified to yield (4.7):

$$L_t^D = \frac{\alpha\theta}{\alpha+\theta}(E\Delta e_t + k + \delta ur_{t-1})^2$$

C.1.2 Proof that (4.9) Greater than (4.11)

To be shown:

$$\frac{\alpha(\alpha+\theta)}{\theta}(k+\delta ur_{t-1})^2 \ > \ \alpha(k+\delta ur_{t-1})^2 \tag{C.4}$$

Successively simplifying:

$$\begin{aligned} \frac{\alpha(\alpha+\theta)}{\theta} &> \alpha \\ \frac{\alpha+\theta}{\theta} &> 1 \\ \frac{\alpha}{\theta}+1 &> 1 \end{aligned} \tag{C.5}$$

C.1.3 Difference Loss Fixed and Loss Discretionary Exchange Rate

$$\begin{aligned} L_t^F - L_t^D &= \alpha(E\Delta e_t + k + \delta ur_{t-1})^2 \\ &\quad -\frac{\alpha\theta}{\alpha+\theta}(E\Delta e_t + k + \delta ur_{t-1})^2 \\ &= \left(\alpha - \frac{\alpha\theta}{\alpha+\theta}\right)(E\Delta e_t + k + \delta ur_{t-1})^2 \\ L_t^F - L_t^D &= \frac{\alpha^2}{\alpha+\theta}(E\Delta e_t + k + \delta ur_{t-1})^2 > 0 \end{aligned} \tag{C.6}$$

Which is equation (4.13).

C.1.4 Derivation of Equation (4.19), Expected Devaluation

Starting with:

$$E\Delta e_t = E(\Delta e_t|\text{Devalue}) \cdot \text{prob}(\text{Devalue}) \tag{C.7}$$

and substituting

$$E(\Delta e_t|\text{Devalue}) \ = \ \frac{\alpha}{\alpha+\theta}(E\Delta e_t + k + \delta ur_{t-1}) \tag{C.8}$$

$$\text{prob}(\text{Devalue}) \ = \ F_t(c_t^*) = \int_{\underline{c_t}}^{c_t^*} f(c)\,dc \tag{C.9}$$

with (C.8) given by (4.6) and $f(c)$ in (C.9) being the probability distribution function describing the beliefs of the public about the possible values of c and their respective probabilities, yields:

$$\begin{aligned} E\Delta e_t &= \frac{\alpha F_t(c_t^*)(E\Delta e_t + k + \delta ur_{t-1})}{\alpha+\theta} \\ E\Delta e_t\left(1 - \frac{\alpha F_T(c_t^*)}{\alpha+\theta}\right) &= \frac{\alpha F_t(c_t^*)(k + \delta ur_{t-1})}{\alpha+\theta} \\ E\Delta e_t\left(\frac{\alpha+\theta-\alpha F_T(c_t^*)}{\alpha+\theta}\right) &= \\ E\Delta e_t &= \frac{\alpha F_t(c_t^*)}{\alpha+\theta-\alpha F_t(c_t^*)}(k+\delta ur_{t-1}) \end{aligned}$$

which equals equation (4.19).

C.1.5 Derivation of Unemployment Equation (4.24)

Starting with:

$$ur_t = \sqrt{\alpha}\left[E\Delta e_t + k + \delta\overline{ur}\right]$$

Substituting equation (4.23), unemployment in steady-state:

$$\begin{aligned} ur_t &= \sqrt{\alpha}E\Delta e_t + \sqrt{\alpha}k + \frac{\alpha\delta k}{1-\delta\sqrt{\alpha}} \\ &= \sqrt{\alpha}E\Delta e_t + \frac{\sqrt{\alpha}k}{1-\delta\sqrt{\alpha}} \end{aligned} \tag{C.10}$$

Again, the last term on the right side of equation (C.10) is unemployment in steady-state, as given by equation (4.23), therefore:

$$ur_t = \overline{ur} + \sqrt{\alpha}E\Delta e_t$$

C.1.6 Derivation of Unemployment Equation (4.28)

Starting with unemployment equation (4.24)

$$ur_t = \overline{ur} + \sqrt{\alpha}E\Delta e_t$$

and substituting expected devaluation from equation (4.19) yields:

$$ur_t = \overline{ur} + \frac{\alpha^{3/2}F_t(c_t^*)}{\alpha+\theta-\alpha F_t(c_t^*)}(k+\delta ur_{t-1}) \tag{C.11}$$

Multiplying both sides by δ, adding k and substituting $ur_{t-1} = \overline{ur}$ yields:

$$k + \delta ur_t = k + \delta\overline{ur} + \frac{\delta\alpha^{3/2}F_t(c_t^*)}{\alpha + \theta - \alpha F_t(c_t^*)}(k + \delta\overline{ur})$$

$$k + \delta ur_t = (k + \delta\overline{ur})\left[1 + \frac{\delta\alpha^{3/2}F_t(c_t^*)}{\alpha + \theta - \alpha F_t(c_t^*)}\right]$$

C.1.7 Derivation of critical value for c (4.30)

Substituting (4.29)

$$E\Delta e_{t+1}(c_{t+1}^*) = \frac{\alpha(c_{t+1}^*)^2 - \alpha(c_t^*)^2}{\theta(c_{t+1}^*)^2 + \alpha(c_t^*)^2}(k + \delta ur_t)$$

into (4.18)

$$c_{t+1}^* = \frac{\alpha}{\sqrt{\alpha + \theta}}(E\Delta e_{t+1} + k + \delta ur_t)$$

yields:

$$c_{t+1}^* = \frac{\alpha}{\sqrt{\alpha + \theta}}\left(\frac{\alpha(c_{t+1}^*)^2 - \alpha(c_t^*)^2}{\theta(c_{t+1}^*)^2 + \alpha(c_t^*)^2}(k + \delta ur_t) + k + \delta ur_{t-1}\right)$$

Rearranging terms:

$$(c_{t+1}^*)^2 - \frac{\alpha\sqrt{\alpha + \theta}}{\theta}(k + \delta ur_t)c_{t+1}^* + \frac{\alpha}{\theta}(c_t^*)^2 = 0$$

Solving for c_{t+1}^*:

$$(c_{t+1}^*)_{1,2} = \frac{\alpha\sqrt{\alpha + \theta}}{2\theta}(k + \delta ur_t) \pm \sqrt{\frac{\alpha^2(\alpha + \theta)}{4\theta^2}(k + \delta ur_t)^2 - \frac{\alpha}{\theta}(c_t^*)^2}$$

Disregarding the negative root and rearranging yields (4.30):

$$c_{t+1}^* = \frac{\alpha}{2\theta}\left[\sqrt{\alpha + \theta}(k + \delta ur_t) + \sqrt{(\alpha + \theta)(k + \delta ur_t)^2 - \frac{4\theta}{\alpha}(c_t^*)^2}\right]$$

Bibliography

Äimä, Kustaa. 1998. "Central Bank Indepence in the Baltic Countries." BOFIT Discussion Paper 4, Bank of Finland.

Alonso-Gamo, Patricia, et al. 2002. "Lithuania: Hirstory and Future of the Currency Board Arrangement." Working Paper 02/127, International Monetary Fund.

Artana, Daniel. 1993. "Some Aspects of the Recent Program." In Liviatan 1993, 41–43.

Arulampalam, Wiji, Alison Lee Booth, and Mark P. Taylor. 1998. "Unemployment Persistence." Working Paper 19, Institute for Labour Research, Essex.

Avramov, Roumen. 1999. "The Role of a Currency Board in Financial Crises: The Case of Bulgaria." Discussion Paper 6/1999, Bulgarian National Bank, Sofia.

Babić, Ante, and Ante Žigman. 2001. "Currency Crises: Theoretical and Empirical Overview of the 1990s." Survey, Croation National Bank, Zagreb.

Baliño, Tomas J. T., et al. 1999. "Monetary Policy in Dollarized Economies." Occasional Paper 171, International Monetary Fund, Washington, DC.

Baliño, Tomás J. T., and Charles Enoch. 1997. "Currency Board Arrangements. Issues and Experiences." Occasional Paper 151, International Monetary Fund, Washington, DC.

Banco Central de la República Argentina. 2002. "Balances Consolidados del Sistema Financiero (serie mensual)." `http://www.bcra.gov.ar/estadistica/estad000100.asp` (September 26, 2002).

Bank of Estonia. 1999. "Chronicle of Monetary Policy of 1998." `http://www.ee/epbe/en/chronicle1998.html` (October 3, 2002).

———. 2000. "Reform of Monetary Policy Operational Framework." *Eesti Panga Bulletin*, no. 5.

———. 2002a. "Foreign Exchange Reserves Backing the Kroon." `http://www.ee/epbe/en/ep_kattevara.en` (October 1, 2002).

———. 2002b. "Monetary Policy Chronicle for the Year of the Monetary Reform." `http://www.ee/epbe/en/chronicle1992.html` (September 29, 2002).

Bank of Lithuania. 2002a. *Annual Report, 2001*. Vilnius.

———. 2002b. "Balance Sheet of the Bank of Lithuania." `http://www.lbank.lt/balance/default.asp?lang=e` (October 1, 2002).

———. 2002c. "International Reserves." `http://www.lbank.lt/ota/default.asp?lang=E` (October 2, 2002).

———. 2002d. "Money Supply." `http://www.lbank.lt/st/default.asp?pid=msupply&lang=e` (October 2, 2002).

Barro, Robert J., and David B. Gordon. 1983a. "A Positive Theory of Monetary Policy in a Natural Rate Model." *The Journal of Political Economy* 91 (4): 589–610.

———. 1983b. "Rules, Discretion and Reputation in a Model of Monetary Policy." *Journal of Monetary Economics* 12:101–121.

Bennett, Adam G. G. 1993. "The Operation of the Estonina Currency Board." *IMF Staff Papers* 40:451–470.

———. 1994. "Currency Boards: Issues and Experiences." Paper on Policy Analysis and Assessment 94/18, International Monetary Fund, Washington, DC.

Berensmann, Kathrin. 2002. *Currency Boards: A Monetary and Exchange Rate Policy Solution for Transition Countries? The Cases of Estonia and Lithuania*. Baden-Baden: Nomos.

Bernanke, Ben, Mark Gertler, and Simon Gilchrist. 1996. "The Financial Accelerator and the Flight to Quality." *Review of Economics and Statistics* 78 (1): 1–15.

———. 1998. "The Financial Accelerator in a Quantitative Business Cycle Framework." Working Paper 6455, National Bureau of Economic Research, Cambridge, MA.

Bernanke, Ben, and Julio Rotemberg, eds. 1996. *NBER Macroeconomics Annual 1996*. Cambridge, MA: MIT Press.

Blanchard, Olivier Jean. 1991. "Wage Bargaining and Unemployment Persistence." *Journal of Money, Credit, and Banking* 23 (3): 277–292.

Blanchard, Olivier Jean, and Francesco Giavazzi. 2001. "Macroeconomic Effects of Regulation and Deregulation in Goods and Labor Markets." Working Paper 8210, National Bureau of Economic Research, Cambridge, MA.

Blowers, G. A., and Alexander McLeod. 1952. "Currency Unification in Libya." *IMF Staff Papers* 2 (3): 439–467.

Boccara, Bruno, and John Chambers. 2002. "Argentina: Stability of Facing the Abyss?" `http://www.ratingsdirect.com` (December 18, 2002).

Bordo, Michael D., and Anna J. Schwarz. 1996. "Why Clashes between Internal and External Stability Goals End in Currency Crises, 1797-1994." Working Paper 5710, National Bureau of Economic Research, Cambridge, MA.

Buch, Holger, and Kai Stukenbrock. 2002. "Currency-Board-System und die Wirtschaftskrise in Argentinien." *Studienwerk der Bankakademie* Volkswirtschaftslehre (June 2002): 7–10.

Bulgarian National Bank. 1998. Regulation No. 6 (on Extending Collateralized Lev Loans to Banks).

———. 2002a. "Balance Sheet of Issue Deptartment." `http://www.bnb.bg/bnb/dd/Balance_issue_dept.nsf/fsWebIndexEN` (October 6, 2002).

———. 2002b. "Monthly Balance Sheet of the Issue Department." `http://www.bnb.bg/bnb/balances.nsf/vWebBSIMEN` (October 6, 2002).

———. [1998] 2002c. Regulation No. 21 (on the Minimum Required Reserves Maintained with the Bulgarian National Bank by Banks).

Bulgarian National Statistical Institute. 2002. "National Accounts." `http://www.nsi.bg/Gdp_e/GdpAll.htm` (October 6, 2002).

Caballero, Ricardo J., and Arvind Krishnamurthy. 2000. "Emerging Market Crises: An Assets Market Perspective." `http://web.mit.edu/caball/www/emerging.pdf` (August 12, 2002).

———. 2001. "International and Domestic Collateral Constraints in a Model of Emerging Market Crises." *Journal of Monetary Economics* 48 (3): 513–548.

———. 2002. "Excessive Dollar Debt: Financial Development and Underinsurance." *Journal of Finance*, vol. forthcoming.

Calvo, Guillermo, and Carmen M. Reinhart. 2000. "Fear of Floating." Working Paper 7993, National Bureau of Economic Research, Cambridge, MA.

Camard, Wayne. 1996. "Discretion with Rules? Lessons from the Currency Board Arrangement in Lithuania." Paper on Policy Analysis and Assessment 96/1, International Monetary Fund, Washington, DC.

Caprio Jr., Gerald, et al. 1996a. "The Lender of Last Resort Function Under a Currency Board: The Case of Argentina." *Open Economies Review* 7:625–650.

Caprio Jr., Gerard, et al. 1996b. "The Lender of Last Resort Function Under a Currency Board. The Case of Argentina." Policy Research Working Paper 1648, World Bank, Washington, DC.

Chang, Roberto, and Anrés Velasco. 2000. "Financial Fragility and the Exchange Rate Regime." *Journal of Economic Theory* 92:1–34.

Chankova, Slavea. 1999. "Currency Board Arrangements: A Tale of Four Countries." mimeo.

Chiu, Priscilla. 2001. "Hong Kong's Experience in Operating the Currency Board System." paper presented at an high-level seminar on exchange rate regimes "Hard Peg or Free Floating?", IMF, Mar 19–20, 2001.

Choi, Woon Gyu, and David Cook. 2002. "Liability Dollarization and the Bank Balance Sheet Channel." Working Paper 02/141, International Monetary Fund, Washington, DC.

Corden, W. Max. 1997. "The Dilemmas of Currency Boards." In Perry 1997, 3–5.

Céspedes, Luis Felipe, Roberto Chang, and Andrés Velasco. 2000. "Balance Sheets and Exchange Rate Policy." Working Paper 7840, National Bureau of Economic Research, Cambridge, MA.

de Loynes, John Barraclogh. 1962. *The West African Currency Board 1912-1962*. London.

Diamond, Douglas W., and Philip H. Dybvig. 1983. "Bank Runs, Deposit Insurance, and Liquidity." *The Journal of Political Economy* 91 (3): 401–419.

Dobrev, Dobrislav. 1999. "The Currency Board in Bulgaria: Design, Peculiarities and Management of Foreign Exchange Cover." Discussion Paper 9/1999, Bulgarian National Bank, Sofia, Bulgaria.

Dobrinsky, Rumen. 2000. "The Transition Crisis in Bulgaria." *Cambridge Journal of Economics* 24:581–602.

Drazen, Allan, and Paul R. Masson. 1994. "Credibility of Policies versus Credibility of Policy Makers." *Quarterly Journal of Economics* 109 (3): 735–754.

Eichengreen, Barry. 1994. *International Monetary Arrangements for the 21st Century*. Washington, DC: The Brookings Institution.

Enoch, Charles, and Anne-Marie Gulde. 1997. "Making a Currency Board Operational." Paper on Policy Analysis and Assessment 97/10, International Monetary Fund, Washington, DC.

———. 1998. "Are Currency Boards a Cure for All Monetary Problems?" *Finance and Development* 35 (4): 40–43.

Enoch, Charles, Anne-Marie Gulde, and Daniel Hardy. 2002. "Banking Crises and Bank Resolution: Experiences in Some Transition Economies." Working Paper 02/56, International Monetary Fund.

Feige, Edgar L., and James W. Dean. 2002. "Dollarization and Euroization in Transition Countries: Currency Substitution, Asset Substitution, Network Externalities and Irreversibility." Working Paper, University of Wisconsin, Madison.

Feige, Edgar L., et al. 2002. "Unofficial Dollarization in Latin America: Currency Substitution, Network Externalities and Irreversibility." In *Dollarizing the Americas*, edited by James W. Dean, Dominick Salvatore, and Thomas Willet. New York, NY: Oxford University Press. (forthcoming) `http://econwpa.wustl.edu:8089/eps/if/papers/0205/0205002.pdf` (September 28, 2002).

Fernandez, Roque B. 1996. "Regulation for a Stable Financial System: Prudential Supervision and Liquidity Management in Argentina." In *Stabilization and Reforms in Latin America: Where Do We Stand?*, edited by Hermann Sautter and Rolf Schinke, 123–146. Frankfurt am Main: Vervuert.

Fischer, Stanley. 1997. "Closing Remarks: What Have We Learned?" In Perry 1997, 19–22.

———. 2001. "Exchange Rate Regimes: Is the Bipolar View Correct?" `http://www.imf.org/external/np/speeches/2001/010601a.pdf` (April 29, 2002).

Fisher, Irving. 1933. "The Debt-Deflation Theory of Great Depressions." *Econometrica* 1:337–357.

Flood, Robert P., and Peter M. Garber. 1984. "Collapsing Exchange Rate Regimes." *Journal of International Economics* 17:1–13.

Flood, Robert P., and Nancy P. Marion. 1997. "Policy Implications of Second-Generation Models." Working Paper 97/16, International Monetary Fund, Washington, DC.

Fung, Andrew. 1999. "Liability and Market Risk Management by a Bank Treasurer in a Modern Day Currency Board System." paper presented at a workshop on "Currency Boards: Convertibility, Liquidity Management and Exit", Hong Kong Baptist University, Oct 9, 1999.

Ganapolsky, Eduardo J. J., and Sergio L. Schmukler. 1998. "Crisis Management in Argentina during the 1994–95 Mexican Crisis. How Did Markets React?" Policy Research Working Paper 1951, World Bank, Washington, DC.

Garber, Peter. 1996. "Comment on Krugman." In Bernanke and Rotemberg 1996, 403–406.

Gavriiski, Svetoslav. 2000. Statement of the BNB's Governor, Mr. Svetoslav Gavriiski at a press conference held at the Central bank on 11 May 2000, `http://www.bnb.bg/bnb/home.nsf/vPages/EUA_SBNBGMSG_EU/$FILE/press-Gavriisky-e.doc` (October 6, 2002).

Gerloff, Axel. 2001. *Wechselkurspolitik in Mittel- und Osteuropa.* Frankfurt am Main, et al.: Peter Lang.

Goldberg, Pinelopi Koujianou, and Michael M. Knetter. 1997. "Goods Prices and Exchange Rates: What Have We Learned?" *Journal of Economic Literature* 35 (3): 1243–1272.

Gosh, Atish R., Anne-Marie Gulde, and Holger C. Wolf. 1998. "Currency Boards: The Ultimate Fix?" Working Paper 98/8, International Monetary Fund, Washington, DC.

Gosh, Atish R., et al. 1997. "Does the Nominal Exchange Rate Regime Matter?" Working Paper 5874, National Bureau of Economic Research, Cambridge, MA.

Government of Hong Kong. [1935] 1997. Exchange Fund Ordinance.

———. [1895] 2001. Legal Tender Note Issue Ordinance.

———. [1986] 2002. Banking Ordinance.

Gulde, Anne-Marie. 1999. "The Role of the Currency Board in Bulgaria's Stabilization." Policy Discussion Paper 99/3, International Monetary Fund, Washington, DC.

Gulde, Anne-Marie, Juha Kähkönen, and Peter Keller. 2000. "Pros and Cons of Currency Board Arrangements in the Lead-up to EU Accession and Participation in the Euro Zone." Policy Discussion Paper 00/1, International Monetary Fund, Washington, DC.

Hanke, Steve H. 1999. "Some Reflections on Currency Boards." In *Central banking, monetary policies, and the implication for transition economies*, edited by Mario Blejer and Marko Skreb, 341–366. Norwell, MA: Kluwer Academic Publishers.

———. 2000. "The Disregard for Currency Board Realities." *Cato Journal* 20 (1): 49–59.

Hanke, Steve H., Lars Jonung, and Kurt Schuler. 1993. *Russioan Curency and Finance: A Currency Board Approach*. London, New York: Routledge.

Hanke, Steve H., and Kurt Schuler. 1992. "Currency Boards for Eastern Europe." Geld und Währung Working Paper 23, University of Frankfurt, Frankfurt, Germany.

———. 1993. "Currency Boards for Latin America." In Liviatan 1993, 13–21.

———. 2000, June. "Currency Boards for Developing Countries: A Handbook." `http://users.erols.com/kurrency/iceg.htm` (May 12, 2001). Slightly updated version of a 1994 study published by ICS Press, San Francisco.

Hanson, James. 1993. "Argentina's Quasi-Currency Board." In Liviatan 1993, 43–48.

HKMA. 1999a. "Exchange Fund and Reserves Management." Fact Sheet 2, Hong Kong Monetary Authority.

———. 1999b. "The HKMA's Role and Policy Objectives." Fact Sheet 1, Hong Kong Monetary Authority.

———. 1999c. "The Linked Exchange Rate System." Fact Sheet 3, Hong Kong Monetary Authority.

———. 2000a. "Hong Kong's Linked Exchange Rate System." Background Brief 1, Hong Kong Monetary Authority.

———. 2000b. *Money in Hong Kong: A Brief Introduction*. Hong Kong Monetary Authority.

———. 2002. Monthly Statistical Bulletin September 2002, Hong Kong Monetary Authority.

Hong Kong Census & Statistics Department. 2002. "Frequently Asked Statistics: GDP and Its Main Expenditure Components." http://www.info.gov.hk/censtatd/eng/hkstat/fas/nat_account/gdp/gdp3_index.html (September 23, 2002).

Hristov, Kalin. 2002. "Fundamental Equilibrium Exchange Rates and Currency Boards: Evidence from Argentina and Estonia in the 90's." Discussion Paper 22/2002, Bulgarian National Bank, Sofia.

IMF. 2000. "IMF Concludes Article IV Consultation with Bulgaria." Public Information Notice 00/32, International Monetary Fund, Washington, DC.

———. 2002a. "Economic and Financial Issues Facing Argentina." Report to the Government of Argentina and the International Monetary Fund, July 29, 2002, http://www.imf.org/external/np/sec/nb/2002/nb0280.htm (September 28, 2002).

———. 2002b. "IMF Concludes 2002 Article IV Consultation with Bulgaria." Public Information Notice 02/82, International Monetary Fund.

———. 2002c. *International Financial Statistics.* Washington, DC: International Monetary Fund.

Irwin, Gregor. 2001. "Currency Boards and Currency Crises." Economic Discussion Paper 65, University of Oxford.

Irwin, Gregor, and David Vines. 1999. "A Krugman-Dooley-Sachs Third Generation Model of the Asian Financial Crisis." Discussion Paper 99/15, Centre for International Economic Studies, Adelaide.

Isard, Peter, Assaf Razin, and Andrew K. Rose, eds. 1999. *International Finance and Financial Crises. Essays in Honor of Robert P. Flood, Jr.* Boston, et al.: Kluwer Academic Publishers and International Monetary Fund.

Jeanne, Olivier. 1999. "Comment." In Isard, Razin, and Rose 1999, 49–54.

Jevons, William Stanley. [1875] 1889. *Money and the Mechanism of Exchange.* New York: D. Appleton and Co.

JPMorgan. 2002. "Argentina." *Data Watch* December 6, 2002:29–30.

Kabakchiev, Bojidar. 2000. "The Currency Board Arrangement Remains Even After Bulgaria's Accession to the EU." Interview given by Mr. Bojidar Kabakchiev, Deputy Governor of the Bulgarian National Bank, http://www.bnb.bg/bnb/home.nsf/vPages/EUA_IUCBA_EU/$FILE/interview-BK-e%.doc (October 6, 2002).

Kenen, Peter B. 1969. "The Theory of Optimum Currency Areas: An Eclectiv View." In *Monetary Problems of the International Economy*, edited by Robert A. Mundell and Alexander K. Swoboda, 41–60. University of Chicago Press.

Kiguel, Miguel A. 2002. "Structural Reforms in Argentina: Success of Failure?" *Comparative Economic Studies* 44 (2): 83–102.

Kiguel, Miguel A., and Nissan Liviatan. 1994. "Exchange-Rate-Based Stabilization in Argentina and Chile." Policy Research Working Paper 1318, World Bank, Washington, DC.

Kiyotaki, Nobuhiro, and John Moore. 1997. "Credit Cyles." *Journal of Political Economy* 105 (2): 211–248.

Knöbl, Adalbert, Andres Sutt, and Basil Zavoico. 2002. "The Estonian Currency Board: Its Introduction and Role in the Early Success of Estonia's Transition to a Market Economy." Working Paper 02/96, International Monetary Fund.

Korhonen, Iikka. 1999. "Currency Boards in the Baltic Countries: What Have We Learned?" BOFIT Discussion Paper 6, Bank of Finland.

Kraft, Vahur. 2001. "Estonia's Upcoming Financial Policy Tasks and Accession to the European Union." *Eesti Panga Buletin*, no. 7:6–8.

Krugman, Paul. 1979. "A Model of Balance-of-Payments Crises." *Journal of Money, Credit and Banking* 11 (3): 311–325.

———. 1996. "Are Currency Crises Self-Fulfilling?" In Bernanke and Rotemberg 1996, 345–378.

———. 1997. "Currency Crises." `http://web.mit.edu/krugman/www/crises.html` (April 9, 1999).

———. 1999. "Balance Sheets, the Transfer Problem, and Financial Crises." In Isard, Razin, and Rose 1999, 31–44.

Kutan, Ali M., and Niina Pautola-Mol. 2002. "Integration of the Baltic States into the EU and Institutions of Fiscal Convergence." BOFIT Discussion Paper 1, Bank of Finland.

Kwan, Yum K., and Francis T. Lui. 1999. "Hong Kong's Currency Board and Changing Monetary Regimes." In *Changes in Exchange Rates in Rapidly Developing Countries. Theory, Practice, and Policy Issues*, edited by Takatoshi Ito and Anne O. Krueger, 403–429. Chicago and London: University of Chicago Press.

Kydland, Finn E., and Edward C. Prescott. 1977. "Rules Rather than Discretion: The Inconsistency of Optimal Plans." *The Journal of Political Economy* 85 (3): 473–492.

La Nación. 2001. Various issues.

———. 2002. Various issues.

Lepik, Ilmar. 1999. "Basic Features of the Estonian Currency Board: Convertibility and Liquidity Management." paper presented at a workshop on "Currency Boards: Convertibility, Liquidity Management and Exit", Hong Kong Baptist University, Oct 9, 1999.

Levy-Yeyati, Eduardo, and Federico Sturzenegger. 2001a. "Dollarization: A Primer." `http://www.utdt.edu/~fsturzen/CHAPTER1.pdf` (April 26, 2002).

———. 2001b. "Exchange Rate Regimes and Economic Performance." *IMF Staff Papers* 47 (Special Issue): 62–98.

———. 2002a. "Classifying Exchange Rate Regimes: Deeds vs. Words." `http://www.utdt.edu/~fsturzen/DW2002.pdf` (September 17, 2002).

———. 2002b. "Levy-Yeyati and Sturzenegger (LYS) de facto classification of exchange rate regimes." `http://www.utdt.edu/~fsturzen/base_2002.xls` (September 17, 2002).

———. 2002c. "To Float or to Trail: Evidence on the Impact of Exchange Rate Regimes." `http://www.utdt.edu/~fsturzen/Marzo2002aer.pdf`, (April 29, 2002).

Liviatan, Nissan, ed. 1993. *Proceedings of a Conference on Currency Substitution and Currency Boards.* Discussion Paper no. 207. Washington, DC: World Bank.

Lu, Ding, and Qiao Yu. 1999. "Hong Kong's Exchange Rate Regime: Lessons from Singapore." *China Economic Review* 10:122–140.

Masson, Paul R. 1995. "Gaining and losing ERM credibility: The case of the United Kingdom." *The Economic Journal* 105:571–582.

McKinnon, Ronald I. 1963. "Optimum Currency Areas." *The American Economic Review* 53 (4): 717–725.

Miller, Jeffrey B. 1999. "The Currency Board in Bulgaria: The First Two Years." Discussion Paper 11/1999, Bulgarian National Bank, Sofia.

———. 2001. "The Bulgarian Currency Board." *Comparative Economic Studies* 43 (1): 53–74.

Ministerio de Economía de la República Argentina. 2002a. "Mercado de Capitales." `http://www2.mecon.gov.ar/infoeco/` (September 27, 2002).

———. 2002b. "Mercado de Trabajo." `http://www2.mecon.gov.ar/infoeco/` (September 27, 2002).

———. 2002c. "Precios." `http://www2.mecon.gov.ar/infoeco/` (September 27, 2002).

Modigliani, Franco, and Merton Miller. 1958. "The Cost of Capital, Corporation Finance, and the Theory of Investment." *American Economic Review* 48:261–297.

Morris, Stephen, and Hyun Song Shin. 1999. "A Theory of the Onset of Currency Attacks." In *The Asian Financial Crises: Causes, Contagion, and Consequences*, edited by Richard Agenor, Marcus Miller, David Vines, and Axel Weber, 230–264. Cambridge: Cambridge University Press.

Mundell, Robert A. 1961. "A Theory of Optimum Currency Areas." *The American Economic Review* 51 (4): 657–665.

Nenovsky, Nikolay, and Kalin Hristov. 1998. "Financial Repression and Credit Rationing under Currency Board Arrangement for Bulgaria." Discussion Paper 2/1998, Bulgarian National Bank, Sofia.

———. 1999. "Monetary Policy under the Currency Board: The Case of Bulgaria." paper presented at a workshop on "Currency Boards: Convertibility, Liquidity Management and Exit", Hong Kong Baptist University, Oct 9, 1999.

Nenovsky, Nikolay, Kalin Hristov, and Mihail Mihaylov. 2002. "Comparing the Institutional and Organizational Design of Currency Boards in Transition Countries." *Eastern European Economics* 40 (1): 6–35.

Obstfeld, Maurice. 1986. "Rational and Self-Fulfilling Balance-of-Payments Crises." *American Economic Review* 76 (1): 72–81.

———. 1991. "Destabilizing Effects of Exchange-Rate Escape Clauses." Working Paper 3603, National Bureau of Economic Research, Cambridge, MA.

———. 1994. "The Logic of Currency Crises." *Cahiers économiques et monétaires*, no. 43:189–213.

———. 1996a. "Comment on Krugman." In Bernanke and Rotemberg 1996, 393–403.

———. 1996b. "Models of Currency Crises with Self-Fulfilling Features." *European Economic Review* 40 (3–5): 1037–1047.

———. 1997. "Destabilizing Effects of Exchange-Rate Escape Clauses." *Journal of International Economics* 43:61–77.

Obstfeld, Maurice, and Kenneth Rogoff. 1996. *Foundations of International Macroeconomics.* Cambridge, MA and London: MIT Press.

Oliva, Maria-Angels, Luis A. Rivera Batiz, and Amadou N. R. Sy. 2001. "Discipline, Signaling and Currency Boards." *Review of International Economics* 9 (4): 608–625.

Pastor Jr., Manuel, and Carol Wise. 1999. "Stabilization and its Discontents: Argenina's Economic Restructuring in the 1990s." *World Development* 27 (3): 477–503.

Perry, Guillermo E., ed. 1997. *Currency Boards and External Shocks: How Much Pain, How Much Gain?* Washington, DC: World Bank.

Pissarides, Cristopher A. 1992. "Loss of Skill during Unemployment and the Persistence of Unemployment Shocks." *The Quarterly Journal of Economics* 107 (4): 1371–1391.

Purroy, Miguel Ignacio. 1997. *Costos y Beneficios de la Rigidez Cambiaria: La Junta Monetaria Argentina.* Caracas: Banco Central de Venezuela.

Ramon-Ballester, Francisco. 1999. "Estonia's Currency Board Arrangement: Performance, Challenges to Sustainability and Prospects for EMU." Working Paper 348, Kiel Institute of World Economics, Kiel.

Randall, Andrew. 2003. "Glossary of the British Empire." `http://freespace.virgin.net/andrew.randall1/beglossary.htm` (April 25, 2003).

República Argentina. 1991a. Ley 23.928 (Ley de Convertibilidad).

———. 1991b. Ley 23.990 (Presupuesto General de Gastos y Cálculo de Recursos de la Administración Nacional para el Ejercicio 1991).

———. 1992. Ley 24.144 (Banco Central de la República Argentina).

———. 1995. Ley 24.485 (Sistema de Seguro de Garantía de los Depositos Bancarios).

———. 2001a. Decreto 1570/2001 (Entidades Financieras. Nuevas Medidas Economicas).

———. 2001b. Ley 25.445 (Ley de Convertibilidad).

Republic of Bulgaria. 1999. Law on Redenomination of the Bulgarian Lev.

———. [1997] 2002. Law on the Bulgarian National Bank.

Republic of Estonia. 1992a. Currency Law.

———. 1992b. Law on the Security for Estonian Kroon.

———. 1993. Law on the Central Bank.

Republic of Lithuania. [1994] 2001a. Law on the Bank of Lithuania.

———. [1994] 2001b. Law on the Credibility of the Litas.

Rivera Batiz, Luis A., and Amadou N. R. Sy. 2000. "Currency Boards, Credibility, and Macroeconomic Behavior." Working Paper 00/97, International Monetary Fund, Washington, DC.

Rogoff, Kenneth. 1996. "The Purchasing Power Parity Puzzle." *Journal of Economic Literature* 34:647–668.

Rohde, Armin, and Ole Janssen. 2000. "Estonia's Monetary Integration into EMU." *Intereconomics* July/August:176–182.

——— 2001. "Osteuropäische Currency Board-Länder und die optimale Integrationsstrategie in die Europäische Währungsunion am Beispiel Estlands." *Osteuropa Wirtschaft* 46 (4): 355–368.

Ross, Märten. 1999. "Estonian Monetary System and Euro." `http://www.ee/epbe/en/art990610/` (October 5, 2002).

Roubini, Nouriel. 2001. "Should Argentina Dollarize or Float? The Pros and Cons of Alternative Exchange Rate Regimes and their Implications for Domestic and Foreign Debt Restructuring/Reduction." `http://www.stern.nyu.edu/~nroubini/asia/argentinadollarization.doc` (January 6, 2001).

Salter, W. E. G. 1959. "Internal and External Balance: The Role of Price and Expenditure Effects." *The Economic Record* 35 (71): 226–238.

Santiprabhob, Veerathai. 1997. "Bank Soundness and Currency Board Arrangements: Issues and Experience." Paper on Policy Analysis and Assessment 97/11, International Monetary Fund, Washington, DC.

Schiff, Jerald, et al. 2001. "Labor Markets in Hard-Peg Accession Countries: The Baltics and Bulgaria." Country Report 01/100, International Monetary Fund, Washington, DC.

Schuler, Kurt. 1992. "Currency Boards." Ph.D. diss., George Mason University, Fairfax, Virginia.

———. 1996. *Should Developing Countries Have Central Banks? Currency Quality and Monetary Systems in 155 Countries.* London: Institute of Economic Affairs.

———. 1999. "The Importance of Being Orthodox." paper presented at a workshop on "Currency Boards: Convertibility, Liquidity Management and Exit", Hong Kong Baptist University, Oct 9, 1999.

Schwartz, Anna J. 1993. "Currency Boards: Their Past, Present, and Possible Future Role." *Carnegie-Rochester Conference Series on Public Policy* 39:147–187.

Starr, Pamela K. 1997. "Government Coallitions and the Viability of Currency Boards: Argentina under the Cavallo Plan." *Journal of Interamerican Studies and World Affairs* 39 (2): 83–133.

Stefanov, Stefan. 1999. "Implications of the Currency Board in Bulgaria." *South East Europe Review for Labour and Social Affairs* 2 (1): 139–156.

Swan, Trevor W. 1960. "Economic Control in a Dependent Economy." *The Economic Record* 36 (73): 51–66.

———. 1963. "Longer-Run Problems of the Balance of Payments." In *The Australian Economy. A Volume of Readings*, edited by H. W. Arndt and W. M. Corden, 384–395. Melbourne: Cheshire.

Tanner, Evan, and Pablo Sanguinetti. 1997. "Structural Reform and Disinflation: Lessons from Argentina's Convertibility Plan." *The Journal of Developing Areas* 51:529–552.

The Economist. 2002a. "Argentina's Collapse. Carving up the Scraps of Power." September 7, 2002:55.

———. 2002b. "The Hole Gets Deeper." vol. September 21, 2002.

Traa, Bob, et al. 1998. "Argentina. Recent Economic Developments." Staff Country Report 98/38, International Monetary Fund, Washington, DC.

Tsang, Shu-ki. 1999. "Legal Frameworks of Currency Board Regimes." *HKMA Quarterly Bulletin* August:50–63.

———. 2000. "Commitment to and Exit Strategies from a CBA." Paper presented on the occasion of a seminar "Currency Boards—Experience and Prospects", held by Eesti Pank, Estonia.

Tsang, Shu-ki, and Yue Ma. 2002. "Currency Substitution and Speculative Attacks on a Currency Board System." *Journal of International Money and Finance* 21:53–78.

Vetlov, Igor. 2001. "Dollarization in Lithuania: An Econometric Approach." BOFIT Discussion Paper 1, Bank of Finland.

Walters, Alan. 1993. "Currency Boards and Their History." In Liviatan 1993, 4–6.

———. 1997. "The Experience of Hong Kong." In Perry 1997, 11–14.

Weber, Axel A. 1998. "Sources of Currency Crises: An Empirical Analysis." Working Paper 25, Oestereichsiche Nationalbank, Vienna.

Williamson, John. 1995. *What Role for Currency Boards.* Washington, DC: Institute for International Economics.

———. 1997. "Features and Implications of Currency Boards: Thoughts about the Argentine Situation." In Perry 1997, 7–9.

Willman, Alpo. 1992. *Studies in the Theory of Balance-of-Payments Crises.* Helsinki: Suomen Pankki.

Wohlmann, Monika. 1998. *Der nominale Wechselkurs als Stabilitätsanker. Die Erfahrungen Argentiniens 1991–1995.* Frankfurt am Main: Vervuert.

World Bank. 1998. "Argentina. The Fiscal Dimension of the Convertibility Plan. A Background Report." Report 16996-AR, World Bank.

———. 2002. *Global Development Finance.* Washington, DC: World Bank.

Wu, Youchang. 2000. "The Multi-Equilibrium Approach to Currency Crises: An Overview." *Economic Science*, no. Sep.–Oct. English translation of originally chinese version.

Xu, Steven. 1998. "Dollarize Hong Kong." *Asiaweek.* Aug 28, 1998.

Yam, Joseph. 1998. *Review of Currency Board Arrangements in Hong Kong.* Hong Kong Monetary Authority.

Permissions

 Every chapter published in this book has been scrutinized by our experts. Their significance has been extensively debated. The topics covered herein carry significant information for a comprehensive understanding. They may even be implemented as practical applications or may be referred to as a beginning point for further studies.

We would like to thank the editorial team for lending their expertise to make the book truly unique. They have played a crucial role in the development of this book. Without their invaluable contributions this book wouldn't have been possible. They have made vital efforts to compile up to date information on the varied aspects of this subject to make this book a valuable addition to the collection of many professionals and students.

This book was conceptualized with the vision of imparting up-to-date and integrated information in this field. To ensure the same, a matchless editorial board was set up. Every individual on the board went through rigorous rounds of assessment to prove their worth. After which they invested a large part of their time researching and compiling the most relevant data for our readers.

The editorial board has been involved in producing this book since its inception. They have spent rigorous hours researching and exploring the diverse topics which have resulted in the successful publishing of this book. They have passed on their knowledge of decades through this book. To expedite this challenging task, the publisher supported the team at every step. A small team of assistant editors was also appointed to further simplify the editing procedure and attain best results for the readers.

Apart from the editorial board, the designing team has also invested a significant amount of their time in understanding the subject and creating the most relevant covers. They scrutinized every image to scout for the most suitable representation of the subject and create an appropriate cover for the book.

The publishing team has been an ardent support to the editorial, designing and production team. Their endless efforts to recruit the best for this project, has resulted in the accomplishment of this book. They are a veteran in the field of academics and their pool of knowledge is as vast as their experience in printing. Their expertise and guidance has proved useful at every step. Their uncompromising quality standards have made this book an exceptional effort. Their encouragement from time to time has been an inspiration for everyone.

The publisher and the editorial board hope that this book will prove to be a valuable piece of knowledge for students, practitioners and scholars across the globe.

Index

www.ingramcontent.com/pod-product-compliance
Lightning Source LLC
LaVergne TN
LVHW051045220926
848485LV00001BA/11